COFFIN'S

OVERTONES
OF
BEL CANTO

PHONETIC BASIS of ARTISTIC SINGING

with

100 Chromatic Vowel-Chart Exercises

by BERTON COFFIN

The Scarecrow Press, Inc.
Lanham, Maryland • Toronto • Oxford

SCARECROW PRESS, INC.

Published in the United States of America
by Scarecrow Press, Inc.
A wholly owned subsidiary of The Rowman & Littlefield Publishing Group, Inc.
4501 Forbes Boulevard, Suite 200, Lanham, Maryland 20706
www.scarecrowpress.com

PO Box 317
Oxford
OX2 9RU, UK

Library of Congress Cataloging in Publication Data

```
Coffin, Berton.
   Coffin's overtones of bel canto.

   Bibliography:  p.
   Includes index.
   1.  Singing--Diction.  2.  Phonetics.
3.  Singing--Studies and exercises.  I.  Title.
II.  Title:  Overtones of bel canto.
MT883.C6          784.9'32              80-21958
ISBN 0-8108-1370-X
```

To the Memory of

PIERRE DELATTRE

Acoustical phoneticist, co-author
and friend whose research and in-
spiration made this contribution
to the art of singing possible.

"Quality is closely allied not only with vowel and consonant sound, regarding their own individual pitch, both of these phenomena being more or less radical and unchangeable. Because of pitch, which must be perfect, we shall see that vowel sounds and colors for expression are modified in relation to pitch. This is an important factor in pronunciation and expression much neglected and too often only partly understood."

> Witherspoon (1925) who was appointed General Manager
> of the Metropolitan Opera in 1935.

"Everything should be made as simple as possible, but not simpler."

> Albert Einstein

"I should recommend philologists who wish to define the vowels of different languages to fix them by the pitch of loudest resonance."

> Helmholtz (1875)

Philologists (linguists) have not done so, but I have defined the vowel-pitches of loudest resonance for the languages of singing. In addition I have set them to music in the form of vocalizes and indicated their use in the modifications of vowels in arias for eight different voice classifications.

> B. C.

TABLE OF CONTENTS

FOREWORD

Is the time right to present a new tool for the teaching of
singing that utilizes many of the discoveries of the late
20th century linked with the teaching of the past? Some
titles have been misnomers, such as the title of the "Talking
Machine." In a way it is true because of certain uses of
wavelengths. But now that we have machines that will read books
aloud to blind people from a printed page, there must be a very
thorough knowledge of language--vowels, consonants, and their
patterns. Since there is synthesized singing by computers both
in the United States and in Europe, it seems that we can better
accept the ideas that all singing is repeated sound (frequency),
its resonation regular (harmonic), or irregular (non-harmonic
noise), and that there are interruptions, intensity variations,
and overtone variations of those sounds which form vowels and
consonants in singing.

It is now well known that vowels have pitch; all singers know
that sung tone has pitch but no extended method has been presented to bring sung pitch and the resonance of vowels into
best relationship. The purpose of this book and the Chromatic
Vowel Chart is to set forth in acoustic phonetics, register and
musical notation, many exercises which will collect and make
the voice stronger and more musical according to the precepts
of Bel Canto.

There are two fundamental points--1) the establishment and use
of the singing voice, and 2) a notation which can be used by
the singer in the performance of songs and opera roles. Simple
explanations are stated with the resonance-vocalises; the
background in greater depth appears in my Sounds of Singing.
The Chromatic Vowel Chart and exercises herein are compatible

ix

with the Vowel Charts and exercises in that text. I believe
the Overtones of Bel Canto: Phonetic Basis of Artistic Singing
will assist the teacher of singing and the singer in finding
his or her true voice. I also believe that it will lead to a
healthy clarity of tone, joy of practice, joy of singing, joy
of listening, and will assist the professional singer in maintaining his or her vocal instrument in the periods when absent
from the teacher of singing. It is to these principles this
book is directed.

Berton Coffin
Boulder, Colorado
June 25, 1980

INTRODUCTION

It has been my privilege to have heard performances in most
parts of the musical world and to have talked with many singers.
I have been interested in their statements that there are few,
if any, good singing teachers in their particular locations. I
heard the same comment when I was President of the National Association of Teachers of Singing, yet I knew my colleagues to be
serious in their art. There are many teachers and coaches who
teach interpretation, and there are many singers who can inter-
pret better than they can sing. I have long suspected that
there is something either very elusive or counter productive in
teaching singing and that the problem may be due to inadequate
tools of our art. We somehow or other have not been able to
sustain voices at a high potential over a long period of time.
A search for the answer has been a compulsion with me for years
and continues to be. I have sponsored or co-sponsored 8 NATS
Workshops, taught vocal pedagogy for 25 years to graduate and
undergraduate students in a university situation, have taught
countless singers here and abroad, and have reached a number
of conclusions.

Artistic performance is a vital, vibrant, and exciting aspect
of our times. It is dependent upon the human spirit, musical
and poetic imagination, health, and the physical events of
vibration and resonation brought about by certain muscular
activities related to the vocal instrument. These vibrations
and muscular activities need to become almost reflexive before
song can really be in sustained flight. Otherwise there are
artistic limitations.

It is my belief that the voice is a musical instrument and that
it may be best formed acoustically by the use of phonetics.
This is made possible by the newly developing field of acoustic

phonetics which has been most completely defined in the collected papers of Dennis B. Fry (Acoustic Phonetics) and the text by
Philip Lieberman (Speech Physiology and Acoustic Phonetics).
When the voice is correctly formed by acoustic phonetics, the
singer avoids many of the muscular problems of hyperfunction
and hypofunction which are pitfalls of his profession. These
may result in stiffness of parts of the vocal tract, hoarseness,
register problems, limitations of range, color, poor vibrato,
malfunction, and disfunction.

The overtones of bel canto are dependent upon a very simple but
invisible phenomenon: Vowels have pitch which act as resonators to sung pitch if they are shaded to allow for greatest
resonance. Various writings have shown how this may be demonstrated, 1) Aiken--The Voice, An Introduction to Practical Phonology, 2) Denes--The Speech Chain, 3) Appelman--The Science of
Vocal Pedagogy, 4) Coffin--The Sounds of Singing, and 5) Sundberg's key article--"The Acoustics of the Singing Voice" in
Scientific American. Interest is growing in this new field and
the future of the teaching and coaching of singers seems to be
very closely involved with Acoustic Phonetics.

It is more effective to form the voice by vibration and resonation than to form it by imagery and descriptions of muscular
action. Fortunately the vocabulary already exists for this new
field. The International Phonetic Association over a period of
many years has developed symbols which represent sounds that
can be differentiated by listeners. I have taken these symbols
and created a Chromatic Vowel Chart by use of a procedure described in The Sounds of Singing. Any who are inquisitive or
dubious can check on the technique of defining vowels by pitch.
Fortunately it is not necessary to go to the "testing station"
to teach vowel colors. A more immediate feedback is available!
When the sounds and their symbols are learned, it is quite
enough to make an intelligent guess in singing and to let the
vibration on the mucous membrane of the vocal tract tell the

singer when best resonance has been found. Thus this technique
of teaching, practicing, and performing partially by-passes the
intellectual. For example, after colors are seen they can be
described by the sense of sight and written in language. Likewise, after vowel colors are heard and felt they can be described by the sense of hearing and notated in the International
Phonetic Alphabet. More important, from the notation vowel
colors can be heard and felt before they are sung.

This text is a way of informing teachers of singing, singers,
and coaches how to utilize to best advantage the resonance characteristic of the human throat. This book is also addressed to
our colleagues, the coaches who are at the interface of language
and music. They are usually one step from actual performance.
They must be keyboard artists and linguists. Few of them have
sung enough to know the sensory feel of vibration in their
throats while singing over orchestral or keyboard instruments
in a performance situation. How can they be expected to know
what the singer's tribulations are--they primarily know music
and language. Frequently they ask for both in absolute values
from the singers with whom they work. Unfortunately they cannot often have both in the upper extensions of singing voices.

Herbert Witherspoon, a great artist, teacher, and former General
Manager of the Metropolitan Opera, whom I quote again, said
(1925, p. 75):

> "Quality is closely allied not only with vowel
> and consonant sound, regarding their own indiv-
> idual pitch, both of these phenomena being more
> or less radical and unchangeable. Because of
> pitch, which must be perfect, we shall see that
> vowel sounds and colors for expression are modi-
> fied in relation to pitch. This is an important
> factor in pronunciation and expression much neg-
> lected and too often only partly understood."

Concerning the effect of vowel shading on diction he stated:

> "The modification of the vowels, and the per-
> fect action of the vocal organs for tone, does
> not injure or make indistinct our pronunciation,

or harm our enunciation and emission. On the
contrary, the obedience to the natural laws of
singing, which causes the slight modification,
is alone possible if we accept this doctrine,
and the result will be far more natural and
spontaneous and true to laws of pronunciation
than if we force the vowels to sound their
"medium-normal" form. It is perhaps the latter
forcing which causes many singers to sing out
of tune on their higher notes." (p. 30)

Why do we hear so much strident, raspy, and out of pitch singing? Frequently because the singer has been coached into absolute language values which conflict with the composer's pitches,
instead of relative language values which are vocal. Very
simply, singing with the best relationship of vibrator and resonator is therapeutic to the singer's throat and his audience.
Furthermore--it releases the singer's spirit for that supra
human endeavor--artistic performance. Whereas our earlier
book, Phonetic Readings of Songs and Arias, provided a real
tool for the singer's language pronunciation, the Overtones of
Bel Canto offers vocalises for specific vocal techniques and
the use of phonetic shadings in the singing of songs and arias.
These can be trained with the reflexes both aurally and kinesthetically through the use of the Chromatic Vowel Chart and related exercises. One of the most important contributions of
this volume is that best singing practices have been notated.

I have frequently been asked how I became interested in the
phonetic approach to the teaching and maintaining of the singing
voice. It probably dates back to my Master's thesis which was
entitled, "Survey and Evaluation of the Various Methods of Voice
Classification," in which I reviewed the literature of Vocal
Pedagogy and elicited opinions and practices from members of
the American Academy of Teachers of Singing and the Chicago
Singing Teachers Guild. It became evident that both register
events and vowel colors on certain notes in the scale were at
the center of voice classification. This concept has always
been present in my teaching and these phenomena observed. The

second influence was my association with Pierre Delattre, the
world famous acoustical phoneticist, who with Lieberman, Cooper,
and Gerstman did basic work on the analysis and synthesis of
vowels, to assist the blind and deaf, at the Bell Telephone Laboratory and the Haskins Laboratory. By the time I met Delattre
their work was solidly established and I was struck by the idea
that there was a register event near the lowest pitch of vowels
around E♮ above middle C. This meant to me that the so-called
"break" at the upper part of the male voice and the lower medium
of the female voice was a phonetic phenomenon and that, if such
was the case, there should be phonetic solutions to it.

After extended research in this country and abroad, my text,
The Sounds of Singing on vowel scales and registers was published in 1977. The Overtones of Bel Canto began as a manual for
the condensed Chromatic Vowel Chart which I was able to build
and utilize from pages 94 and 109 of The Sounds of Singing.
The greatest problem was one of notation and the solution was
not evident until I found a way to notate register events,
pitch, and vowel color in the same exercise. Perhaps the phenomena of register and vowel are best understood when the vocal
instrument is likened to a trumpet, the vowels are likened to
the fingering (changing of tube length), and the registers
likened to the pinching or loosening of the lips to obtain the
higher and lower modes of vibration. It will be seen that there
are very impressive and extensive inter-relationships between
the vibrating source and the resonating system. My inquisitive-
ness in wanting to know "why" has led me to the acoustics and
phonetics laboratories to find out how much of the phenomena
are acoustical and how much muscular. I have been happy to not
let scientific measurement stand in the way. I have been interested in the art of singing and how things work. This text
contains very little science, per se, just observable and usable
coordinations. If I have contributed to a higher singers' art
and have extended singers' careers, I have achieved my purpose
in presenting this rather complete vowel-pitch-overtone approach based on Italianate singing.

ACKNOWLEDGEMENTS

I am indebted to many specialists in the area of sound and phonetics related to this book which forms the keystone of two other texts, Phonetic Readings of Songs and Arias, and Sounds of Singing. It all began in 1959 with the late Dr. Pierre Delattre, French linguist, in the Sound Laboratory at the University of Colorado-Boulder and with him in the Phonetics Laboratory at the University of California-Santa Barbara. Additional work was done in the Boulder Sound Laboratory with Hans-Heinrich Wängler, German phoneticist. Later consultations with Dr. Fritz Winckel of the Technical University of West Berlin were most helpful.

I am greatly indebted to Dr. Johan Sundberg of the Royal Institute of Technology of Stockholm, Sweden, who demonstrated resonance tracking on a new singing synthesizer. Many observations were clarified in this consultation. I am also indebted to Dr. Werner Deutsch, Sound Laboratory, Academy of Sciences, Vienna, in the preparation of Sonagrams for overtone analysis, and for consultations. I am indebted to Joseph Olive of the Bell Telephone Laboratory, Summit, New Jersey, for his demonstration of computerized singing with vowels, pitch, and consonants. This reinforced several ideas and caused me to discard others as to the nature of singing. It showed what was acoustically possible without muscular play and provided a better understanding of the muscular actions and limitations in singing.

My grateful thanks go to opera artists and advanced singers with whom I have been able to further develop the art of singing in my work in the United States and in Europe. Finally, without the hundreds of singers we have heard in over 70 opera houses in more than 375 performances this work would be of little

xvi

value. The concentrated listening to live singing is essential.
I have been greatly assisted by my soprano-concert manager wife,
Mildred Coffin, whose eyes and ears have amplified my senses in
forming this text on _bel_ _canto_. She and Myra Jackson have been
my patient typists; and Robert Snyder and Donald Ridley have
been of great assistance in proofing this book for which I am
very grateful.

THE INTERNATIONAL PHONETIC ALPHABET

(Revised to 1979)

		Bilabial	Labiodental	Dental, Alveolar, or Post-alveolar	Retroflex	Palato-alveolar	Palatal	Velar	Uvular	Labial-Palatal	Labial-Velar	Pharyngeal	Glottal
CONSONANTS (pulmonic air-stream mechanism)	Nasal	m	ɱ	n	ɳ		ɲ	ŋ	ɴ				
	Plosive	p b		t d	ʈ ɖ		c ɟ	k g	q ɢ		k͡p g͡b		ʔ
	(Median) Fricative	ɸ β	f v	θ ð s z	ʂ ʐ	ʃ ʒ	ç ʝ	x ɣ	χ ʁ		ʍ	ħ ʕ	h ɦ
	(Median) Approximant		ʋ	ɹ	ɻ		j	ɰ		ɥ	w		
	Lateral Fricative			ɬ ɮ									
	Lateral (Approximant)			l	ɭ		ʎ						
	Trill			r					ʀ				
	Tap or Flap			ɾ	ɽ				ʀ				
(non-pulmonic air-stream)	Ejective	p'		t'				k'					
	Implosive	ɓ		ɗ				ɠ					
	(Median) Click	ʘ		ʇ ʗ									
	Lateral Click			ʖ									

DIACRITICS

- ̥ Voiceless n̥ d̥
- ̬ Voiced s̬ t̬
- ʰ Aspirated tʰ
- ̤ Breathy-voiced b̤ a̤
- ̪ Dental t̪
- ̫ Labialized t̫
- ̡ Palatalized t̡
- ̴ Velarized or Pharyngealized ɫ, ɫ
- ̩ Syllabic n̩ l̩
- ͡ or ͜ Simultaneous s͡f (but see also under the heading Affricates)
- ˔ or ̝ Raised e˔, e̝, e̝ w
- ˕ or ̞ Lowered e˕, e̞, e̞ ʁ̞
- ̟ Advanced u+, u̟
- ̠ or - Retracted i̠, i-, t̠
- ̈ Centralized ë
- ̃ Nasalized ã
- ˞ r-coloured a˞
- ː Long aː
- ˑ Half-long aˑ
- ̆ Non-syllabic ŭ
- ˒ More rounded ɔ˒
- ˓ Less rounded y˓

OTHER SYMBOLS

- ɕ, ʑ Alveolo-palatal fricatives
- ʆ, ʓ Palatalized ʃ, ʒ
- ɼ Alveolar fricative trill
- ɺ Alveolar lateral flap
- ɧ Simultaneous ʃ and x
- ʃˢ Variety of ʃ resembling s, etc.
- ɪ = ɩ
- ʊ = ɷ
- ɜ = Variety of ə
- ɚ = r-coloured ə

VOWELS

	Front		Back
Close	i	ɨ	ɯ
	ɩ		
Half-close	e	ə	ɤ
Half-open	ɛ		ʌ
	æ	ɐ	
Open	a		ɑ

Unrounded

	Front		Back
Close	y	ʉ	u
	ʏ		ɷ
Half-close	ø	ɵ	o
Half-open	œ		ɔ
Open	ɶ		ɒ

Rounded

STRESS, TONE (PITCH)

ˈ stress, placed at beginning of stressed syllable: ˌ secondary stress: ˉ high level pitch, high tone: ˍ low level: ˊ high rising: ˏ low rising: ˋ high falling: ˎ low falling: ˆ rise-fall: ˇ fall-rise.

AFFRICATES can be written as digraphs, as ligatures, or with slur marks; thus ts, tʃ, dʒ: ʦ ʧ ʤ: t͡s t͡ʃ d͡ʒ. c, ɟ may occasionally be used for tʃ, dʒ.

Fig. 1. Reproduced by permission of the International Phonetic Association.

CHAPTER **I**

THE INTELLIGIBILITY OF LANGUAGES IN SINGING

<u>Vowel Sound Tracks</u>. Language is understood by means of sound tracks made by the human voice. Understanding the nature of the voice has come so far that it will soon be possible for anyone to have a voice synthesizer as reasonably as a video-tape machine. Business, military, and language specialists have been using related devices for years. Now hearing will be believing especially after a person has synthesized speech in his own home. How does the speaking voice work? By means of varying the resonances of the vocal tract which form the vowels. A rough concept can be gained of the system in the illustration from Chiba and Kajima (1958), Fig. 2. The concurrence of resonance frequencies make the vowel sounds; the combinations are all important. One, or two, or three resonances without the other will not work for distinct linguistic perception. The interplay of all the resonances is necessary. Consonants are interruptions or quick changes of those resonances.

It will be noticed that the lower frequencies of the vowels can be checked against the numbers on the bottom of the Chromatic Vowel Chart. The important speech signals fall above middle C at 250 Hz. In sing-

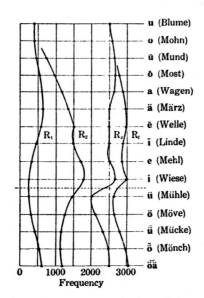

Fig. 94. Formant Diagram of the German Vowels (after Thienhaus)

Fig. 2. Chiba & Kajiama

From THE VOWEL by Chiba & Kajiyama. ⓒ 1958, Phonetic Society of Japan.

1

ing, we are most interested in the lower resonance, R^1, and overtone relationships to the sung tone. This is involved with the fullness, quality, limpidity, and intonation of the singing voice. The diagonals of the Chromatic Vowel Chart indicate the harmonic relationship of the sung pitch and the resonance of the vocal tract. Vowel pitch and sung pitch can fight each other or they can work together. This is a system of acoustical cooperation and will bring the greatest yield a voice can give. The lower resonances and their harmonic tracks can and have been charted for your use.

On the Chromatic Vowel Chart, Track I is the actual lower Resonance of Vowels, R^1. Pitches on Track 2 will resonate the Vowel Scale, R^1, by their second harmonic overtone, on Track 3 by their third harmonic, etc. You will understand much more by your sense of vibration. The concurrence of harmonics and the Resonances falling between c^3 and the top of the piano must rely on your ear. The vowel colors used to center and build the voice are shown on the next page. They include most of the sounds of the IPA Rounded and Unrounded Vowel Triangles of the IPA (see p. xviii) which are basically made up of variations of the Front [i] and Back [u] Vowels. In singing there must be a Middle or Neutral Series in which there is neither Fronting or Backing of the tongue. I have created a Neutral Series for which I have modified the IPA slightly. ʌ, carat, is the unrounded Neutral Vowel--the vowel we snore on--which when rounded proceeds through (ʌ), ʊ to ə which I have used as the most rounded vowel since it is the most rounded symbol. This enables me to notate the pipings of the non-vowel which is most easily sung in melismatic passages of treble voices. This form allows the throat to act most like an organ pipe. All other vowels are according to the usually accepted values.

2

Fig. 3.   VOWEL SYMBOLS

Typewritten	Script	Printed on Chromatic Vowel Chart

		Acoustical Phonetics	**Approximate Pronunciation**
		Front Vowels	
a	ɑ	ɑ	front Ah, Italian A, corners back, *mine.*
æ	æ	æ	as in American *last.*
ɛ	ɛ	ɛ	as in American *let.*
e	e	e	first vowel sound in *may.*
ɪ	ɪ	ɪ	American, *fit.*
i	i	i	as in American, *feet.*
		Neutral Vowels	
ʌ	ʌ	ʌ	lateral (open) schwa, *fun.* Sheltered Ah.
ʊ	ʊ	ʊ	half rounded (half closed) schwa, *pull.*
ə	ə	ə	rounded (close) schwa, Fr. *le.*
		Back Vowels	
ɑ	ɑ	ɑ	lateral Ah, corners back, and jaw down, *shout.*
ɒ	ɒ	ɒ	dark Ah, *father.*
∪	∪	∪	our coinage of the lateral ɔ, rotated 90 degrees. (Bright *awe*). *joy.*
ɔ	ɔ	ɔ	as in American, *awe* (Dark *aw*).
ɤ	ɤ	ɤ	O with lips either drawn back or neutral. (Bright O), *jovial.*
o	o	o	The German ∪, *ohne.* (Dark O).
ɯ	ɯ	ɯ	[u] with lips either drawn back or neutral. (Bright U).
u	u	u	as in English *pool.* (Dark U).
		Umlaut Vowels	
œ	œ	œ	lips rounded [ɛ], Ger. *Götter*, Fr. *coeur.*
ø	ø	ø	lips rounded [e], Ger. *schön*, Fr. *peu.*
ʏ	ʏ	ʏ	lips rounded [ɪ], Ger. *Hütte.*
y	y	y	lips rounded [i], Ger. *fühl*, Fr. *du.*

The Symbol (ʌ). The Neutral Vowels have been defined by three symbols [ʌ, ʊ, and ə]. Traditionally [ʌ] has been described as accented schwa and [ə] as unaccented. However, in my acoustic definition I have used [ʌ] to denote the open neutral sound which has a resonance from Notes 32-36. When the lips are rounded, the pitch is lowered; I have defined [ʊ] as having the resonance between Notes 26 and 29. When the lips are rounded to the closed resonance of Notes 23-25, I have defined the sound as [ə]. I have, in addition to the phonetics in the Sounds of Singing, used the symbol (ʌ) to denote the Neutral Vowel which resonates Notes 30, 31, and 32--I will call it the half rounded ʌ .

<u>Nasalization</u> is indicated by ~ as in æ̃, ɔ̃, ɑ̃, ɛ̃.

OTHER SYMBOLS

22 A number indicates the note number on which the exercise begins when the Chart is correctly placed on the piano for the singer's voice classification.

(ɛ) A circle with a vowel in it indicates that the vowel is to be sung behind the hand over the mouth. The mouth is open, the soft palate is lowered so that there is vibration against the hand and through the nasal turbinates.

(oɔ) Two vowels encircled indicate that vowels change behind the hand while both mouth and nasal passages vibrate. When the hand is removed, our X-Ray motion picture study indicates the palate returns to its up and back position. In the process the upper swallowing muscle (superior constrictor) has been relaxed in such a manner that there is more harmonic overtone--the basis of study in singing. G. B. Lamperti as quoted by W. E. Brown (1931) stated, "Tone and breath 'balance' only when harmonic overtones appear in the voice and not by muscular effort and 'voice placing'." Non-harmonic overtone is noise. Real Voice Building and Tone Placement come through strengthening those physical musculatures in the vocal tract, larynx, and posture muscles which assist in phonating and resonating the harmonic overtones of the singing voice.

ᕁ∾ <u>Turn</u>. The turn is used frequently in this text at the end of phrases to center the resonance and to find the balanced breath support by the lifted sternum. This is the <u>appoggio</u> or leaning against the chest of many Italian schools and differs from the outward abdominal press of many German schools. There is a short pause before each turn during which breath should <u>not</u> be taken. According to DeReske (Leiser 1934), the chest will ring on low notes if the pressure of the breath is lessened. The reason is simple, it does not take as much accelerator pressure to run an engine at low speed--there are fewer explosions per second--the same is true with singing.

<u>Pitch</u>. Most of this text was written in Vienna at a pitch of A-444 Hz. It is workable as low as 435 Hz.

Fig. 4. <u>The Chromatic Phonetic Alphabet Used</u>.

a	*a*	mine--ma<u>i</u>n. Italian Ah between æ and ɑ.
ɑ	*ɑ*	Bright Ah--Cheeks up, corners of lips back and chin down, sh<u>ou</u>t.
ɒ	*ɒ*	Dark Ah--<u>fa</u>ther
ã	*ã*	d<u>an</u>s, French nasal
æ	*æ*	<u>fa</u>st
b	*b*	<u>b</u>ack
ç	*ç*	i<u>ch</u>, German. <u>h</u>uman, English
d	*d*	<u>d</u>o
ḓ	*ḓ*	dentalized d, <u>D</u>on--do<u>n</u>
ɛ	*ɛ*	<u>e</u>bb
ɛ̃	*ɛ̃*	pl<u>ai</u>n, Fr. nasalized ɛ or æ
e	*e*	first sound in m<u>a</u>y, me<u>i</u>
ə	*ə*	pursed lips l<u>e</u>, Fr.
f	*f*	<u>f</u>it
g	*g*	<u>g</u>ave
h	*h*	<u>h</u>ot
hw	*hw*	<u>wh</u>ite
i	*i*	<u>ea</u>t
ɪ	*ɪ*	<u>i</u>t
j	*j*	<u>y</u>es
dʒ	*dʒ*	<u>j</u>ust
k	*k*	<u>k</u>eep
l	*l*	<u>l</u>ow
ḽ	*ḽ*	dentalized l, <u>l</u>ingua
ʎ	*ʎ*	<u>gl</u>i, It. Tongue touching lower gum line of front teeth.
m	*m*	<u>m</u>y
ɱ	*ɱ*	i<u>nf</u>ra, It. Lower lip pressing against upper front teeth.
n	*n*	<u>n</u>ow
ṉ	*ṉ*	Dentalized n, <u>N</u>i<u>n</u>a, It.
ɲ	*ɲ*	It. o<u>gn</u>i with tongue touching lower gum line of front teeth
o	*o*	b<u>oa</u>t, without diphthong
ɤ	*ɤ*	Open O, between <u>o</u> and <u>ɔ</u>
ɔ	*ɔ*	<u>aw</u>e. Dark aw.
ɔ̃	*ɔ̃*	Fr. non. Nasalized <u>ɔ</u> or <u>o</u>
ↄ	*ᴜ*	(My symbol) bright <u>aw</u>. Between <u>ɔ</u> and <u>ɑ</u>, j<u>oy</u>.
œ	*œ*	Fr. c<u>oeu</u>r, ɛ with rounded lips
ø	*ø*	Ger. sch<u>ö</u>n, e with rounded lips
p	*p*	<u>p</u>et
pf	*pf*	Ko<u>pf</u>, Ger.
r	*r*	<u>r</u>ed
ř	*ř*	rolled r, <u>r</u>osa It. ˇ indicates roll
ɾ	*ɾ*	One flip of r, <u>Br</u>itish
s	*s*	<u>s</u>ee

5

ʃ	ʃ	show		ʌ	ʌ	fun, accented neutral vowel
t	t	tell		v	v	voice
t̪	t̪	dentalized t, mo<u>t</u>o It.		w	w	win
θ	θ	thin		y	y	i with lips rounded. Fr. d<u>u</u>, Ger. f<u>ü</u>hl
ð	ð	this				
u	u	pool		ʏ	ʏ	I with lips rounded, Ger. H<u>ü</u>tte
ɯ	ɯ	bright <u>u</u>, with lips unpuckered between u and ʊ		z	z	zeal
				ʒ	ʒ	pleasure
ʊ	ʊ	pull		x	x	Ger. a<u>ch</u>, soft palate fricative.

All singers, sooner or later, are called upon to sing in a foreign language be they American, Italian, German, French, English or other. A singer's study can be facilitated by learning to use <u>all</u> of the sounds of singing--the various colors of vowels and the various gradations of consonants. Singers should be able to use the non-explosive consonants of the Italian language to reduce interference with vocal cord vibration. For further explanation see The Sounds of Singing.

Now that the Vowel Charts and acoustical phonetics are being used abroad as well as in the United States, I have received numerous requests to include sample words for the IPA in Italian, German and French. I present those which are in our text, Phonetic Readings of Songs and Arias, Coffin, Errolle, Singer, and Delattre, 1964.

Phonetic Symbol	As found in Italian words
a	casa.....ka<u>z</u>a
ɛ	ecco.....ɛk:ko
e	che .....ke
i	mi .....mi
o	voce.....votʃe
ɔ	oggi.....ɔdʒi
u	muto.....m<u>u</u>to

From PHONETIC READINGS OF SONGS AND ARIAS by Coffin, Errolle, Singer and Delattre. © 1964, Pruett Press, Inc.

6

Phonetic Symbol	As found in French words	Phonetic Symbol		As found in German words
ɑ	âme......ɑm	long	a:	Kahn.....ka:n
a	Madame...madam	short	a:	Mann.....man
e	nez......ne	long	ɛ:	währen...vɛ:rən
ɛ	plaire...plɛr	short	ɛ	weg......vɛk
i	qui......ki	long	e:	Teer.....te:r
o	nos......no	short	e	der......der
ɔ	porte....port		ə	baden....ba:dən
u	jour.....ʒur	long	i:	Sieb.....zi:p
ø	deux.....dø	short	ɪ	in.......ɪn
œ	fleur....flœr	long	o:	Rose.....ro:zə
y	du.......dy	short	ɔ	Gott.....gɔt
ɑ̃	dans.....dɑ̃	long	u:	Kuh......ku:
ɛ̃	pain.....pɛ̃	short	ʊ	unter....ʊntər
ɔ̃	non......nɔ̃	long	ø:	Löhne....lø:nə
œ̃	un.......œ̃	short	œ	Götter...gœtər
ə	petit....pəti	long	y:	Lüge.....ly:gə
		short	ʏ	Müller...mʏllər
			ae	Mein.....maen
			ao	Haus.....haos
			ɔø	treu.....trɔø

All languages must be modified chromatically to make the musical languages of singing. A complete Chromatic Vowel Chart would need to have more symbols than are available. However, by the use of phonetics and numbers to indicate the degree of opening I have formed a system which will equalize the voice muscularly and acoustically.

Degrees of Vowel Openness. <u>The</u> <u>Variable</u> <u>Lower</u> <u>Resonance</u> <u>of</u> <u>the</u> <u>Vocal</u> <u>Organ</u>. The vocal tract has an extremely long lower resonance of 18 half steps, from about f^1 to $b\flat^2$ depending on voice classification. (Vary the placement of the arrow for the various voice classifications.) There is a workable range of 15 half steps, which means that there is 6.6% change of opening for each half step. The [o] with the 6th degree of opening is 6.6% more open than the [o] with 5, and the [o] with 7 is about 13% more open than the [o] with 5. Openness occurs by jaw lowering, corner backing of the lips, head raising, and movements of the tongue [see Delattre's Fig. 6]. Closing is gained by lip rounding, jaw closing, movements of the tongue, and head lowering. These are controlled by ear, muscle memory, and reflex. Basically the tuning system of vowels should be trained with great elasticity. By such movement muscular strength will develop. There are several interesting observations that can be made:

- Some vowels tune very narrowly--2 or 3 half steps. Others tune more broadly--the vowel [ʌ] sounds over 5 half steps. This vowel is of great help in tuning difficult <u>ah</u> sounds in songs and arias.

- It will be seen that there are 4 different vowel colors for each degree of openness from 1 to 14 and 2 from 15 to 18. Degree of opening #16-18 are so open that spreading occurs when these sounds are on high pitches. Degrees of opening #1-2 are so closed that there is danger that the lower resonance will not be heard; in such cases the sounds are lacking in loudness. Use a vowel with a larger degree of opening which will place the voice in a lower register.

- In these studies much "rhyming" is done on the same degree of openness. It is best to rhyme the Front and Neutral, and the Umlaut with Front, Neutral, and Back Vowels. [ɑ] is dark Ah (precede by w) and [a] is a bright vowel (precede by j or y). Thus, rhyme the [wɑ, ja] or [wɑ, ya] where they appear on the Chart as gold vowels.

8

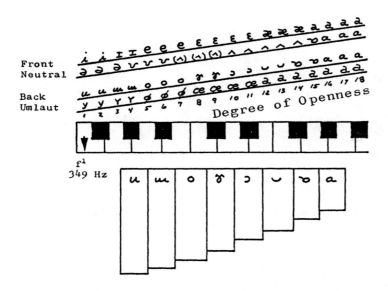

Fig. 5. Degrees of Openness and Relative Pitch.

The Vocal Organ. In Fig. 5 we have portrayed the vowel system
of the singing voice as being somewhat analogous to organ pipes
with the [u] having the longest pipe and the lowest frequency,
and the [ɑ] having the highest. When the [u] vowel is seen on
an oscilloscope, there is a long wave which can be progressively
shortened until it becomes [ɑ]. Some schools of singing seem
to freeze to a position for vocalization such as an [o] or an
Ah which is acoustically inferior to using the complete vowel
scale, within muscular limits. In the vocal organ there are
four ranks of vowels, Front, Neutral, Umlaut, and Back, which
are analagous to the Reed, Flute, String, and Diapason stops on
the pipe organ. Each organ stop can have a 2, 4, 8, or 16 foot
pitch. This is somewhat analagous to the harmonic overtone relationship of registers in the vocal organ indicated by the
numbers at the end of the diagonals of the Chromatic Vowel Chart
--only they indicate the harmonic relationship of resonance to
sung pitch. See Figs. 10 and 11.

9

[i] and [y] have a reduced amount of lower resonance, R^1. They are mostly R^2, R^3, or R^4.

[u] and [ə] have a small amount of overtone.

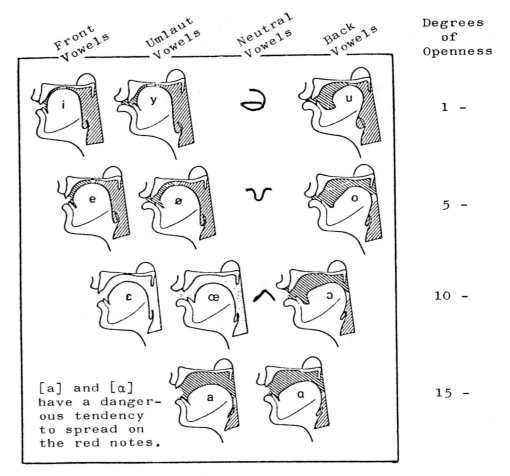

Front Vowels   Umlaut Vowels   Neutral Vowels   Back Vowels   Degrees of Openness

1 -

5 -

10 -

15 -

[a] and [α] have a dangerous tendency to spread on the red notes.

The Neutral Vowels, which I have added in bold letters, have been given chromatic definition.

Use [j] to form the front Ah [a].

From "La radiographie des voyelles française et sa corrélation acoustique," by Delattre. The French Review, O. 1968. Permission of French Review.

Use [w] to form the back Ah [α].

Fig. 6. Delattre's Resonance Spaces of French Speech.

10

The Voice as a Stopped Pipe. The voice acts as a stopped pipe which is open at the lips and closed at the vocal cords. Of course the cords are together only part of the time in their cycle but the duration of the sound above 150 Hz is such that there can be a standing wave (Fant 1960). The most important resonance for fullness of sound is the lowest, R^1, on which the diagonals of the Chromatic Vowel Chart are based. The next most important are R^2 and R^3 which are variable and distinguish the difference between Front, Neutral, Umlaut and Back Vowels. The tongue, jaw, lips, soft palate and head posture manipulate in such a way as to change the height of resonance for the different vowels shown in Fig. 1. The stopped pipe resonates at the same time a 1/4th wavelength, R^1; the 3/4 wavelength, R^2; the 5/4 wavelength, R^3; and the 7/4 wavelength, R^4. The lower the sung pitch, F^0, the more resonances there can be. As pitch ascends the number of resonances diminishes. Hence high sounds are pure with few overtones while the pitches of low male voices are richer in overtones.

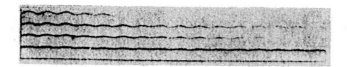

--Lily Pons (soprano); "Caro Nome" (Rigoletto, Act I).
  RCA Victor Record No. 14203-A (2 in.)

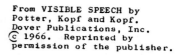

From VISIBLE SPEECH by
Potter, Kopf and Kopf.
Dover Publications, Inc.
© 1966. Reprinted by
permission of the publisher.

--Lawrence Tibbett (baritone); "Largo al Factotum" (Barbiere di
  Siviglia, Act I). RCA Victor Record No. 14202-B (2-1/2 in.).
  The second note is in Falsetto, other notes in Chest Voice.

Fig. 7. Overtone comparison of a Female and a Male Voice.

The Very Variable Pipe. I have shown how the stopped pipe of
the vocal tract can be lengthened and shortened. In addition,
it has the capability of varying its bore--there are large bore
brass instruments, small bore brass instruments, and ones in between. The mechanism for varying the bore has not been system-
atically discussed or taught to my knowledge. Two qualities
can be associated with the size of bore. Garcia (1894, p. 11)
said there are . . . "the clear (bright), or open, and the dark
or closed. These two opposite qualities are obtained princi-
pally through the agency of the larynx and the soft palate.
The movements of these two organs are always in contrary
direction. The larynx rises when the soft palate falls, and
when the larynx falls, the soft palate rises. The high vault
produces the dark timbres, the lower arch the clear ones. The
arch rises when we are in the act of yawning, and falls when we
are in the act of swallowing." I will tell a way of bringing
about the small bore for bright or clear singing--the use of
the open mouth hum, Ⓐ , in which the hand over the open mouth
causes the soft palate to lower and as a consequence the tongue
rises towards it. Fig. 14 shows the velar-pharyngeal axis.
The axis is lengthened for sombre timbre and for full sonority;
the axis is shortened for clear timbre. It is also shortened
for whistle register, for head register and for the beginning
and ending of the messa di voce. The learning of this phenomenon and the identification of how it may be obtained and used
is one of the most important parts of this text. The infinite
variability of the bore and the length of the vocal tract add
great interest and color to singing. This will overcome the
fatigue of singing and listening to singing which is all through
the same bore. The voice is a flexible instrument and lives
best on change. Keep changing the types of exercises to automate the controls and to strengthen the muscles involved with
giving the various sounds. Unless you vary your singing you
will become fatigued and your audience will believe your singing to be colorless. I hope this text will help to establish
multi-color singing which seems to be quite rare today. A base-
ball pitcher has to have three or four good pitches; very few

12

can stay in business on just a fast ball. With a change of
pace, the fast ball will also appear to be faster--keep your
audience guessing but know what you are doing yourself! These
exercises are for instrumental acoustics within the muscular
structure of the human throat. For further development of this
point, see The Sounds of Singing, p. 204, and Chapters IV and
V of this text.

Knödel Remover. When a singer attempts to sing with a fixed or
set resonator, problems ensue. The Italians seem to train
predominantly on the [Ah] Vowel. The German schools train on
Round Vowels for aesthetic or linguistic reasons--the Umlaut
series in their language makes for a more muted tone which has
been called a Knödel because it sounds like a dumpling is stuck

The tongue hump is in
front of the axis for
Front vowels:

i e ɛ æ ɑ

The tongue hump is in
front of the axis for
Umlaut vowels:

y ʏ ø œ ʊ

There is a variable upward and
downward pull. The upward is in
the direction of the elevator
muscles. The downward is in the
direction of the depressors.

There is little or
no tongue hump for
the Neutral vowels:

ə ʌ

(After Fritzell)

The tongue
hump is
back of the
axis for
the Back
vowels:

u ɯ o ɔ ʊ

ɒ ɑ

Fig. 8.   Crossover Exercises
          from Sounds of Singing, p. 207.

in the throat. A variable use of the vocal tract will overcome
this tendency and the heavy breath pressure required to obtain
forced resonance. There is an axis over which the tongue continually passes in speech called the Velopharyngeal Axis. When
vowel series are continually changed, the muscular systems of
the throat become supple and strong. Neck muscles do not become
fatigued and there is an exhilarating sense of free vibration
when tuning is proper. I believe this is the proper basis of
singing. When there is a Knödel, do a great deal of practice on
Crossover exercises (changes between Vowel Series) and Yodel exercises (changes between sung pitches having the same resonator).

The indicated spaces of Fig. 6 make a variation of resonances
which have the frequencies shown in Fig. 2. Following the exercises use these phenomena to place and amplify the voice in
songs and arias. You will know when things are right because
there will be a free flowing vibrato. If the vibrato is irregular there is a fight going on between vocal cord vibration, vocal
tract resonation, and the breath. Since [i], [y], and [u] have
the same lower resonance I advocate alternating them to find the
best resonator for them. I call this technique, "rhyming." In
rhyming vocalises the overtones change but the lower resonance
should stay the same for optimum placement and fullest sound.
See Fig. 9 a, b, and c. i, y, u (and ə); e, ø, o (and ʊ); ɛ,
œ, ɔ (and ʌ) rhyme on the Vowel Chart. Placing one of the
"rhyming" vowels helps place the others. Although Fig. 9. is of
speech, the highness of the energy is relatively the same in
singing.

The example at the top of the page shows how the three resonances of the speaking voice are affected by consonants, all of
which are included in the Sieber vocalizes--da me ni po tu
la be. [b] and [d] affect mainly R^1; [m], [n], and [l] affect
all three resonances. The vocalizes are valuable for the flexibility of pronunciation which they activate.

Rhyming.

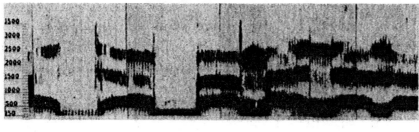

a b̠ a a d̠ a a m̠ a n̠ a a l̠ a

Fɪɢ. 3. Spectrograms of [b], [d], [m], [n], [l], showing the frequency of formant 1 rising from left to right in three steps: [b d], [m n], [l]. (Scale is disposed for reading measurements at center of formants.)

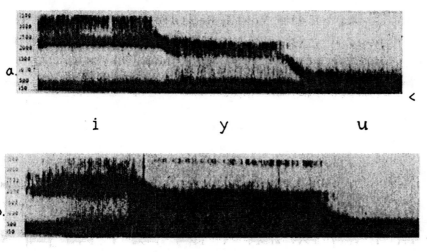

i   y   u

e   ø   o

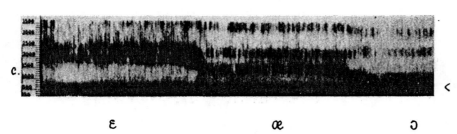

ε   œ   ɔ

Fig. 9. Spectrograms showing the lowering of formant 2 frequencies, either by lip rounding: [i]–[y], [e]–[ø], [ε]–[œ]; or by tongue backing: [y]–[u], [ø]–[o], [œ]–[ɔ]. (Scale is disposed for reading measurements at center of formants.)

From "The Physiological Interpretation of Sound Spectrograms" by Delattre. PMLA 66, 1951. Reprinted by permission of the Modern Language Association.

15

<u>Registers</u> - <u>Resonance</u> <u>Tracks</u>

The purpose of this text is to introduce ways of applying
optimum resonation to many techniques of singing. This is done
by training the phonetic relationship of vowels to sung pitch
and the register events which singers may or may not feel in
their throats. Schematics of the registers are shown with most
of the exercises. The terms of the Registers for the <u>Female</u>
<u>Voice</u> are derived from those used by the early castrati, speci-
fically, Head (H), Middle (M), and Chest (C). Acoustically I
have identified others, the Whistle, by (W). I have called the
heavily underlined diagonal the Vowel Register (V) because it
is the lower resonance, R^1, of the Vowels. The Mixed Voice I
identify with (X) and for poetic reasons I have defined the
very low Chest Register in women (K), which stands for Kellar.
(Most of this book was written in Vienna!) The register schematic for Female Voices in this text is indicated in full.

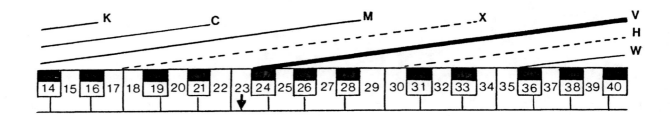

Fig. 10. Schematic of Registers for Female Voices

The terms for <u>Male</u> <u>Voice</u> are a bit more difficult. I have
called the register extending to about b♭¹ the Upper Register
(it seems a bit quaint to call it Middle although that is
traditional). The Vowel Register (V) is used for Falsetto and
full voiced close vowels on High Notes. The Mixed Voice (X)
is a mixture of Upper Voice (U) and Vowel Register (V). I
have used the term Chest (C) for the register ending at about
e♭¹. All other registers below are forms of Chest Voice. I
have used the numbers from the Chart instead of inventing
names, so the vowels on Registers 4, 5, and 6 are resonated

16

by the 4th, 5th, and 6th harmonics of sung pitch. I have used
(L) for Low Voice which seems logical.

The action of the registers is a bit like a channel. Vowels in
certain channels act in certain ways. I have indicated registers by their abbreviations over the exercises to assist in
setting up the voice. I am sure that your sense of vibration
will tell you much more about registers, channels, pipes, and
grooves. After all, what is in a name--it is the action with
which we are concerned. The schematic of registers for Male
Voices in this text is shown in full.

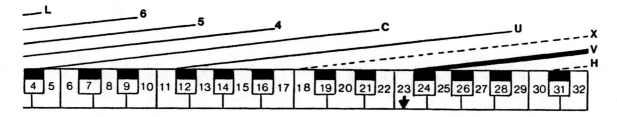

Fig. 11. Schematic of Registers for Male Voices.

It is of interest that the counter-tenor is in mid-position on
these charts, further indicating that all of human singing is
based on the same acoustical events. The human voice in toto
is a 10-track system of which each of the voice classifications
partakes in its own way. The idea is not new since it comes
directly from Manuel Garcia II, (1841), although it has recent-
ly been neglected.

Register Transitions, Track Switching

A well known deceased European teacher of singing told his singers to select a spot on the stage floor and look at it when
singing high notes. This practice has undoubtedly shortened the
careers of many fine singers. It is a single track teaching of
singing. Nothing is so boring or vocally devastating. The
acoustical nature of the voice was unknown to this person. I
have shown that there are 15 available degrees of opening of the
vocal tract, 4 Vowel Series and a 10-tract system which forms
the singing voice in toto. Switching Tracks is done like

17

yodeling (or as on a bugle, by lip slurring). And, the
yodeling can be done from the same degree of opening on one
track to the same on another. Or it can be from any of the 15
on a track to any of the 15 on another track. At the Congress
of the Collegium Medicorum Theatri in Vienna, April 21, 1979,
Dr. E. Loebell of Berne, Switzerland told me, "I even tell my
medical students that they should yodel because this is the
most hygienic thing they can do. It makes everything loose
and if you can yodel you have no difficulties with your voice,
whatsoever." Yodels allow the switching of tracks (which are
registers) with greatest ease. There are many yodels large and
small interspersed in the Exercises so that the voice is always
kept flexible.

The changes in speech can be at the rate of about 10 consonants
and vowels per second--so the voice has the ability to move
very fast. It is difficult to see all that happens. The mouth
opens and closes like the pupil of an eye, only much faster.
The opening and closure is in all directions from the center.
It is like a leaf shutter on a camera which has the same ability
to move from center position to a large opening very quickly.
In singing, when moving about 5 degrees of opening, there is an
opening of the mouth in all directions including the upper
teeth raising while the lower teeth drop. A backward head
movement gives a space in which the depressor muscles can work.
Let me say that with the vowels coded in Gold on the Chromatic
Vowel Chart, the head is raised and the jaw lowered. With those
in Blue--closed--the head lowers towards the rising chin. This
is a resonance tracking device. I have pictures of famous
singers with their heads back for high notes on open vowels.
They form a Who's Who--Caruso, Gigli, Schipa, Gedda, Tucker,
Merrill, Rysanek, Sills, Pavarotti, Sutherland, Chaliapin,
Tibbett, Nilsson, and others. With the number of TV presenta-
tions of opera being given, the teachers and singers will do
well to observe what is happening. Resonance Tracking is
occuring, hence with video tape replay closer study can be made
of how singers use the tracks or channels. Show me a singer

who sings with his head in one position and I will show you a
singer who is stuck in the throat and has a limited range. The
voice is an elastic instrument, which in singing can be based
on Chromatic Phonetics gained through various degrees of openness of the vocal tract.

CHROMATIC VOWEL CHART FOR VOICE BUILDING AND TONE PLACING

Fig. 12.

Vowel Shading for Loudest Resonance
Berton Coffin

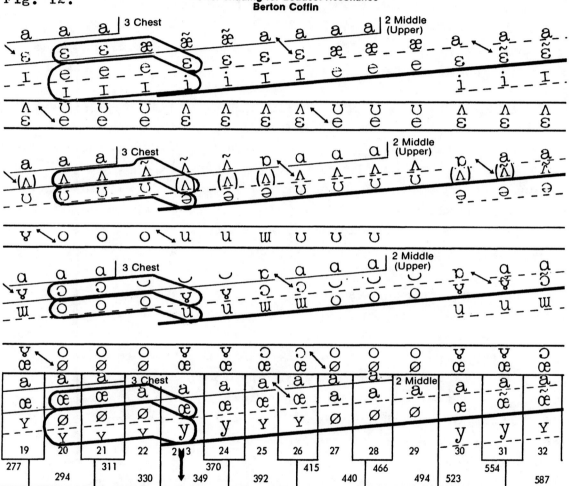

There are loops on the Chromatic Vowel Chart on Notes #20, 21,
22, and 23. This is a point of register transition in Male
Voices and in Female Voices if Chest Register is employed. In
the upper of the two loops the color is green on Notes #20 and
#21. Note #22 is in yellow and is precarious--in case of doubt
use the close form of the vowel which is on the lower loop. On

19

Notes #20, 21, and 22 are the open and close forms of vowels which exist in most languages and should be used for linguistic intelligibility. Dr. van Deinse says that in this area the thyroid cartilege and cricoid cartilege have reached their closest approximation and the change in vowel timbre is a muscular necessity. Singing in the gold, on Notes #22, 23, and 24, unless in quick runs, is fatiguing to the throat muscles. Poor transition at this passaggio has been referred to as a break. The answer is to train the mixed voice through this area which will eliminate the yodels of heavy female voices in this area and give the male voice its upper extension.

Breath Management and Resonance Tracking. The singing formed by this text is that of great International singing in which the greatest attention is paid to natural physical function. It is not related to the heavily muscular, provincial approach of fixed support with a fixed resonator which can lead only to forced resonance, impeded vibrato, and a lack of freedom. Singers of those schools speak of relaxation--they must because those approaches are overly tensed. A system built on acoustic-phonetic principles makes a highly efficient use of the breath since the cords themselves are regulators of the breath flow. As the Italians have spoken of little more than appoggio, I will have little to say on breath support other than that it is variable. It appears that as one sings up a track on the Vowel Chart there is usually an increase of breath pressure. When there is a shift from one track to another, there is also a subtle shift of breath pressure. The bulging eyes and red faces seen in male singers on Track 2 become less when a shift is made to Track 1.5, Mixed Voice. By like token, in Female Voices, the breath effort at the top of Track 1 becomes less when a shift is made to Track .67, Head Voice. In both cases the singer is in a gear which allows the voice to ascend higher with brilliance, taking the place of fatness of tone. This is somewhat like the shift from the A to the E string of a violin. The shift of harmonics is a very workable technique by which the range of vocal instruments can be extended.

Many singers have come to worship fatness of sound but most of them are singing without their "E strings," or upper register. This is destructive to the singing voice. In effect, it is the same as racing an engine at high speed instead of changing gears so that the RPM of the engine can be reduced.

On ending notes in the middle and low part of voices I have used the turn, ⸜∾ , as a device for retaining the appoggio action of the breath. It was used by William Shakespeare in the <u>Art of Singing</u>, 1921. He was a student of Francesco Lamperti. This is related to what Lamperti called <u>nota mentale</u>. He believed that a phrase should end as though there were a mental note to be heard after it. The technique is very useful when ending phrases on lower notes after fatiguing high notes. It teaches a balanced breath to the end of the phrase.

For further statements on the breathing of the various schools of singing, I recommend Richard Miller's <u>English</u>, <u>French</u>, <u>German</u> <u>and</u> <u>Italian</u> <u>Techniques</u> <u>of</u> <u>Singing</u>.

<u>Practice Procedures</u>.

- Place the arrow according to your voice classification ($\frac{1}{2}$ step above the so-called break of the voice if it is known). <u>All exercises have the note number indicated on which to begin the exercise. This is a transposing device for the different voice classifications</u>.

- <u>DO</u> TRAIN THE VOICE ON WHAT IT CAN DO. Do <u>not</u> train on what the voice cannot do.

- Think the vowel change and sing the pitch, that is all. This is unlocalized singing--free and easy if the pitches and vowels are within your physical limits. All tuners-- the tongue, jaw opening or closing, soft palate and head movement should be left free to do their tuning. Let them float. A set position is a stuck position. It is possible to say "more open or less open," "close more," etc., but it is difficult to say which element of the machine to change without upsetting the coordination.

- Practice for no more than 30 minutes at a time with intervals of rest. The maximum should be no more than three times a day.

- Keep moving from one part of the voice to another, continally changing exercises.

- Work all vowel series, continually alternating them in vocalizes so that all muscular systems of the voice will be activated; and the singing voice can quickly and effectively sing languages. Tosi (1723, p. 29), "Let him [the student] study on the three open Vowels, particularly on the first [Ah], but not always upon the same, as is practical now-a-days; in order that . . . from this frequent Exercise he may not confound one with the other, and that hence he may the easier come to the use of the Words." The practice of chromatic vowels should enable a person to sing well in all languages.

- Shade any sustained vowel if necessary so that it will resonate freely.

- Continually go from one register of the voice to another, blending them by switching tracks.

- Students can remember only two vowels at a time in vocalizes--call out to them the 2 vowel colors on which you wish them to sing. Learning will occur more quickly if they can see the symbol of the sound before they sing it--visual and aural reinforcement.

- Exercises with more than two vowels should be read by the singers while singing. They are too involved to be remembered.

- Learning will occur much more quickly if the student is encouraged to tape the lessons.

- The Exercises are in bold hand script for legibility at a distance and for a pattern of phonetic symbols which can be imitated in the singer's scoring of songs and arias for performance. (See pp. 89-94 and 157-162.)

- Never look down at music on the piano--it deprives the head of its tuning postures. Either have your music on a music stand or be seated while reading from the piano. Many teachers do this to deactivate the muscles of the legs and to call more upon the muscles of the chest and torso.

- Sing the moving part of exercises twice so that the voice will have a chance to correct itself. For example --

●●● Allow the sensors of the throat to do their work!

F

CHAPTER II

THE FEMALE VOICE

Registers of the Female Voice. Mathilde Marchesi (1905 p. iii)
said "This (the registers) is the Alpha and Omega of the formation and development of the female voice, the touchstone of all
singing methods, old and new." She was Professor of singing
in Vienna 1854-61 and 1868-78. 1869 is memorable because it
was the year in which the Vienna State Opera opened. I believe
she was the first teacher of singing in the Vienna Conservatory
although she is best known for her famous school in Paris. She
was the most emminent teacher of female voices of all time.
She stated "Unfortunately, it is owing to this ignorance of the
limits and the treatments of these three registers of the female
voice that there are so many imperfectly trained singers, who
struggle against the faults and difficulties of a mechanism
wrongly used, and so many unequal voices, which possess sets of
weak and heterogeneous tones, commonly called breaks. These
breaks, however, are only tones wrongly placed and produced."
This text shows how the various registers can be strengthened
and equalized. It is all a matter of playing games with different overtones which have been clearly defined in Chapter V
in this book. The procedures herein are definitive and vital
ways in which to place the voice in vibration and resonance.
Singers will understand more than ever before that the larynx
and the resonators form a single system and that they work together or fight each other, depending on how the singer relates them.

What is a register? It is a variable position which will make
the harmonic diagonals on the Chromatic Vowel Chart. Each has
its own particular quality which can be sensed by the singer
and listener. The Vowel Register is uniquely metallic, the

23

F

Head Voice is noticeabley "fluty." The Chest Register is strong
and masculine. The Mixed Voice is a combination of the Middle
Register and the Vowel Register and has a timbre of its own.
Marchesi did not teach the Whistle Register although her student
Emma Calvé used it, having learned it from one of the Castrati,
Mustafa (Pleasants, 1966, p. 304). They are all here for your
use, I hope you enjoy them!

Open Your Mouth Correctly! Mancini (1777, p. 89) made a statement, "...it is very important for him who wishes to sing to
know how to open the mouth; because upon the opening of the
mouth depends the clearness of the voice." Does this mean that
he wished to have a clear tone or a pure Italian vowel--they are
not synonymous! He later said, "I have finally fixed a general
rule . . . every pupil must shape his mouth for singing, just as
he shapes it when he smiles. The upper teeth show a little and
are slightly separated from the lower ones." He indicated that
the exaggerated opening of the mouth gives a voice which is
throaty, since the fauces are under strain, and lacking in clearness and facility. He said the person would sing " . . . with
a suffocated, crude and heavy quality." This approach is discussed on page 84.

Sundberg (1974) has shown that the opening for vowels changes
with pitch for optimum resonation. In my experience I have
found that when the degree of openness of the mouth is allowed
to adjust to resonate sung pitch the voice is clearer and the
vibrato will spin. There is in effect sympathetic resonation
with less breath effort required of the singer. I have found
that the vocal tract has 15 usable degrees of openness which
are shown on page 27. It is a marvelous page to warm up on
(page 101 for Male Voices). Keep moving around on the page and
kinesthetically sense the vibration.

F

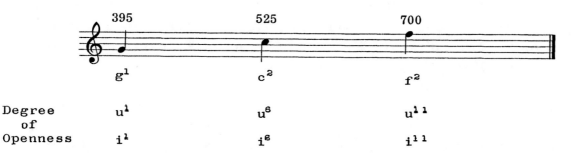

F_0 IHzI   395   525   700

Fig. 13. Photos of the lip opening of a soprano singing the
          vowels (u) and (i) (upper and lower series) at the
          fundamental frequencies (F_0) indicated. The lip and
          jaw opening are seen to increase with rising funda-
          mental frequency. Sundberg 1977. <u>Music Room and
          Acoustics.</u>
                                          Timbre" by Johan Sundberg.
                                          Reprinted by permission of
                                          the author.

395   525   700

g^1 c^2 f^2

Degree u^1 u^6 u^{11}
  of
Openness i^1 i^6 i^{11}

In my observations [u] with the 6th degree of opening sounds
like [ɤ] and [u] with the 11th degree of opening sounds like
[ʊ]. [i] with the 6th degree of opening sounds like [ɛ] and
[i] with the 11th degree of opening sounds like [æ]. Either the
degrees of opening or the vowel color can be used by the singer.

The same phenomena exist for all voices in the same locations
when the Chromatic Vowel Chart is set properly for the singer's
voice classification. However, if the voice does not center in
on the resonance, there is a probability the singer's voice
classification is incorrect and the arrow of the Chart should
be moved. In case of doubt, place the arrow a little lower.

The Use of Chromatic Phonetics. One of the best ways to
establish resonance of the singing voice (placement) is to
rhyme all vowels of the same degree of openness which have
been coded green, gold and blue on the keyboard sized Vowel
Chart. Vowels in green have been notated on Passaggio Lines I
and II. The complete list of rhymes is indicated here. Do
not rhyme the 16th, 17th and 18th degree of opening on high
notes. To find the bright Ah [a], precede with [j]. To find
[α], precede with [w].

Space Chart. Tune the indicated vowels on charted pitches to
find correct space. DO NOT SUPERIMPOSE SOME SET SPACE CONCEPT
ON THE THROAT. The vowel timbre and sense of feel will tell
when the microscopic tuning of resonance is optimal--that can
be remembered. A voice with a set position is out of tune and
out of resonance, like an organ rank with only one size of pipe
for all notes. The same size resonator for all vowels is false
according to acoustical phonetics. Degrees of openness are
gained by movements of the lips, tongue, jaw, soft palate and
head. They should be allowed to move as they wish.

Breath. When the best resonance is heard and felt the singer
will notice that less breath pressure is required. He should
hold back on the breath. This is the famous lutte vocale or
"vocal struggle" of which Francesco Lamperti (1890, p. 33)
spoke. Forced resonance requires a forced breath pressure.
Sympathetic resonance is part of a self sustaining oscillatory
system (Benade 1977, p. 360).

Couplings. All of the vowels of the same degree of opening
couple with the possible exception of the Back Front group in
the last column of Fig. 14. 26

F

Fig. 14. Rhyming-Tone Placing Chart
by Degrees of Openness

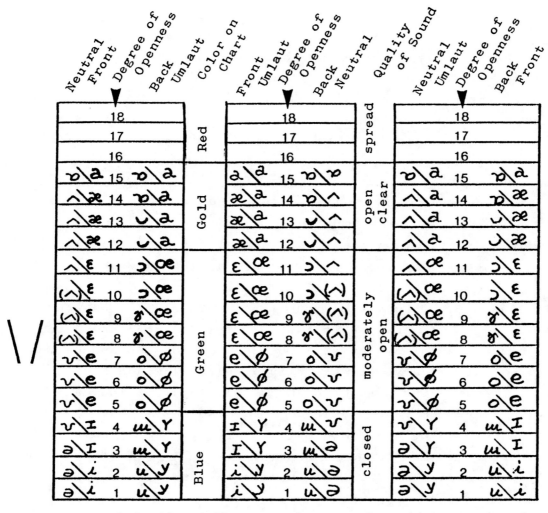

Yodel back and forth on the same degree of opening on the Chart
below--continually changing tessitura.

Place the arrow on the correct note for your voice classification.

The Nature of Vowels. There is a "medieval" concept that vowels are somewhat like a colored paint that can be spread on any sung pitch indiscriminately. It has long been known that such is not the case! Sundberg has shown that when vowel resonances are set on a computer and a soprano scale is run with the vowel resonances staying the same, the vowel color will change to the ear. When [u] and [i] come to the top of a scale they change in quality to a mousey sound which singing teachers know as whistle register. When the lower resonance is run to match the pitch, the "voice" becomes louder, changes vowel quality and the high notes become a bit shrill. Singing teachers say they should be rounded--or the mouth slightly closed. In ascending scales resonators must open to match pitch--in descending they must close, so I will use symbols to indicate the manner of opening and closing of vowels in the exercises. \\// indicates that the vowels open in ascending and close in descending. //\\ indicates that the vowels close in ascending and switch tracks.)(indicates the exercise is narrow in the middle and wide at the top and bottom. () indicates the vowels are closed on the low and high notes and more open in the middle. || indicates the vowels are the same opening. ⁊\ indicates the top note opens and closes before descending. /\ indicates the lower note closes and opens before or after going up. \/ indicates the lower note opens and closes before or after going up. In long scales there are double openings }} and closings or double closings and openings. }{ These concepts of opening and closing }{ will be helpful in your exercises, songs and arias, and will almost become automated in your singing. With the televising and video taping of outstanding singers these actions can be studied in slow motion and stop frame. Observe the phenomena of tuning which comes about by a combination of ear and kinesthetic feel of the throat. When this is done leading singers become great enough to sing in the large halls and over heavy accompaniment.

F

Sing Resonant Vowels on the Same Pitch (spelling). Sing vowels
on the same pitch while slowly spelling vertical columns to find
loud and easy resonance. Test by moving lips, jaw and tongue
microscopically to find the center of resonance. Memorize the
vowel color and the pitch to place that note in your voice. The
sensations of the mucous membrane of your vocal tract will tell
you the best placement. Sing other vertical columns on the Vowel
Chart. Continuously change vowel series and pitches. Turn on
the vowels to help find the center of resonance--indicated by
∞.   Alternate with scalewise and arpeggio exercises.

> Place the arrow on the proper note for your voice classification.
> Go by note numbers and musical design and <u>not</u> by the notes
> written. The note numbers are a transposing device for the
> different voice classifications.

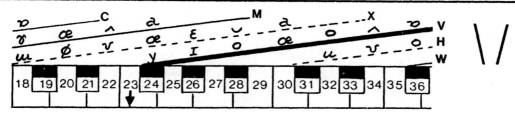

Nota Bene: Spell from the top down on Note #30 and below, and
             from the bottom up above Note #30!

a - as the first sound in l<u>ig</u>ht
ɒ - as in f<u>a</u>ther
℧ - is between [ɔ] and [ɒ]
ɤ - is between [o] and [ɔ]
ɯ - is between [u] and [o]

SW - Super Whistle Register
 W - Whistle Register
 H - Head Register
 V - Vowel Register
 X - Mixed Register
 M - Middle Register
 C - Chest Register

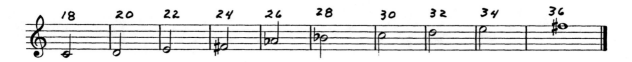

29

Resonance Tracking or Piping--Middle Voice. Leap to the lower
vowel and pitch in the exercise to know its placement before
singing the passage to and from it. The vowel series have been
changed from exercise to exercise. Front Vowels only make the
voice harsh. Back Vowels only make the voice hooty. Continually change vowel series in vocalization.

Vocal cords cannot have a strong, free and easy swing unless
there is the momentum of regular vibration. Irregular vibration or barking sounds are injurious to the vocal cords and
will not penetrate the orchestral screen.

The arrow ↓ or ↑ is a fail-safe device for reminding the
singer in which direction the exercises are written. When sung
in the wrong direction the exercises will misplace the voice.
After singing as written, then reverse the direction.

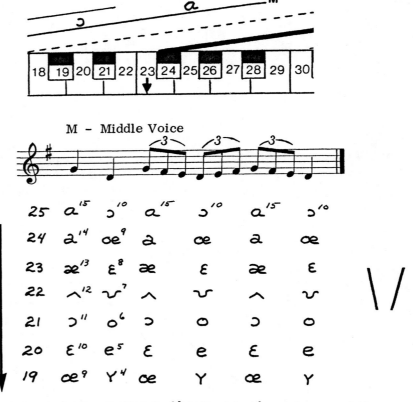

Go by the note number on your Chart at the piano with arrow in
proper position for your voice classification.

F

Resonance Tracking--Middle Voice, Variations.

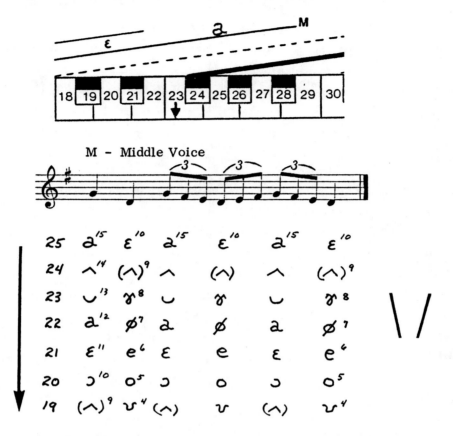

M - Middle Voice

Exercises crossing from one Vowel Series to another.

Say only the first two vowels to the singer, then play the
notes. If the lesson is recorded, the singer can then practice
with the tape. This can be done on all one or two-vowel
exercises.

31

F

<u>Coordinating the Chest and Laryngeal Muscles</u>. In Tomograms of
the larynx the vocal cords look like wedges. They have an intrinsic musculature which can make them very firm. When this is
done the voice assumes a bright metallic sound since the "vocal
wedges" touch and make short, discrete puffs--very much like
puffs from the lips of brass instrumentalists. The cords are
also capable of waving at each other in such a way as to make
fluty sounds. Both laryngeal techniques should be taught and
used in singing.

First I will give a Garcia type exercise for the firm sounds.
Beginning on the vowels "ah" and "eh" as in the words "alma,
sempre" attack the vowels on one note beginning on Note #14.
Proceed note by note as high as Note #20. This will bring about
the ringing quality characteristic of these notes because the
lips of the vocal cords are brought in close contact by the
sphincter action in the larynx. These "happy attacks" should
be practiced for one or two minutes at a time, but can be repeated two or three times a day. (Based on Garcia, 1911,
p. 14.) This can be carried higher in other registers.

I have found that short, vigorous actions of the arms as though
striking timpani while singing the indicated vowels will assist
in giving nerve impulse and coordination of the muscles of the
chest and of the larynx. In such a manner sing the following
vowels on the Note numbers and registers indicated.

14	ɑ ɛ ɑ ɛ	18	ɣ ɛ	22	ʊ æ	25	ɔ ɛ
15	ʊ æ ʊ æ	19	ɣ ɛ	23	ʌ æ	26	ɔ ɛ
16	ʌ ɑ ʌ ɑ	20	ɔ ɛ	24	ʊ æ	27	ʊ æ
17	ʊ æ ʊ æ	21	ɔ ɛ			28	ʌ ɑ
	Chest		Middle			Mixed	

Alternate this with exercises on p. 35. These opposites are
the basis of dramatic and lyric contrasts in singing.

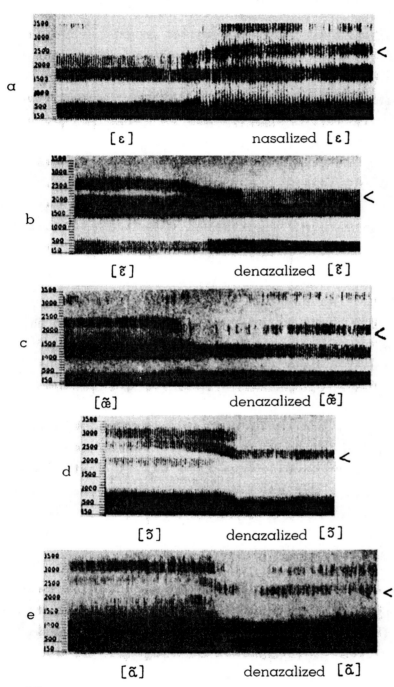

a   [ɛ]   nasalized [ɛ]

b   [ɛ̃]   denazalized [ɛ̃]

c   [œ̃]   denazalized [œ̃]

d   [ɔ̃]   denazalized [ɔ̃]

e   [ɑ̃]   denazalized [ɑ̃]

Fig. 15. Spectrograms showing the 300 cycle shift of formant 3 when the velum is lowered (from left to right) as in *a*, or raised as in *b, c, d, e*, all other organs being kept as immobile as possible. (Scale is disposed for reading measurements at center of formants.)

Nasality.

Example a. shows that the vowel [ɛ] when nasalized has a <u>higher</u> 3rd resonance and a <u>weaker</u> 1st resonance in speech.

Example b. shows that the French vowel [ɛ] when denasalized as in English or Italian has a <u>lower</u> 3rd resonance and a <u>stronger</u> first resonance.

Examples c, d, and e show the same occurrences when the French vowels [œ̃], [ɔ̃], and [ɑ̃] are denasalized.

This is of great value to male and female singers in their upper passaggios and allows them to shift from the resonance used in the center of their voices to that of their higher notes. The following nasal exercises are given to assist in these transitions.

Further explanation can be found on pp. 37 and 193.

From "The Physiological Interpretation of Sound Spectrograms" by Delattre. PMLA 66, 1951. Reprinted by permission of the Modern Language Association.

<u>Development of the Head Voice Register--Whistle.</u>
There are several reasons for training the Whistle and Super
Whistle in the Female Voice. Most important is the necessity
of establishing a mechanism to hold up the other end of the
bridge at the passaggio. This bridge turns out to be Head
Voice on Track .67. This register is a bit like an overdrive
and allows the singer to have an extension of range as the overdrive gives an extension of speed without burning out the car's
motor. This extension gives the high C^1s and D^1s to sopranos
and the highest register to lyric and coloratura sopranos. The
highest classifications should not be striven for. The way the
voice responds will show what the eventual classification will
be, not the determination of a singer or the pre-programming of
a teacher of singing.

<u>Vowel Behind the Hand.</u> "Do not hum but sing as though you are
humming with your mouth open" is one of the most familiar of the
G.B. Lamperti quotations (1931, p. 104). Place the palm of the
hand (or back of the hand) over a small opening of the mouth and
sing the indicated vowel. (u) means to sing the [u] behind the
hand. Likewise the (i) and (y). The small ʰ indicates that
the sound should begin with a small puff of air through the nose.
My X-ray motion picture studies show that the tongue takes the
vowel positions behind the hand. This is a way of training nasality and tongue positions for Head Voice. There will be a much
smaller sound and resonator in the Super Whistle which begins on
Note #42. Lily Pons brought the teeth close together for this
register.

This register was called the Flageolet by Anna Lankow of Berlin
(1902) and <u>voce di capelli</u> (voice of the hair) by Rossini who
did not like the quality. It is related to the upper sound of
those who use the two register approach to singing. It should
be related to vowels and the intervening registers used by
classical schools of singing in developing seamless scales.
There is also the Super Whistle which extends to c^4 in some
voices. The intervals of the beginning of each of the registers is harmonic.

F

Whistle Register--The Preparation for Head Voice. Whistle while pronouncing vowels behind the hand.

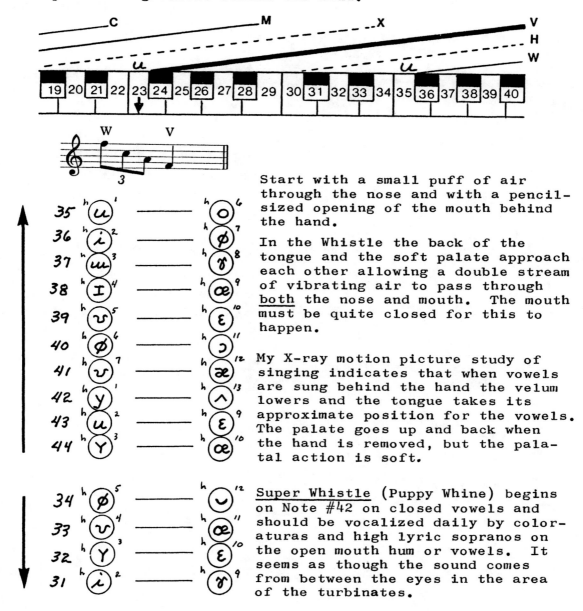

Start with a small puff of air through the nose and with a pencil-sized opening of the mouth behind the hand.

In the Whistle the back of the tongue and the soft palate approach each other allowing a double stream of vibrating air to pass through both the nose and mouth. The mouth must be quite closed for this to happen.

My X-ray motion picture study of singing indicates that when vowels are sung behind the hand the velum lowers and the tongue takes its approximate position for the vowels. The palate goes up and back when the hand is removed, but the palatal action is soft.

Super Whistle (Puppy Whine) begins on Note #42 on closed vowels and should be vocalized daily by coloraturas and high lyric sopranos on the open mouth hum or vowels. It seems as though the sound comes from between the eyes in the area of the turbinates.

Variation: While singing vowels behind the hand when coming down from the highest notes, switch to the green vowels in Head Voice, the green vowels on the Vowel Register of the Chart, and the green vowels in Mixed Voice.

F

Resonance Tracking, Vowel Register Exercises on the Same Vowel
Series.

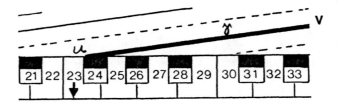

Sing the indicated vowel
behind the hand to feel the
vibration in the turbinates.
Remove the hand quickly to
hear the vowel, then pro-
ceed with the exercise,
nasalizing the upper note
in the passage. Exposed
notes in runs should be
tuned in <u>both</u> pitch and
resonance.

Alternate with the vowels
in the exercises on the
opposite page.

Improvise similar vocalizes
on the Vowel Register from
the Chromatic Vowel Chart.
Make singing a musical
language.

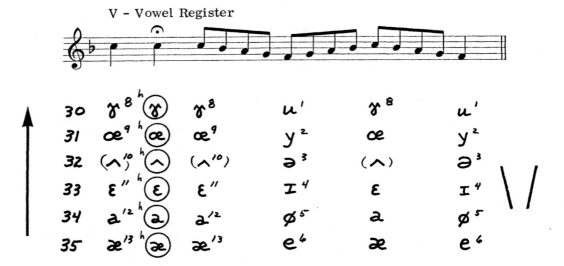

If the arrow is placed too high on the piano for your voice it
will close too late. If it is too low the voice will close too
soon. It is better to have it too low than too high.

F

<u>Resonance Tracking--Crossover Exercises on the Vowel Register.</u>

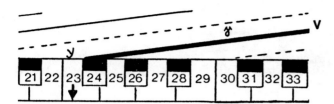

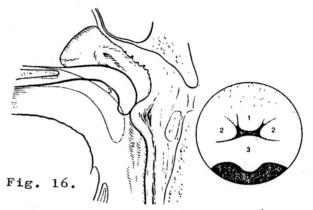

From STIMME UND SPRACHE by
Günter Habermann, © 1978,
Georg Thieme Verlag. Re-
printed by permission of
the publisher.

When vowels are sung against the palm or back of the hand <u>with the mouth open</u>, the soft palate is forced to open to the lower position. In this position the pillars of the fauces (2) and the soft palate and uvula (3) can be trained to move upward and downward, and the air stream can be taught to divide through both the nose and mouth in singing when necessary. This opening facilitates the high notes, is necessary for the French Nasals and in <u>sotto voce</u> when the vowel tract is reduced in size. Hold hand over the mouth long enough to hear and feel the high vibration in the turbinates then remove hand, keeping that memory of vibration in the tone. This is education of the soft palate.

Fig. 16.

(Haberman after Tarneaud.)

Illustration of Nasal and Denasalized Sound. 1. Passavant cushion, 2. Pillars of the fauces, 3. Soft palate and uvula.

37

F

Low Notes for Female Voices (and Counter-Tenors).   Chest

Voice.

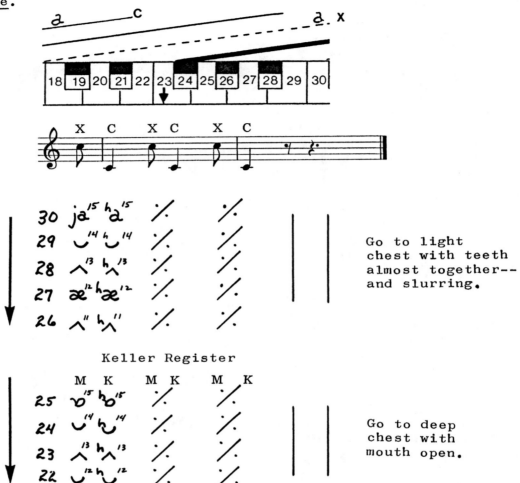

Also yodel other vowels at the octave, working primarily with
vowels in gold. The low notes are most sonorous on back vowels.
Alternate the high and low positions on the low note to train
the full and smaller sounds of chest voice.

Alternate between these two pages--to establish the chest register and to blend it with the registers above.

F

Contrast of Low Larynx Chest Sound and High Larynx Chest Sound.
Transitions to and from Chest and Keller Registers.

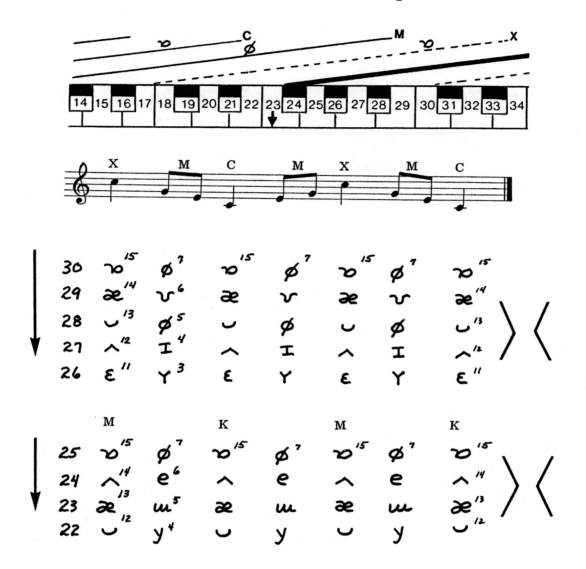

This exercise teaches the singer to protect the register change
with the lips.

Keep the Chest Voice <u>up</u> (↑) in the first low note and give the
low larynx chest sound (↓) on the last note.

F

Strengthening the harmonics and musculature of the Mixed Voice.
Know where you are going before you get there. On the same note
sing the first vowel and then the second which is the opening at
the bottom of the run. Then sing the run. Sing other exercises
on different vowel series on the Chromatic Vowel Chart.

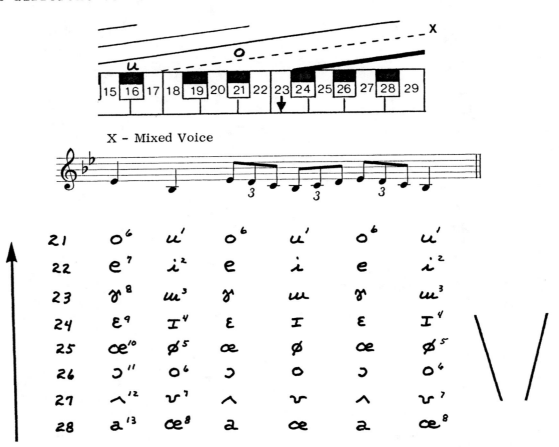

X - Mixed Voice

Keep the Mixed Voice more closed than marked or it will be un-
stable and not be compressed enough.

The voix mixte register exists in Male and Female Voices in the
same place on the Vowel Chart, between the Middle and the Vowel
Register. This is the reason Mezzo Sopranos and Tenors sound
alike on these same notes. It is the same register.

F

Strengthen the Central Area of the Female Voice by Training the Mixed Voice. The same exercise crossing over between various vowel series.

X - Mixed Voice

"In studying Italian vocal scores we are forced to the conclusion that in the days of the Old Masters the 'voix mixte' was cultivated to an extremely high degree; it would have been impossible, otherwise, for singers to make use of their high range as continually and skillfully as was called for, and yet have remained active in their art at what in our time seems a remarkable age. Nowadays, when the art of using the 'voix mixte' belongs, apparently, to the realm of fable, we can harly find a singer capable of interpreting the old Italian compositions; we overcome this difficulty simply by contemptuously shrugging our shoulders at 'Italian acrobatic feats,' and content ourselves with bellowing out high tones with as much dignity as possible. Only a few seem to appreciate that the modern dearth of brilliant tenor voices is to be sought in the non-cultivation of the 'voix mixte.'" August Iffert of Dresden, Germany as translated by Lankow (1902, p. 37).

F

<u>Yodels at the Fourth with Whistle Register.</u> Yodel downward
from Whistle on the same vowels and same mouth opening.

Yodel on the same
degree of opening.

Yodel on the same
degree of opening.

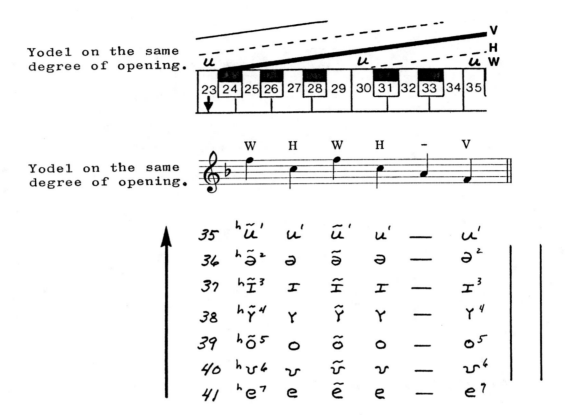

"From the physiological and phoniatric viewpoints it may be
said that correctly formed yodeling represents a natural use
of the voice. A good yodeling style cannot harm the vocal
organ. Similar to any other vocal performances, yodeling may
be produced correctly or with faulty technique. Most of the
yodelers studied in the course of these investigations were
excellent artists. Several of them had performed for 25 or 30
years without ever suffering from vocal disorder....yodeling
belongs among the physiologically natural styles of artistic
singing." Luchsinger (Switzerland) and Arnold, p. 110.

A dimple forms under the larynx in the Whistle because of the a
action of the oblique crico-thyroid muscle, see p. 186.

F

<u>Yodels at the Fourth with Whistle Register.</u> Yodel downward from
Whistle on different vowels with the same degree of opening.

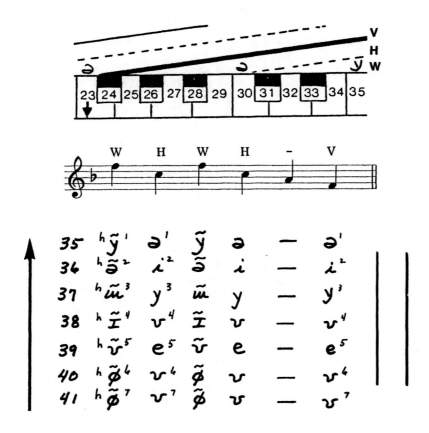

The larynx raises and lowers somewhat for pitch and for vowel.
In the case of a yodel on the same vowel the mouth position
will remain in very nearly the same position but the larynx
will be found to make slight adjustments in height for pitch.
This is excellent for training a flexible positioning of the
larynx and for the changing of registers. The vowels and
pitches given have harmonic relationships.

43

F

<u>Dimple Falsetto to Head Voice</u>. <u>Build the Head Voice</u>.

Marchesi, the famous teacher of female voices, said that sopranos should enter head voice at f#^{2}. Stratton (1966) described Marchesi's students as using "blown tone." Head Voice
sounds like a flute tone and has air in it. Feel as though you
are blowing across the embouchure of a flute--also feel as
though you are blowing your nose at the same time. Obtain
this by inhaling through both nose and mouth at the same time
in a double pronged inhalation. This register is sung with
half a dimple under the larynx--both crico-thyroid muscles being
used. The careers of Marchesi's singers were so long that they
did not have enough time left to learn how to teach their art.
Thus they were unable to hand down their tradition.

F

Vowel Register to Head Register Transitions.

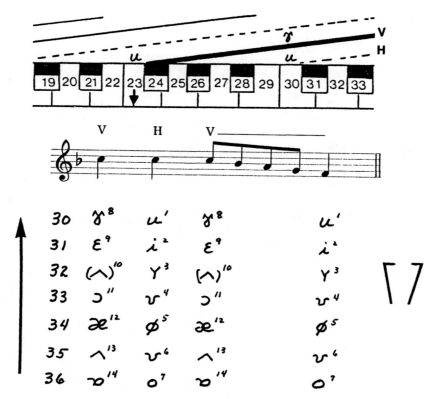

Close to go to Head Voice. When descending on Vowel Register go
from open to more close.

Use dimple falsetto on the second note.

I am of the opinion that vocal masters of the past were listening to the play of overtones in the voices which they were
training--it is they who developed the term, "registers." And,
I know that better and faster results are obtained when a somnambulistic approach is taken in this acoustical type of singing rather than a rational, analytical, or intellectual one. To
some singers vocalizing in this manner is their form of daily
meditation. It sensitizes the thresholds of perception. Teaching by overtones leads more towards the art than the science of
singing. It is the intuitive which inspires, not the mechanistic.

45

F

Yodels between Mixed, Vowel and Head Registers. The same vowel appears a 5th below and a 5th above the Vowel Register. The 5th below finds and develops the Mixed Voice; the 5th above finds and develops the Head Voice.

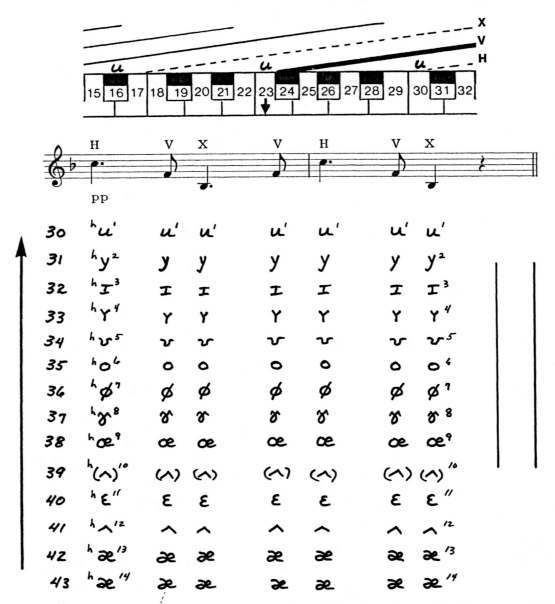

Variation: Begin exercises on the third note--singing upward from the lowest note.

F

Embellished Yodels between Mixed, Vowel, and Head Registers.
The longer exercise crosses over between varied vowel series
for continuation of tone. Practice lightly and fast. This
will build the Head Voice and facilitate register transitions.
Blowing the breath in Head Voice has the effect of reducing
breath pressure. This helps the tone to spin.

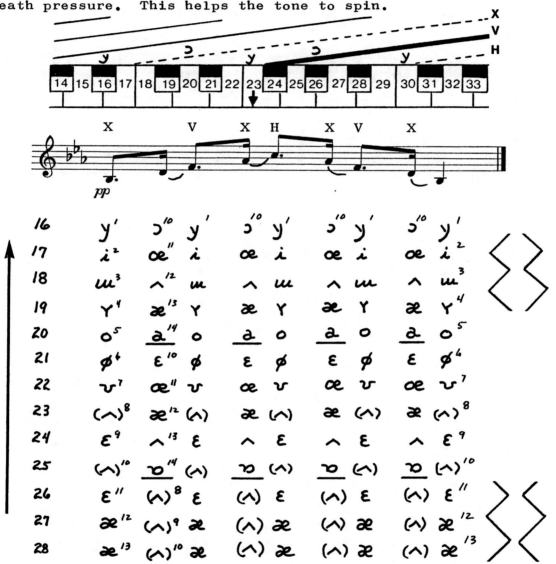

Notice: There is a register change below the underlined vowels.
Repronounce and have a feeling of disconnection between the short and long notes.

F

Resonance Tracking in Arpeggios.

Close the Vowel between the lower and the upper notes. This
exercise is especially helpful in narrowing or collecting the
lower passaggio. See Martinelli's statement p. 108.

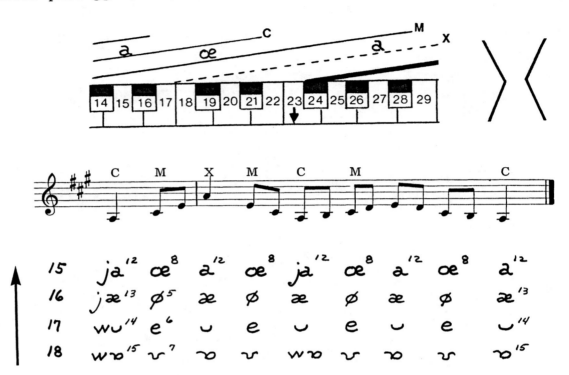

Also blend the low voice by arpeggios in a descending progression.

Also sing from Mixed Voice to Chest Voice in the arpeggio by
beginning after the bar. Touch the Chest Voice lightly so
that the voice will have an easy transition to Middle Voice
and back in the five note run.

F

Bridging the Mixed and Chest Voice.

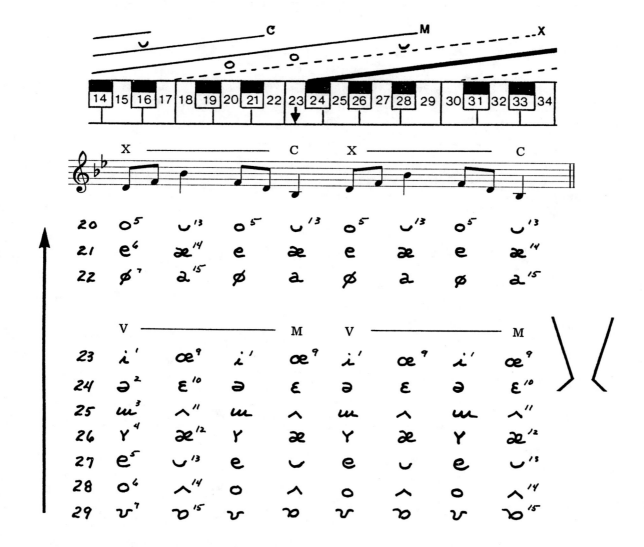

Think the gold vowels in the mouth.

Use opposite phonetics and exercises. Move from page to page
and jump from one note number to another instead of always moving half step by half step up and down the scale. The number
of sequences in music is rarely more than three--this would be
a good principle to follow in exercises. Use contrasts in forming and training the voice.

49

F

Register Transitions in Lower Passaggio. Strengthening the
lower passaggio. Narrow at bottom and top, wide in the middle.

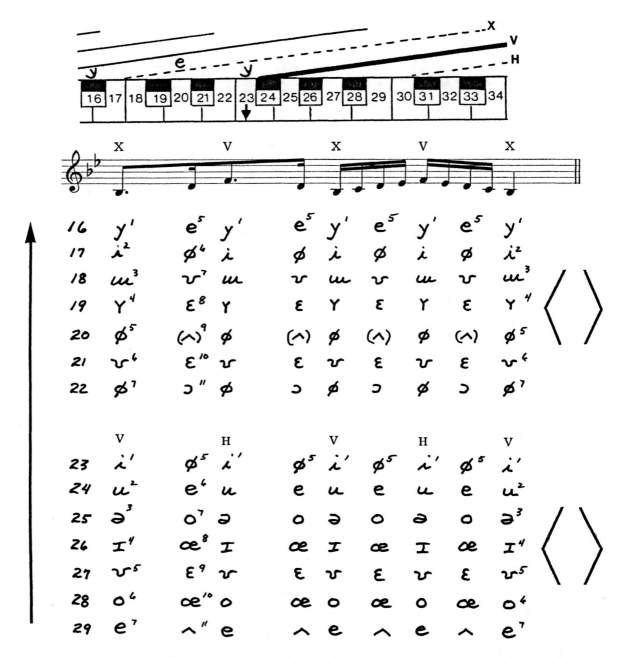

Alternate these with the "open-close-open" exercises on opposite
page.

F

Register Transitions--Favorable Vowels. Narrow in middle, more open at the top and bottom.

Alternate these with the "close-open-close" exercises on opposite page.

F

Strengthen the Lower Passaggio by Switching Tracks. On the same vowel series, switch tracks and make a transition from the Vowel Register through the Mixed Voice to the Chest Register. These switches of tracks in the voice are similar to lip slurs between modes of vibration on brass instruments. Become very flexible in these subtle changes to avoid a big "break" and to give a smooth line. There are small yodels between each of these notes.

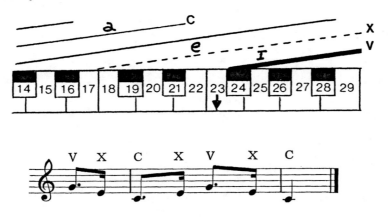

(The heavy lines indicate that there is a register change.)

Vibrator and resonator (source and system) are <u>one</u>; train them both and most aspects of the voice will synchronize. This means that the interaction of the resonator and the vibrator seems to take care of the air flow and the registers.

F

Strengthen the Lower Passaggio--Varied Vowel Series. Go to a
low position of the larynx on the first low note and then keep
the last note up--train two colors. Tilt the head back to help
the chest notes on vowels which have 11 to 15 degrees of opening. Strengthen the passaggio to chest voice by switching
tracks while crossing between varied vowel series.

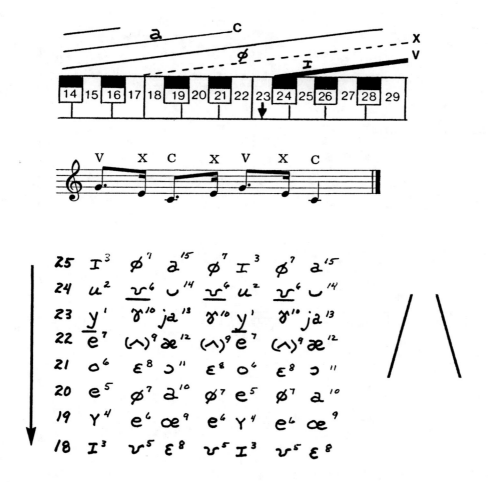

Keep the Chest Voice "up" in the first low note and give the
low larynx chest sound on the last note. Develop both colors
of voice. The lower chest sound is easier in medium and low
voices and is used for dramatic effect and over heavy orchestra-
tion. It is not used as much in the high voices but should be
developed nevertheless for their "dramatic" sound.

F

Equalizing Registers.   Strengthening the Vowel and Head Registers by yodels of the twelfth on the same vowels.   Although the vowels are the same, the vocal tract will shift slightly because of pitch.

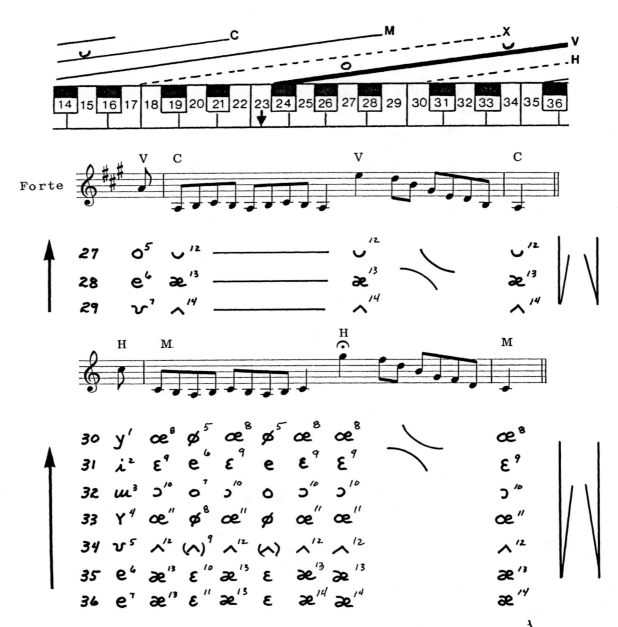

Protect the vowel by slightly closing in descending
This hides the subtle register changes which occur—watch this
in the good singers.

54

F

Equalize the Registers--develop Head Voice.

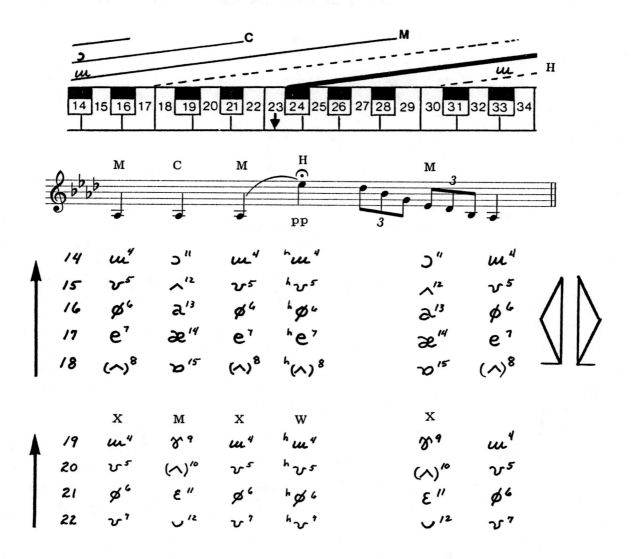

Change dynamics by changing registers. Get into the stratosphere by using whistle voice.

F

Resonance Tracking on the Vowel Register--same Vowel Series.
Voice amplification and placement by resonance tracking in descending patterns on the same vowel series. Create other vowel sequences for yourself from the Chromatic Vowel Chart.

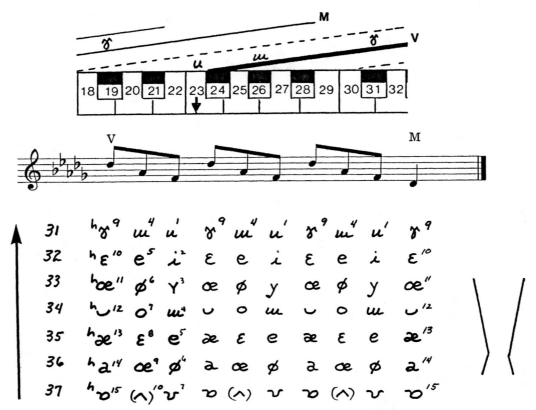

Head Voice. Sing the first three vowels behind the hand to shorten the velopharyngeal axis. Ease up on the breath. When the turbinates are vibrating it feels like the notes are being sung between the eyes.

Variation: Reverse the last four notes and repeat.

56

F

Register Tracking on the Vowel Register--Alternating Vowel
Series. Voice amplification and placement with various vowel
series to give best continuity of tone.

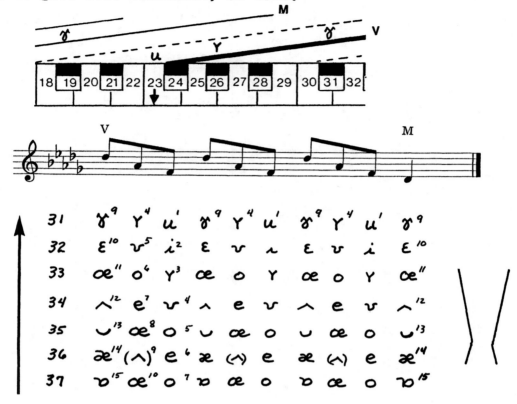

Head Voice. Allow air to vibrate both in the mouth and in the
turbinates. Start with a smaller position and a slight h.

Variation: Reverse the last four notes and repeat.

Develop reflex of closing the resonator in descending.

F

Strengthen the Female Middle Voice--same Vowel Series. These
exercises are constructed so there is more pinch of the glottis
at the lower part of the exercise. This should be practiced
daily by all female voices from coloraturas to contraltos.

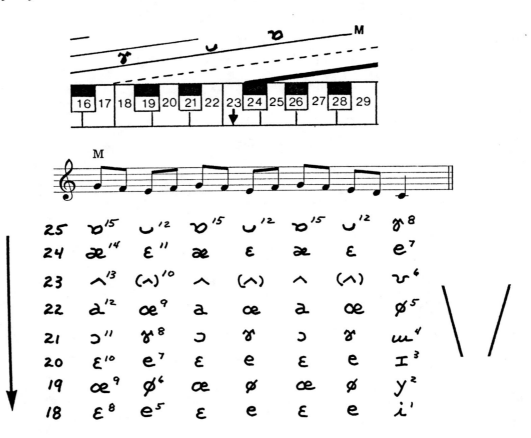

Watch a mirror to see the play of the lips, jaw, and tongue to
assist the tunings of the vocal tract to become automatic.
Also sing in minor keys.

"The inner muscles of the larynx (those directly connected with
the action of the vocal cords) cannot function properly and
freely in producing vibration and pitch of the voice until the
outer muscles of throat and neck are busy with pronunciation of
word and resonance of tone....These inside muscles are compell-
ed to do double duty if the outside muscles connecting the head
with torso do not know and perform their allotted work."

G.B. Lamperti, p. 41.

F

Strengthen the Female Middle Voice--Alternating Vowel Series.
The Female Middle Voice needs to be strengthened daily--many
have only a gasp in this Register. This is probably due to an
abuse of Chest Voice in speech, in pop, yelling, heavy breath
support, pushed singing or simply a lack of development.

Keep the sternum up for the last note. Do not go into Chest
Voice. Train the voice in both ways to strengthen the Middle
Voice and to have Chest Voice when it is desired. Aesthetics
vary from country to country and in various types of music.

Variation: reverse the last bar.

As you come down an overtone diagonal on the Chart, the vowel
becomes smaller and smaller.

59

F

Piping on Augmented Triad, Whole Tone, and Chromatic Scales.
Resonance tracking on the same Track and the same Vowel Series--
gives a continuous vibration of the lower resonance. Vowels are
usually different at the interval of a Major 3rd on the Chromatic Vowel Scale. After the Augmented Triad and Whole Tone
Scales have been sung, heard and felt, fill in the half steps
to hear and feel the subtle gradations in the Chromatic Vowel
Scale. Chromatic phonetics are a necessity to the singer--
linguistic phonetics in singing cause atrocious sounds and problems. I have warned of this in the Foreword of Phonetic Readings of Songs and Arias which was published 15 years ago. Now
I can tell the singer what should be done to make the best
wedding of language and music. In the process, this is a discipline which will build a healthy and beautiful voice. Exercises on Notes #18-22 are in Mixed Voice. Exercises from
Notes #31-36 are on the Vowel Register. When sung well the
exercises feel like a gentle massage.

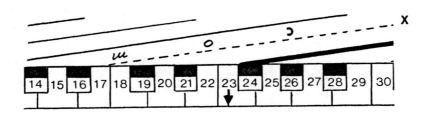

60

F

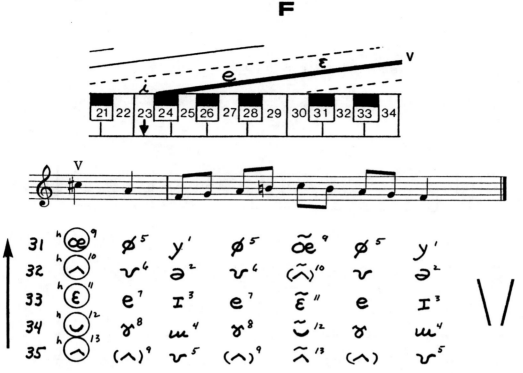

Alternate singing ascending and descending exercises. Ascending passages will tend to carry up weight, descending passages will tend to bring the lighter quality down into the voice.

Variation: Begin exercise after the bar.

Educate the senses of vowel color, the feel of vibration, and the degrees of opening--this text is written for the senses.

F

Run between Head, Vowel, and Mixed Register Resonances--Favor-
Vowels on the exposed notes. Sing _mezzo voce_.

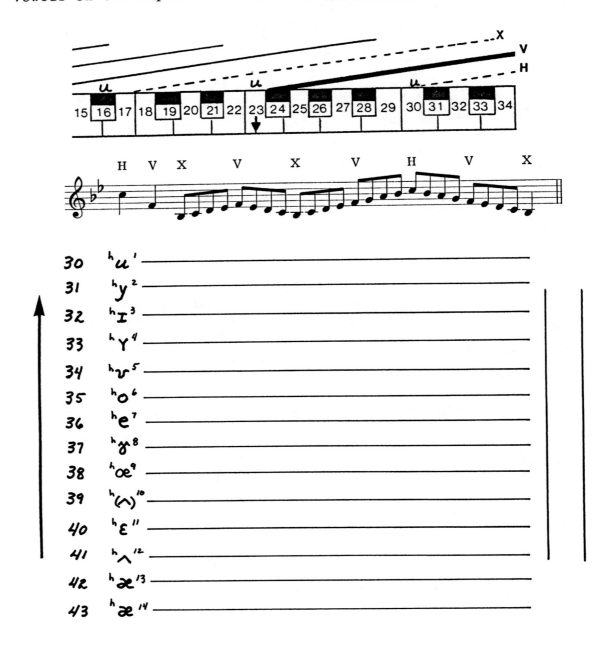

In singing the runs go between the same vowels on the exposed
notes. Memorize the feel.

F

Run on the Resonance, then run to the tuned Resonance of the
High Notes. Sing legato and also repronounce the vowels in
such a way that they almost detach.

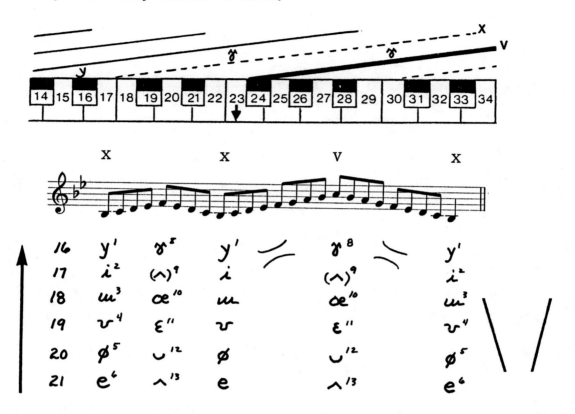

It is impossible to tune the resonance to sung pitch on every
note--but exposed notes which need emphasis can be brought out
simply by tuning the resonance with a favorable vowel. Otherwise the voice feels like it is drifting about and is insecure.
Between the exposed notes the resonance can usually be allowed
to make a gradual change in the degrees of openings indicated.

63

F

Strengthening the Mixed Voice in the Lower Passaggio--Piping.
Place and strengthen the Mixed Register while resonance tracking on the same Vowel Series. Allow the vowel on the 3rd to
find its place by feel.

Notes #31-37 place and strengthen the Vowel Register while
resonance tracking on the same Vowel Series. Sing others from
the Vowel Chart.

Variations: Segment and repeat different parts of the exercise.

64

F

Place and Strengthen the Mixed Voice. Crossover exercises between various vowel series.

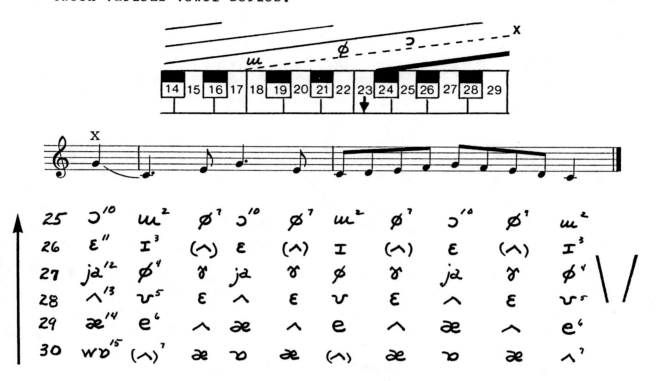

25	ɔ¹⁰	ɯ²	ø⁷	ɔ¹⁰	ø⁷	ɯ²	ø⁷	ɔ¹⁰	ø⁷	ɯ²
26	ɛ¹¹	ɪ³	(ʌ)	ɛ	(ʌ)	ɪ	(ʌ)	ɛ	(ʌ)	ɪ³
27	ja¹²	ø⁴	ɣ	ja	ɣ	ø	ɣ	ja	ɣ	ø⁴
28	ʌ¹³	ʊ⁵	ɛ	ʌ	ɛ	ʊ	ɛ	ʌ	ɛ	ʊ⁵
29	æ¹⁴	e⁶	ʌ	æ	ʌ	e	ʌ	æ	ʌ	e⁶
30	wɒ¹⁵	(ʌ)⁷	æ	ɒ	æ	(ʌ)	æ	ɒ	æ	ʌ⁷

Notes #31-37 place and strengthen the Vowel Register while crossing over between varied Vowel Series.

31	ʰⓞₑ	y²	e⁶	̃œ⁹	e⁶	y²	e⁶	̃œ⁹	e⁶	y²
32	ʰⓔ	ɪ³	ʊ⁷	̃ɛ¹⁰	ʊ	ɪ	ʊ	̃ɛ	ʊ	ɪ³
33	ʰⓞ	ɯ⁴	ɛ⁸	̃ɔ¹¹	ɛ	ɯ	ɛ	̃ɔ	ɛ	ɯ⁴
34	ʰⓐₑ	e⁵	(ʌ)⁹	̃æ¹²	(ʌ)	e	(ʌ)	̃æ	(ʌ)	e⁵
35	ʰⓐ	ø⁴	ɛ¹⁰	̃a¹³	ɛ	ø	ɛ	̃a	ɛ	ø⁶
36	ʰⓞₑ	ʊ⁷	œ¹¹	̃ʌ¹⁴	œ	ʊ	œ	̃ʌ	œ	ʊ⁷

Variation: Segment and repeat different parts of the exercise.

The upper resonance of the voice is related to the higher spaces in the vowel tract. This is found by using the vowel behind the hand, ʰⓞₑ, etc.

65

F

Bridging the Registers by small yodels.

Relieve the work done by
a particular set of vowel
muscles by crossing from
one vowel series to
another.

Sing the exercise slowly and repeat in faster tempo. Blow air
through the vocal cords for Head Voice. This reduces breath
pressure so the ribs should be raised and the waist thinned.

66

F

Continually change tessituras of vocalization so the voice does not become fatigued. The play of the tongue in these opposite phonetics establishes elasticity and strength in all areas of the voice.

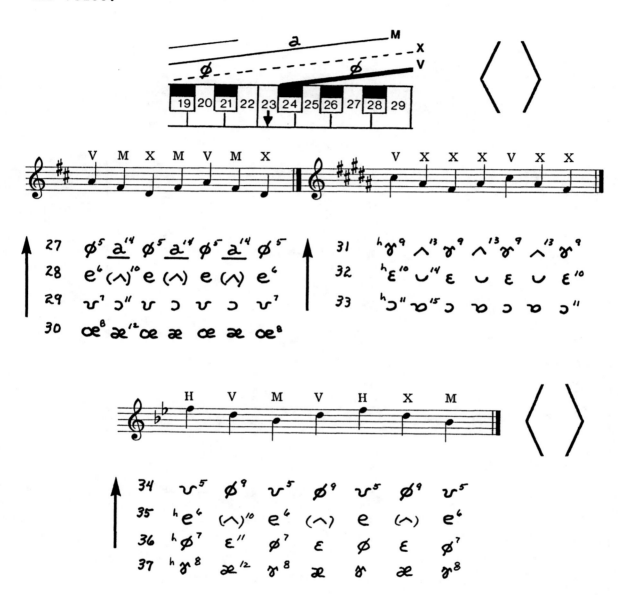

Hold the breath back in Head Voice.

Variation: Fill in with runs on a repeat of the exercise.

F

Floating Head Voice. Yodel to Head Voice. Portamento. Keep
the air moving on sotto voce. There must be more breath flow
so an eddy effect can occur. See p. 195. Let things fall into
place. Let the mouth close slightly on upper notes.

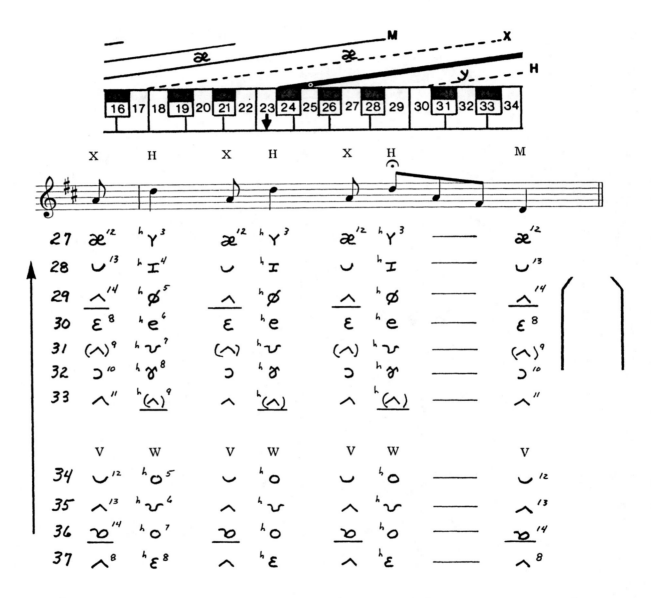

Also pant lightly through both nose and mouth--double pronged
inhalation. This lowers the palate so that the vibration can
be high. Trying to get the palate high throws the voice into
the mouth and destroys high vibration.

F

Head Voice for High Notes. Round the top notes to Head Voice--
there will be a resultant purity of tone (see p. 212). Keep
the air moving and bite the upper note.

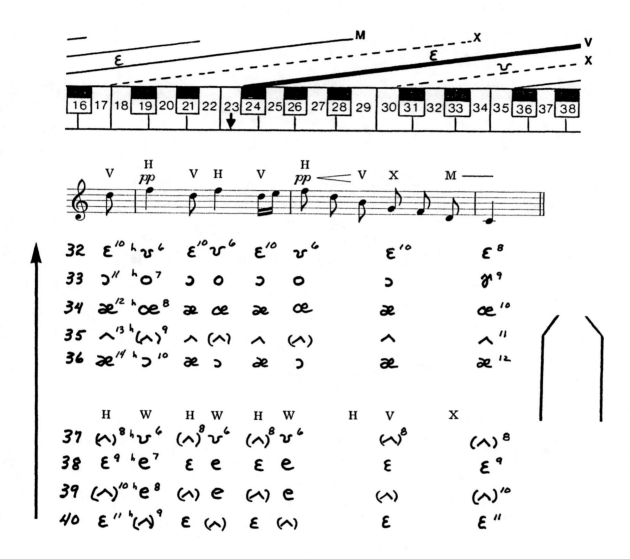

Let the tone find the right slot. On the <u>pianissimo</u> high notes
the vocal cords probably do not touch each other in vibrating--
merely wave at each other. Later trill on the third high note,
still later make a <u>messa di voce</u>. This quality of tone was called "blown tone" by Stratton, 1966. The closing of the mouth for
Whistle Register was a Lily Pons technique.

69

F

Crescendo on Vowel Register.

On the Vowel Register the voice will be more metallic. Do not practice this exercise to excess!

This is a favorite sound of Italian operatic composers in climactic passages. It approaches the limits of the voice. Precede it by exercises using Head Voice.

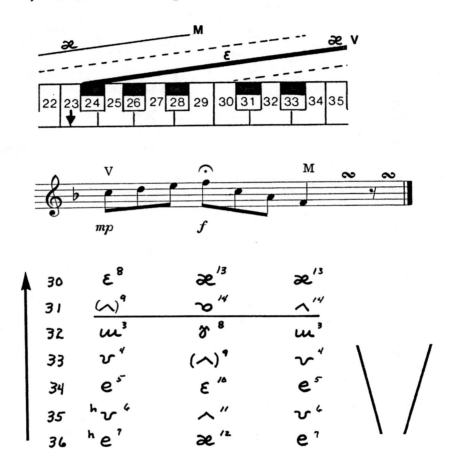

On the Vowel Register the voice will be more metallic. Practice this exercise within reason. In case of a "tickle" in the vocal cords use a slight [h] (which increases the air flow) and move the exercise faster without dwelling so long on each tone. This type of sound is sometimes required for dramatic effects but it tends to "spread" the voice--do it infrequently. Notice the Register change below the heavy line.

70

F

Turns, Rounding and Dynamic Contrasts of High Notes. There is
a rounding (closing) which should occur at the upper passaggio
of the female voice so that it can be extended into the high
register. The muscular adjustment of the laryngeal muscles
and vocal folds can be brought about by timbre changes which
can easily be controlled by the ear.

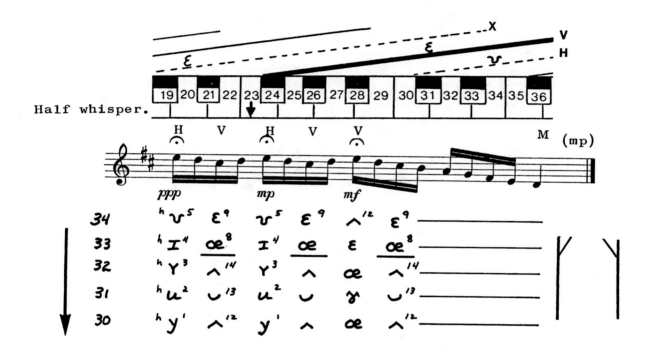

Start on dimple Head Voice. Pant through both the nose and a
pencil-size opening of the mouth to prepare for the Whistle.
Then sing the ppp sound, sending the vibrating air through both
the nose and mouth. Hardly hear the flute-like sound. Have a
very short distance between soft palate and back of tongue.
Use much air-flow but little breath pressure. "Fly it!"

For mp singing lengthen the velopharyngeal axis to allow more
resonation.

For mf singing, show the teeth and hold the head back progressively on Degrees of Opening 12, 13, and 14. Let the breath go!

F

Yodels at the Fifth on Related Vowels of the Same Resonance
Pitch. Mixed to Vowel to Medium Registers.

If the vowels have the same degree of opening the voice will
yodel between registers.

F

Agility, Resonance Tracking to High Voice with Track Switching.
Closing, reopening and closing in descending scales.

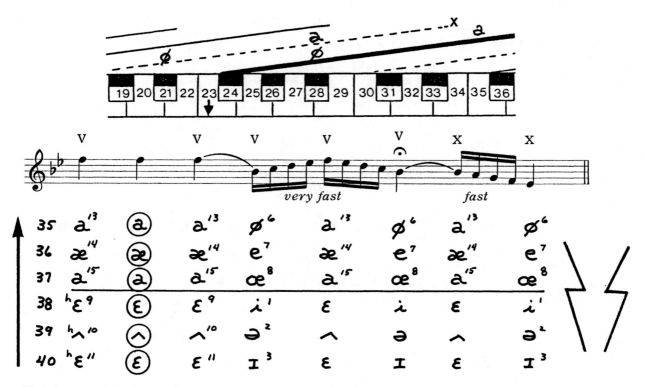

35	a^{13}	(a)	a^{13}	$ø^{6}$	a^{13}	$ø^{6}$	a^{13}	$ø^{6}$
36	$æ^{14}$	(æ)	$æ^{14}$	e^{7}	$æ^{14}$	e^{7}	$æ^{14}$	e^{7}
37	a^{15}	(a)	a^{15}	$œ^{8}$	a^{15}	$œ^{8}$	a^{15}	$œ^{8}$
38	$^{h}ɛ^{9}$	(ɛ)	$ɛ^{9}$	$ɪ^{1}$	$ɛ$	$ɪ$	$ɛ$	$ɪ^{1}$
39	$^{h}ʌ^{10}$	(ʌ)	$ʌ^{10}$	$ə^{2}$	$ʌ$	$ə$	$ʌ$	$ə^{2}$
40	$^{h}ɛ^{11}$	(ɛ)	$ɛ^{11}$	$ɪ^{3}$	$ɛ$	$ɪ$	$ɛ$	$ɪ^{3}$

Notice register change to Head and Vowel Registers between
Notes #37 and 38.

Variation: Reverse the exercise to train opening, closing and
reopening in ascending scale--train the senses of feeling and
hearing so this type of tuning modification occurs. Watch it on
video tape with slow motion and stop frame. Resonating air
pressures probably guide the best singers to this phenomenon.
It leads to a reinterpretation of the "pure vowel" theory--a
pure tone in which there is not disruptive noise because of conflict of resonance pitch and vibrator pitch. Such statements as,
"It was almost in tune" or "It was in tune but not in pitch"
probably refer to this phenomenon.

Teach the play of the resonators in agility for purity of sound
which comes from harmonic agreement of resonance with sung pitch.

F

Agility. Head Voice to Mixed Voice to Middle.

The head voice is the youth of the voice. However care should also be taken to equalize the voice in the middle and very low. There must also be strength there. Move from one part of the voice to another to keep all areas active and elastic.

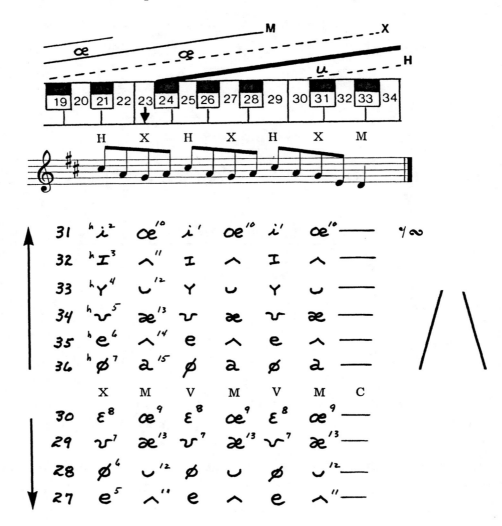

It may help the singer to think that the H (Head Register symbol) above a musical example could stand for ʰ aspiration on the beginning of a tone.

F

<u>Agility in Head Voice</u>. Use various articulations. Transition
to lower voice. Also sing the upper third chromatically to
develop a seamless voice.

Also sing chromatics on the second and third groups.

Keep the chest up on the turn.

F

<u>Agility Voice Placement Exercise</u>.   Head Voice to Middle Voice.

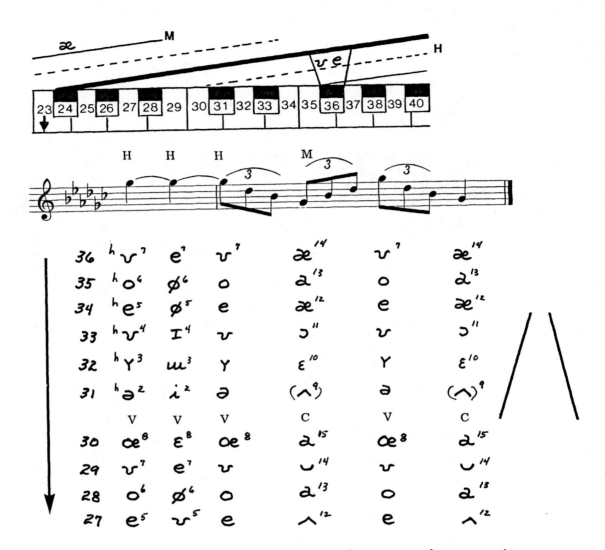

The head position will stay pretty much the same when varying
vowels on the upper note of the same register.

F

Agility Voice Placement Exercise.   Vowel Register, Head Voice to Middle Voice.

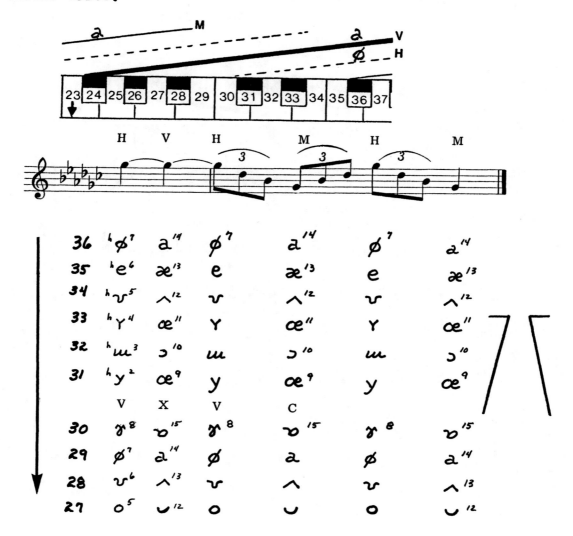

Make a crescendo and diminuendo on the first three notes by changing vowels which give a register shift. A very valuable exercise for timbre exploration over the upper passaggio.

The head position will raise when going from the medium position to the open position on the first note. This assists in resonation and is seen in the international singers.

F

Bridging the Mixed, Middle and Head Registers.
Ease up on the breath for Head Voice. This is an exercise
which will lead to floating high notes. Precede by p. 35.

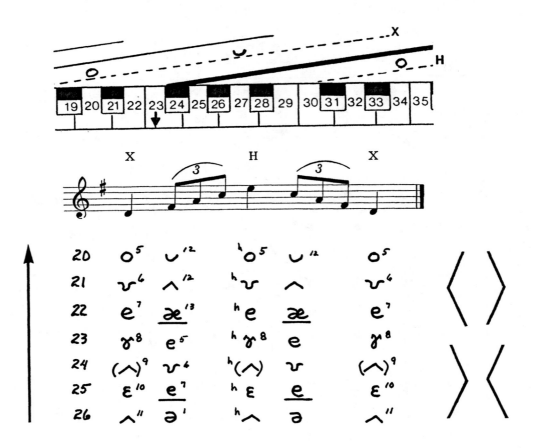

F

Floating High Notes.

Flexible resonators require a flexible breath. Move from one exercise to another frequently changing tessituras.

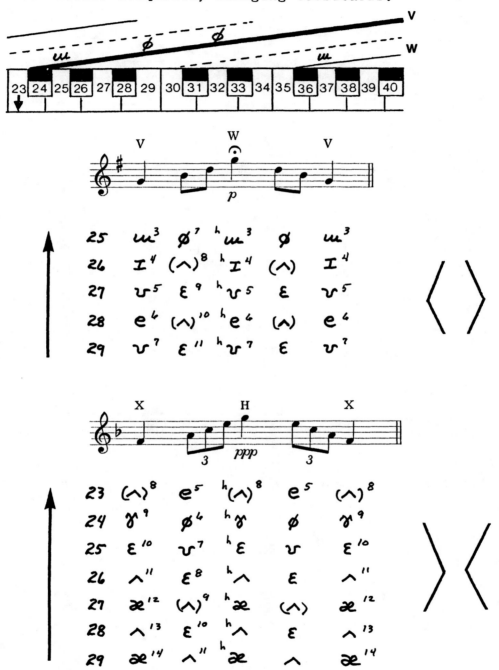

Widen the ribs for Head Voice, ease up on the breath pressure and feel like you are sighing through the tone--more air flow.

F

Arpeggios to Upper Notes.

Register transitions with hour-glass and diamond exercises.

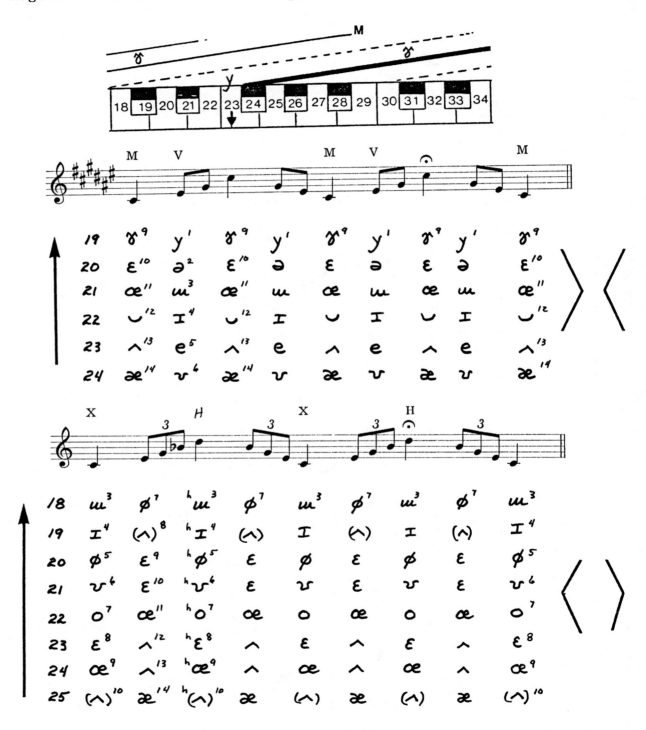

F

Agility with Piping. Crossover exercises. Favorable vowels, Vowel Register to Mixed Register, Head Register to Vowel Register.

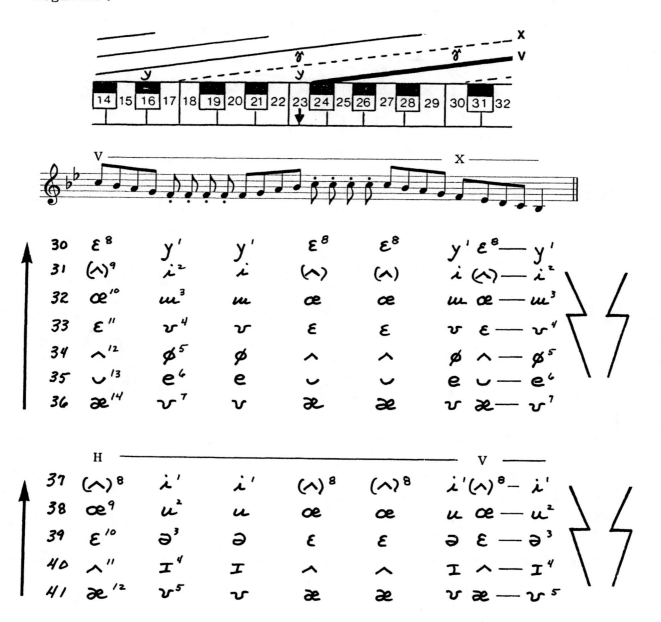

Close, reopen and close in descending scales--noticeable in many of the better treble voices. The use of staccati is an antidote for locked breath (only for Female Voices).

Use inhalation through both nose and mouth for Head Voice.

F

Yodel and Piping of Scales.   Always have proper resonance tuning on exposed notes.

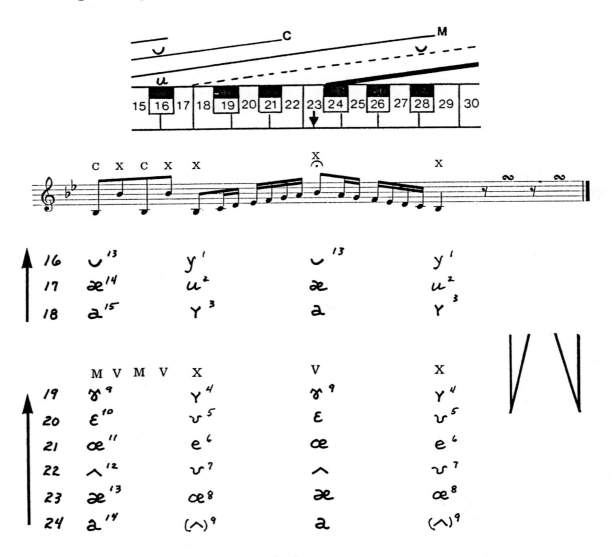

In the exercises on Notes #16-18 the runs are on the same track.

In the runs on exercises on Notes #19-24 there is a switch of tracks between the low and the high notes. However the singer will already know the sound of the vowel to which she is running because of the yodels on the first notes. The switch of tracks will hardly be noticed by the singer and listener but will be more agile if the notes are lightly articulated or pulsated.

82

F

Turning into Head Voice.   Switching from Head Voice to the
Vowel Track.   (Closing for Head Voice.)

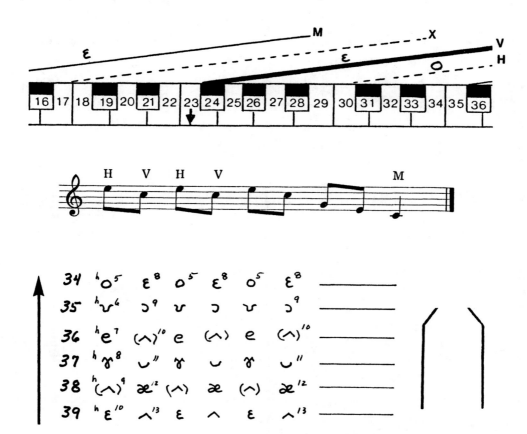

Say only the first two vowels to the singer(s), then play
the pitches.

Also, trill on the 5th note.

Very Light, Bright Ah [a]. Agility Exercise on uncoupled Ah.
Shorten the velopharyngeal axis by inhaling through both nose
and mouth, with the mouth almost closed. Such imaginary ways
as "inhaling a rose" or thinking of the instant just before a
sneeze can be used to accomplish the same thing. Sing the exercise on a very light Ah with a high degree of openness. This
is uncoupled singing. Keep the voice flexible and light so that
it will move. This exercise should also be used by the heavier
voices to keep them light and as an antidote for heaviness.
This is Mancini's approach to mouth opening, see p. 24.

a (Loose lipped)

Bright Ah. For brilliant singing the head is back and the
upper teeth show. Keep larynx up on the last note!

a (Loose lipped)

a (Loose lipped)   Pacchierotti 1838.

These exercises can be sung on the same vowel but have a "soft
focus" in camera terms. Allow the jaw and lips to play as they
wish. The exercises on the opposite page have tuned vowel resonances on the exposed notes and there is a "clear focus." In
camera work both are artistically valuable as they are in
singing.

Variation: Sing exercises on opposite page with loose lipped
            [a] as well as with the indicated phonetics.

F

<u>Agility and Education of the Soft Palate</u>. Before singing the
following exercises place the hand over the mouth and inhale in
and out on the vowel indicated, eg in the exercise beginning on
Note #18 [œ]. This is the "nasal connection" of which the
German soprano, Lilli Lehmann, spoke, p. 252.

"Put the palate into the nasal position, the larynx
upon [œ]; attack the lowest tone of the figure with
the thought of the highest; force the breath, as it
streams very vigorously forth from the larynx, toward the nose, but allow the head current entire
freedom, without doing away with the nasal quality;
and then run up the scale with great firmness. In
descending ... [adjust i and e] very close to
each other, so that the scale slides down, not a
pair of stairs, but a smooth track ... The pressure
of the breath against the chest must not be dimin-
ished, but must be unceasing."

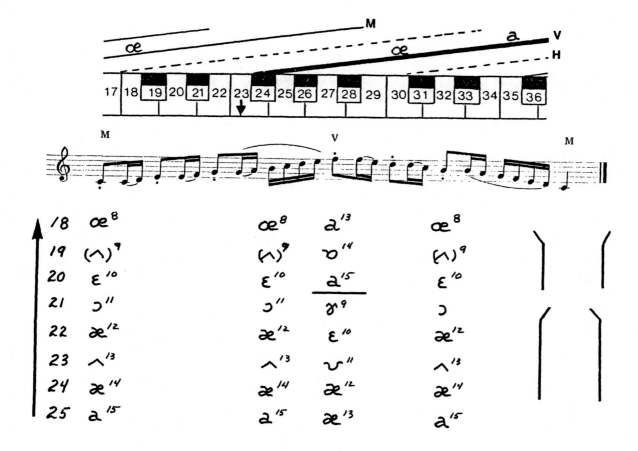

85

F

Scored Vocalizes.

Score vocalizes before using. Too much uncoupled Ah diminishes
and fatigues the voice. You do not need to notate the registers.

B. Lütgen. Vol. 1.

Panofka
Op. 85, p. 7

Many teachers do not use formal vocalizes because there is a
feeling that they are counterproductive. It is my belief the
problem is that the same vowel on all notes utilizes the same
set of muscles without relief and also that the sung pitches and
and resonance pitches do not agree. The effectiveness of the
Sieber vocalizes with the Graun syllables, is due to the alternating labial and dental consonants with different vowels.
Also solfeggi on do re me etc., utilize different vowels
but the consonants are less beneficial. F. Lamperti made special comments about how the solfeggi and the articulation of
consonants should be used. He thought they should preceed and
accompany studies of vocalization. He wrote on the breath and
said he would write on pronunciation--but the work seemingly
was never finished. "He who knows how to breathe and pronounce
knows how to sing," is a well known old Italian statement.

86

DIPHTHONG CHART			
αe	αo	ɔø	ei
Sing across on the same pitch so that there is a continuity of resonance. Each diphthong should have a diminuendo ⟩.			
40	ʌɛ	ɔo	ɔœ	ɛe
39	ʌɛ	ɔo	ɔœ	ɛe
38	ʌɛ	ɔɣ	ɣœ	ɛɪ
37	ʌɛ	ɒɣ	ɣœ	ɛɪ
36	ʌe	ɒo	oø	æe
35	ʌe	ʌo	◡ø	æe
34	ʌe	ʌo	◡ø	æe
33	ʌɪ	ʌɯ	ɔœ	ɛɪ
32	ʌɪ	ʌɯ	ɔœ	ɛɪ
31	ʌɛ	ʌə	ɣœ	ɛi
30	ʌɛ	ʌə	ɣœ	ɛi
29	æe	ʌo	◡ø	æe
28	æe	ʌo	◡ø	æe
27	æe	ʌo	◡ø	æe
26	ʌɛ	ʌɔ	ɔœ	ɛɪ
25	ʌɛ	ʌɔ	ɔœ	ɛɪ
24	ʌɛ	ʌɣ	ɣœ	ɛi
23	ʌɛ	ʌɣ	ɣœ	ɛi
22	ʌe	ʌʌ	◡ø	eɪ
21	ʌe	ʌo	ɔœ	eɪ
20	ʌe	ʌo	ɔœ	eɪ
19	ʌɪ	aɣ	ɣœ	ɛɪ
18	ʌɪ	ɒɣ	ɣœ	ɛɪ
17	ʌe	ʌo	◡ø	ei
16	ʌe	ʌo	◡ø	ei
15	ʌe	ʌo	◡ø	ei
14	ʌɛ	ʌɔ	ɔœ	ɛɪ

Fig. 17.

Diphthongs are glides which should be harmonic or they will be weak. They may occur between vowels on the same Track with the same or different vowel series, or on different tracks.

French and German are more rounded than English. English has 1/3rd rounded vowels--both French and German have 2/3rds of the vowels rounded. For long notes in singing, where standing waves are necessary, the rounded glides of diphthongs should be used in all languages. Diphthongs are <u>directions</u> of vowel shift--go to the nearest harmonic. This page should be practiced and used as a reference.

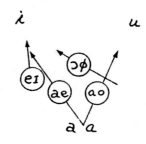

87

FRENCH NASAL CHART

With the nasal passage left open so that the air vibrates through both mouth and nose.

	ã	ɛ̃	ɔ̃	œ̃	
40	ɔ̃	ɛ̃	õ	ʌ̃	40
39	ɔ̃	ɛ̃	õ	ʌ̃	39
38	(ʌ̃)	ɛ̃	ɣ̃	(ʌ̃)	38
37	(ʌ̃)	ɛ̃	ɣ̃	(ʌ̃)	37
36	ʊ̃	æ̃	õ	(ʌ̃)	36
35	ʊ̃	æ̃	õ	(ʌ̃)	35
34	ʊ̃	æ̃	õ	(ʌ̃)	34
33	(ʌ̃)	ɛ̃	ɔ̃	œ̃	33
32	(ʌ̃)	ɛ̃	ɔ̃	œ̃	32
31	(ʌ̃)	ɛ̃	ɣ̃	œ̃	31
30	(ʌ̃)	ɛ̃	ɣ̃	œ̃	30
29	ʊ̃	æ̃	õ	ʌ̃	29
28	ʊ̃	æ̃	õ	ʌ̃	28
27	ʊ̃	æ̃	õ	ʌ̃	27
26	(ʌ̃)	ɛ̃	ɔ̃	œ̃	26
25	(ʌ̃)	ɛ̃	ɔ̃	œ̃	25
24	ʊ̃	æ̃	ɣ̃	œ̃	24
23	ʊ̃	æ̃	ɣ̃	œ̃	23 →
22	ʊ̃	æ̃	õ	œ̃	22
21	ɔ̃	ɛ̃	õ	œ̃	21
20	ɔ̃	ɛ̃	õ	œ̃	20
19	(ʌ̃)	ɛ̃	ɣ̃	œ̃	19
18	(ʌ̃)	ɛ̃	ɣ̃	œ̃	18
17	ʊ̃	æ̃	õ	œ̃	17
16	ʊ̃	æ̃	õ	œ̃	16
15	ʊ̃	æ̃	õ	œ̃	15
14	(ʌ̃)	ɛ̃	ɔ̃	œ̃	14

Delattre

Fig. 18. Nasal Vowels
Notice the velum is lowered and the base of the tongue raised.

In nasal vowels the soft palate is allowed to open which creates a weaker R^1 (lower resonance). Nasal vowels assist the passaggio notes to head voice. If even one of the nasal passages is obstructed there is a cul de sac sound which makes passaggio notes difficult. Professional singers attempt to cancel performances when the nose is temporarily closed because of a cold or allergy. If there is a permanent partial closure of either nasal passage it should be repaired by a singer's doctor for reasons of health and good resonance. See p. 193.

The Scoring of Songs and Arias. Thus far the previous chapter
has been concerned with the formation and reinforcement of singing voices. The real test is what occurs in public performance.
On all long and/or exposed notes the resonator and vibrator
should be in overtone relationship. Since sung pitch has wavelength and vowels have wavelength, the voice will be much clearer, stronger, and will carry better if the two sets of wavelengths agree harmonically. This I have already stated and hope
the singer has established in his or her throat. Some "natural"
singers do this by imitating the sounds of good singers on certain notes. I have notated colors for those singers who need
added assistance.

The examples given are all operatic because they are written
for very specific voice classifications. Songs are transposed
and sung on differing pitches by different voices. To notate
a song for all voice classifications would be an exercise in
futility. However, a study of how scoring of arias for specific voices is done will show singers the way to score the
vowels for their individual throats in any music they sing.

I will classify voices by arrow placement--fortunately composers were writing for specific voices which could do certain
things on certain notes--otherwise they were changed (sometimes by the singer). Thus I will give examples for sopranos
whose arrow is on A♭--called A♭ soprano. Other examples are
for G soprano, F♯ mezzo soprano, and E♮ contralto.

Scoring a song or aria may appear to be tedious but so is fingering wind instruments. The phenomenon is the same; control
the resonance and help the vibrator. Scoring can be done just
on exposed notes or rather completely; score enough of the
vowels to give you successful performances. Your use of the
Chart will improve your hearing and feeling, and will give you
an overtone control of your bel canto.

F

Scoring can be done only in questionable spots. The example is for soprano with the arrow on g[1].

G Soprano

Or scoring can be done more extensively.

Or scoring can be rather complete according to individual needs of the singer. I will score the examples rather completely. Watch the numbers and notice the opening and closing; frequently most of the opening is on the inside of the mouth being done by the tongue where it cannot be seen. The numbers assist the singer in resonance tracking and in knowing whether an overtone shift is occuring (register change).

It is usually not necessary to score all vowel-pitch sounds although one very successful European singer is doing so. Usually it is sufficient to score those spots which bother--this is the background of scoring for the voice--like fingering for the trumpet. Notice the critical tunings are usually above c^2.

Register	Vowel Openings	G Soprano
X	α^{15}	Back <u>ah</u> because follwed by palatal fricative [x].
H	e^6	Head voice--the nearest vowel to [ɪ]. Rounded vowel [ø]^6 is an option.
V	ε^{11}	[ɛ] for correct pronunciation. [œ] is an option. Slightly round the lips.
H	$(\wedge)^9$ $\phi^6 \phi^7$	Slightly round [e] for Head voice; use [e]^7 for [ɪ] on c#^{2}.
H	$\phi (\wedge)^9$	Use [ø] for [ɪ] and then change the resonance to [ʌ]^9 on the neutral pipe series on top for purity of tone.

91

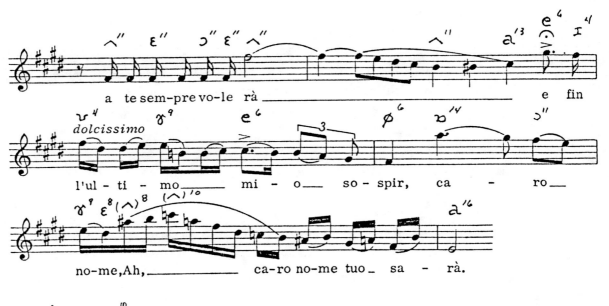

a te sem-pre vo-le rà _____ e fin

dolcissimo

l'ul - ti - mo _____ mi - o ___ so - spir, ca - ro ___

no-me, Ah, _____ ca-ro no-me tuo _ sa - rà.

Register	Vowel Openings	
		A♭ Soprano
M	ɔ ɛ″	Keep all of the vowel in Middle voice opening.
V	ʌ″	Sing [ʌ] not [a]¹⁸ which would be white and loose vocal tract resonance. Run on pipe series and end on [a]¹³.
H	e⁶ ɪ⁴	Play with Head voice diminishing to dolcissimo. There is no resonant [i] on c#₂; sing the nearest thing [e]⁶.
V	ɒ¹⁴	Back Ah because of [k] sound; sing the <u>c</u> without explosion
V	ɔ″	Proper vowel pitch.
H	(ʌ)⁸- ʌ″	Go up the pipe series.

92

J'i-rai   chez mon a - mi Lil-las Pas - tia.

tra la   la   la   la   la   la   la   la   la   la   la.

F# Mezzo Soprano

Register

Vowel Openings

F# Mezzo Soprano

V	$\varepsilon^8 (\wedge)^9$	There is no resonant [i] on c#^{2}. Sing [ʌ] which keeps the same overtone.
X	a^{13}	This interval has the same vowel opening. Depending on taste and country in which this is sung, the lower chest note can be sung in high or low chest position--the latter giving a more robust, masculine tone.
C	a^{13}	
v^6	$\wedge''$	By slightly rounding the lips on the acciacatura the singer goes to Head voice for the last note. Option is a red [a] which is more like a last gasp.

93

vol - te a me par - lò____   tre vol te a me, a me par - lò!

Si - len - zio!   Si - len - zio!

E♮ Contralto

This is an example which involves both Head and Chest Register for Contralto.

Register	Vowel Openings	
H	(∧)⁹ ∅⁵	for Head Voice at the top.
C	α¹⁶	par
X	ᴜ¹²	lò. Future tense is open vowel in Italian. Passage from α¹⁶ to ᴜ¹² is a yodel but is pp so it should not be obvious.
X	e⁷	me is close vowel in Italian.
M	∧" ∧¹⁴	Use sheltered <u>ah</u> on the same register with the vowel opening when it goes up. Future tense
M	ɤ⁹	should be [ɔ] but it would be a "wolf tone"-- not resonant and fighting. Your only choice is to shade it--use [ɤ].
X	ε"	Silεnzio is mixed voice on the upper note.
C	ε"	Silεnzio on low note--full chest voice; it is what they have all been waiting for.

M

CHAPTER III

THE MALE VOICE

Registers of the Male Voice. The form of the Male Voice has
best been described by Manuel Garcia II in the Art of Singing
(ab. 1855, p. 11) undated, Ditson. His vowel-pitch relationships for male voices have been transposed to the Chromatic
Vowel Chart nomenclature with the arrow set at $f\#^1$ for tenors
and at $e\flat^1$ for bass. The baritone voice was not established
at that time. I think that the Garcia Vowel Scale is unknown
and happens to be a description of the Caruso Vowel Scales on
page 97. They can be used for all Male voices since they give
a clue to how vowels close and switch tracks in ascending. The
following statement may be a bit tedious to read but it is exact
and vital to all male singers! I have used brackets [ ] to
indicate how Garcia's statement refers to the Chromatic Vowel
Chart. He heard and knew the effects of the overtone relationships to the Italian vowels.

"(Men) should attack their chest voice (on A and E Vowels)
Note #7 or 8. The sounds Notes #13, 14, 15, 16, 17 for basses
and Notes #12, 13, 14, 15 for tenors offer a phenomenon worthy
of attention. Unless care be taken, it becomes very difficult
to produce them of a clear quality; the larynx always tending
to render them sombre [the A overly darkened rather towards
Track 3], and then they are a source of trouble to the singer.
The only way to combat this tendency and give firmness to a
voice, is to employ clear timbre [Track 4], emitting the Italian
A and E with more and more openness [vowels on the same Track
open in ascending]. (Men) should begin to round gently at
Note #16 [move down to Track 3] for the actual clear quality
would be too thin. The reader will remark that the word
rounding, [Track 3], and not closing [Track 2] is used here.

This applies to the sounds on Notes #19, 20, 21 [round by switching to Track 2]. From Note #22 the two qualities agree, but the closed timbre [Track 1 Vowel Register] in these sounds should not be practiced until a pupil has mastered the bright timbre [Track 1.5], which is difficult to attain in this part of the vocal scale [Mixed Voice]. If this caution be neglected, there is risk of the voice being veiled or muffled." [After Track 1.5 is practiced on the green, then sing Track 1, the Vowel Register. Track 1.5 will be the easiest to sing from Note #23 upwards because the vowels are neither too open nor too closed. On Track 1 there will be great resonance since the vocal cords are vibrating at the frequency of the resonator.]

"The bright timbre alone [high Resonance [1] of the vocal tract] can make the voice light and penetrating, but though it may communicate its character to the entire compass, it is especially in this tenth of the chest register, viz Notes #6-#21, that its effects are pleasing. Voices should, without exception, abandon it upon reaching Note #22 [where the vocal tract has a harmonic change--switch to Track 1.5 Mixed Voice]; nor should tenors use it above Note #23 in the chest register as it renders the tone disagreeable. Generally, tenors will take up the falsetto [Track 1.5 Mixed Voice] at Note #19 and continue it upwards as far as Notes #28 and #29. Between Notes #19 and #23 these voices experience great difficulty in firmly enunciating sounds, the timbre of which should be neither too shrill or too muffled . . . [sing the vowels on Track 1.5 and Track 2]. However accomplished a singer may be, the sounds on Notes #24, 25, 26, 27, 28 in the clear timbre [Track 2], will always appear shrill, even when heard in a very large room (hall), and will resemble a boy-chorister's voice. Therefore, they should never be used except in the close timbre [Track 1 or Track 1.5]."

Now look at the Caruso Vowel scales [all back Vowels] in relationship to this. Garcia and Caruso were both trained in Naples; perhaps this Scale came from teachers of that city.

M

Caruso Exercises with vowel-pitch relationship. These exercises
are for an F# tenor and are copied exactly as they appear in
Caruso and the Art of Singing by Fucito and Beyer (1929, p. 152).
They clearly indicate Caruso's approach to the passaggio but all
are on Back vowels which tend to make the voice heavy. Other
voice classifications should use these exercises with correct
arrow placement within the range suitable to them. (See Caruso
Scale on the Chromatic Vowel Chart.)

[Notes #6-8]

This exercise went higher and higher but always went to [o]
between b♮ and f♮ and to [u] on f# and above.

[Notes #9-12]

Caruso always used [u] on the higher note.

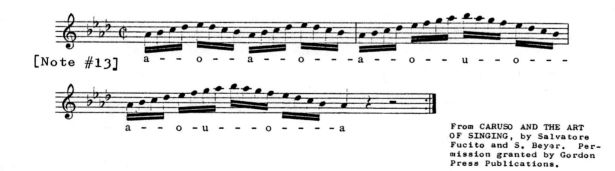

[Note #13]

From CARUSO AND THE ART
OF SINGING, by Salvatore
Fucito and S. Beyer. Per-
mission granted by Gordon
Press Publications.

Other exercises went to [o] around d^1 and above and [u] on f#^{1} and above.

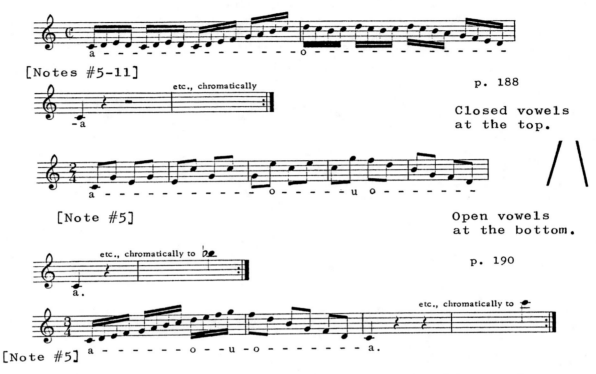

[Notes #5-11]

p. 188

Closed vowels
at the top.

[Note #5]

Open vowels
at the bottom.

p. 190

[Note #5]

I believe his exercises were a tool for tuning his vowel resonance to his sung pitch. This is the reason for including the
Caruso Vowel Scale on the Chromatic Vowel Chart where it can be
moved up and down for use by all voices, including Female Voices.
It is especially important for the passaggio on Notes #20 to 23
which are encircled on the Chart. They have been called "pivot"
notes by some singers.

Forms of Openings--Male Voices. In ascending scales resonators
must open to match pitch--is descending they must close, so I
will use symbols to indicate the manner of opening and closing
of vowels in the exercises.

M

$\bigvee$ indicates that the vowels open in ascending and close in descending. $\bigwedge$ indicates that the vowels close in ascending and switch $\bigwedge$ tracks. $\rangle\langle$ indicates the exercise is narrow in the middle and wide $\rangle\langle$ at the top and bottom. $\langle\rangle$ indicates the vowels are closed on the low and high notes $\langle\rangle$ and more open in the middle. $\|$ indicates the vowels are the same opening. $7\sqsubset$ indicates the top note opens and closes before descend- $7\sqsubset$ ing. $\diagup\diagdown$ indicates the lower note closes and opens before or after $\llcorner\lrcorner$ going up. $\diagdown\diagup$ indicates the lower note opens and closes before or after $\diagdown\diagup$ going up. With the televising and video taping of outstanding singers these actions can be studied in slow motion and stop frame. Observe the phenomena of tuning which comes about by a combination of ear and kinesthetic feel of the throat.

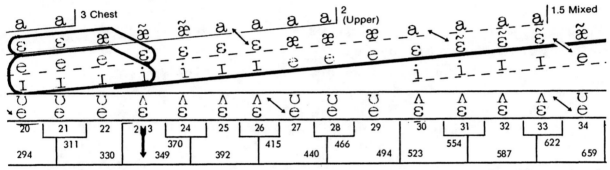

Fig. 19. The Loop Section and Passaggio Lines of Chart.

Fig. 19 shows the loop section of the Chromatic Vowel Chart. Singers can go through this area in two ways--closed or open. The Caruso scales go through this passaggio on the close back vowel. Other vowels may be used. The [æ] over Note #22 is precarious as is the [ɛ] over Note #23 which should be sung half [e]. Generally speaking male singers have an easier transition to the upper extension if the lips are slightly rounded.

Rhyming by Crossover Tunings. One of the best ways to establish resonance of the singing voice (placement) is to rhyme all vowels of the same degree of openness which have been coded green, gold and blue on the keyboard sized Vowel Chart. Vowels in green have been notated on Passaggio Lines I and II.

99

The complete list of rhymes is indicated here. Do not rhyme the 16th, 17th and 18th degree of opening on high notes. To find the bright AH [a], precede with [j]. To find [ɑ], precede with [w].

Space Chart and Tone Placing Chart. Tune the indicated vowels on the charted pitches to find correct space. DO NOT SUPERIMPOSE SOME SET SPACE CONCEPT ON THE THROAT. The vowel timbre and sense of vibration on the lips and in the chest will tell when the microscopic tuning of resonance is optimal--that can be remembered. A voice with a set position is out of tune and out of resonance, like an organ rank with only one size of pipe for all notes. The same size resonator for all vowels is false acording to acoustical phonetics. Degrees of openness are gained by movements of the lips, tongue, jaw, soft palate and head. They should be allowed to move as they wish. (G.B. Lamperti, 1931, p. 112, "Any arbitrary use of the throat, other than procuring a tone's pitch or a word's color, is detrimental to control of the voice. Do not yawn.")

Breath. When the best resonance is heard and felt the singer will notice that less breath pressure is required. He will feel an open chest and widened ribs. The diaphragm is always lifted up in singing; this takes the weight off of the vocal cords. The only time the diaphragm descends is when breath is taken. He should hold back on the breath. This is the famous lutte vocale or "vocal struggle" of which Francesco Lamperti (1890, p. 33) spoke. Forced resonance requires a forced breath pressure. Sympathetic resonance is easy and is a part of a self-oscillating system (Benade 1977, p. 173).

Couplings. All of the vowels of the same degree of opening couple with the possible exception of the Back to Front group in the last column of the next page.

Round the (ʌ) vowel on the 8th, 9th and 10th degrees of opening. I will call (ʌ) the half-rounded ʌ.

Fig. 20.

Rhyming – Tone Placing Chart
by Degrees of Openness

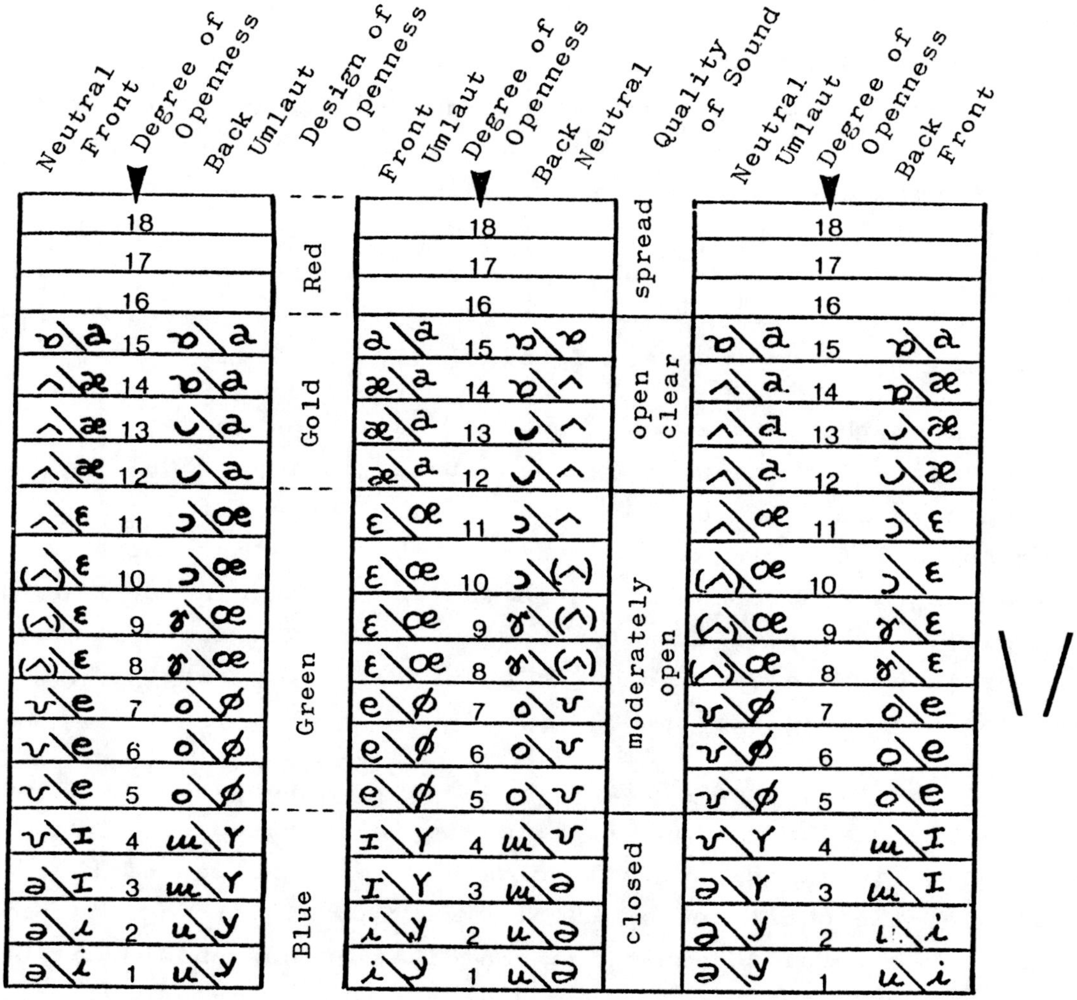

Yodel back and forth on the same degree of opening on the Chart below—continually changing tessitura.

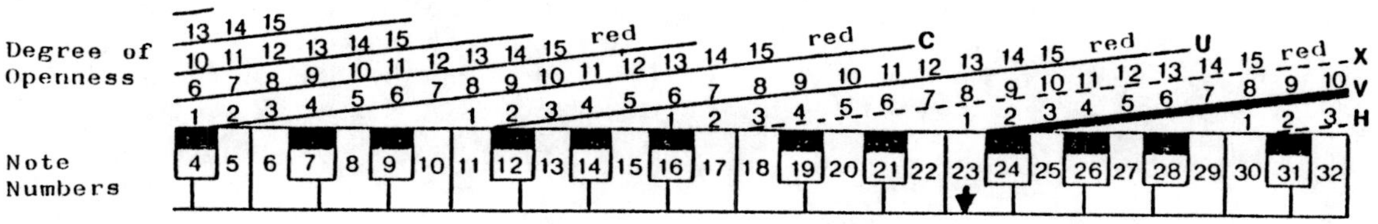

Place the arrow on the correct note for your voice classification.

M

Coordinating the Chest and Laryngeal Muscles.

Howard (1886) has referred to the vocal cords as vocal shelves--
this form can be seen in the many tomograms of the larynx which
are readily available. They also look like wedges. They have
an intrinsic musculature which can make them very firm. When
this is done the voice assumes a bright metallic sound since the
vocal wedges touch and make short, discrete puffs--very much
like brass instruments. For metallic sounds think of flying
wedges. They are also capable of waving at each other in such
a way as to make fluty sounds. First I will give Garcia's exercise for the firm sounds. Coffin (1977, p. 72).

Beginning on the vowels "ah" and "eh" as in the words, "alma,
sempre," attack the vowels on one note beginning on Note #7.
Proceed note by note to #15 on α ε α. These attacks "will
bring out all the ring of the voice. The notes must be kept
full and equal in force. This is the best manner of developing
the voice. At first, the exercise must not exceed two or three
minutes in duration," Garcia (1894, p. 14). The range of the
exercise is from Garcia (1872, p. 11).

I have found that short, vigorous actions of the arms as though
alternately striking timpani while singing the indicated vowels
will assist in giving nerve impulse and coordination of the
muscles of the chest and of the larynx into higher registers.
It is very helpful to establish coordination but should not be
used more than one or two minutes at a time. Sing on the gold
and green vowels to Note #21.

7	v^{13} ε	14	$⊃''$ ε	
8	v^{14} ε	15	$∧^{12}$ æ	
9	v^{15} ε	16	$∪^{13}$ a	
10	$∧^{12}$ æ	17	$∧^{14}$ æ	
11	$∧^{13}$ æ	18	$γ^8$ ε	
12	$∪^{14}$ a	19	$(∧)^9$ ε	
13	$(∧)^{10}$ ε	20	$⊃^{10}$ ε	

Use this as a contrast to
the whistle type of vibration in Falsetto voice
(p. 106) with which it is
blended for Mixed Voice,
p. 112.

<u>Ringing and Veiled Sounds</u>.   "If after every explosion the glottis closes completely, each impinges sharply on the <u>tympanic membrane</u>, and the sound heard is bright and ringing. But if the glottis is imperfectly closed [slightly], and a slight excape of air unites the explosions, the impressions upon the tympanum are blunted, the sound being then veiled . . . Coupled with the theory of <u>timbres</u> [clear and sombre see upper left hand corner of the Chromatic Vowel Chart] and that of the breath, it puts the singer in possession of all the "tints" of the voice, and indeed initiates him into all the secrets of voice-production." Garcia 1894, p. 7.

The ringing sounds are gained through the exercises on page 102, the veiled, ethereal, air-flow sounds are gained through the exercises on page 107 and anywhere that I have indicated an attack which begins with a small ^{h}. Both types of vocalization should be practiced daily. Mackinlay (1908, p. 131) said that Garcia found that "the exhaustion of the air contained in the chest is more rapid in the proportion of four to three in the production of a head [when compared with] than a chest note."

―――――――――――――

I am of the opinion that vocal masters of the past were listening to the play of overtones in the voices which they were training--it is they who developed the term, "registers." And, I know that better and faster results are obtained when a somnambulistic approach is taken in this acoustical type of singing rather than a rational, analytical, or intellectual one. To some singers vocalizing in this manner is their form of daily meditation. It sensitizes the thresholds of perception. Teaching by overtones leads more towards the <u>art</u> than the <u>science</u> of singing. It is the intuitive which inspires, not the mechnaistic.

M

Sing Resonant Vowels on the Same Pitch (spelling). Sing vowels on the same pitch while slowly spelling vertical columns to find loud and easy resonance. Test by moving lips, jaw and tongue microscopically to find the center of resonance. Memorize the vowel color and the pitch to place that note in your voice. The sensations of the mucous membrane of your vocal tract will tell you the best placement. Sing other vertical columns on the Vowel Chart. Continuously change vowel series and pitches. Turn on the vowels to help find the center of resonance--indicated by ∞. Alternate with scalewise and arpeggio exercises.

Place the arrow on the proper note for your voice classification. Go by note numbers and musical design and not by the notes written. The note numbers are a transposing device for the different voice classifications.

ɒ - as in father
ʊ - is between [ɔ] and [ɑ]
ʌ - as in luck
ʊ - as in pull
ɯ - is between [u] and [o]

V - Vowel Register
X - Mixed Voice
U - Upper Voice
C - Chest Voice as are
    4, 5, 6, and L

Nota Bene: Spell from the top down on Notes #16 and below, and from the bottom up above Note #16!

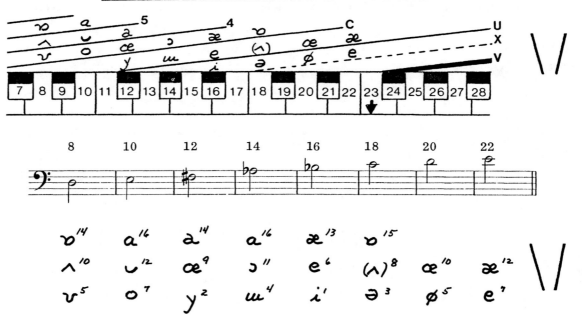

104

M

Resonance Tracking for Chest and Upper Voice.

Know where you are going before you get there. On the same note sing the first vowel and then the second which is the opening at the top of the run. Then sing the run. Sing other exercises on different vowel series on the Chart.

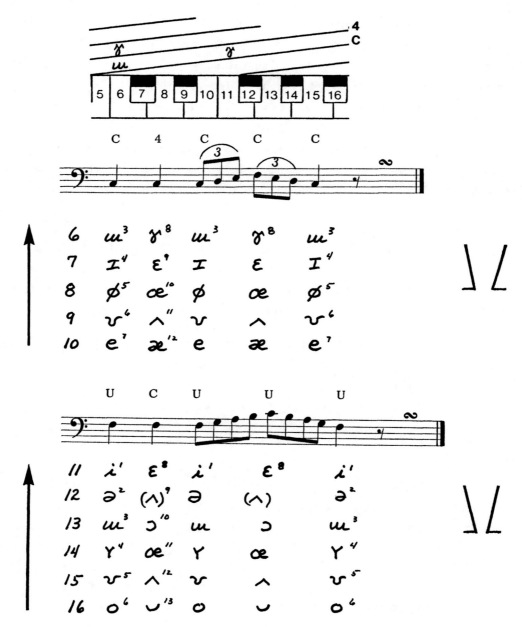

Find the greatest vibration on the first two notes by slight movements of the tongue, lips and/or jaw then proceed with the exercise.

M

Development of the Mixed Voice Register--Falsetto.

There are several reasons for training the Falsetto and Super Falsetto in the male voice. Most important is the necessity of establishing a mechanism to hold up the other end of the bridge at the passaggio. This bridge turns out to be Mixed Voice on Track 1.5. This register is a bit like an overdrive and allows the singer to have an extension of range as the overdrive gives an extension of speed without burning out the car's motor. This extension gives the high C to tenors, and in many cases is the way in which supposed baritones become Helden Tenors and basses become Helden Baritones. These classifications should not be striven for. The way the voice responds will show what the eventual classification will be, not the determination of a singer or the pre-programming of the teacher of singing.

"Do not hum but sing as though you are humming with your mouth open," G.B. Lamperti (1931, p. 104). Place the palm of the hand over a small opening of the mouth and sing the indicated vowels. ⓤ means open mouth hum on [u], etc. ⓞ means open mouth hum on the vowel behind the hand on [ɔ], etc.

Notes #30, 31, and 32 in Super Falsetto feel like they are right between the eyes and the sound is very small. Super Falsetto (Head Voice) helps establish the high C and comes in on Note #30 where Head Voice begins in Female Voices.

The Mixed Voice is an overtone phenomenon of Vowel and Upper Registers, see p. 210. Establish the Falsetto first so that the Mixed Voice can be strengthened. "Natural voices" find this by imitating Mixed Voice sounds in recordings, but most voices need to be assisted in this by training.

Both Falsetto (Track 1) and Super Falsetto (Track .67) are made possible by the oblique crico-thyroid muscle (see p. 188) which forms a dimple under the larynx. The dimple Falsettos allow the highest extension of the Male Voice.

M

<u>Preparation for Mixed Voice.</u>   <u>Falsetto with Vowels behind the</u> <u>hand</u>.

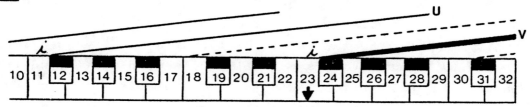

F

See p. 33 for discussion
of nasality.

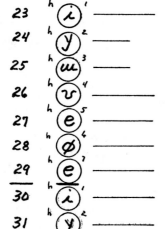

23 ⁿ ⓘ ¹ ————————
24 ⁿ ⓨ ² ————————
25 ⁿ ⓤ ³ ————————
26 ⁿ ⓥ ⁴ ————————
27 ⁿ ⓔ ⁵ ————————
28 ⁿ ⓞ̸ ⁶ ————————
29 ⁿ ⓔ ⁷ ————————
30 ⁿ ⓘ ¹ ————————
31 ⁿ ⓨ ² ————————
32 ⁿ Ⓘ ³ ————————

Start with a small puff of air through
the nose and with a pencil-sized opening of the mouth behind the hand.

My X-ray motion picture study of singing indicates that when vowels are
sung behind the hand the velum lowers
and the tongue takes its approximate
position for the vowels. The palate
goes up and back when the hand is removed in Upper and Chest voice, but
the palatal action is soft. It must
remain partly open in Falsetto because the back of the tongue and the
soft palate must approach each other
allowing a double stream of vibrating air to pass through <u>both</u> the nose
and mouth. The mouth must be quite
closed for this to happen.

26 ⁿ ⓒⓔ ¹¹ ————————
25 ⁿ Ⓞ ¹⁰ ————————
24 ⁿ ⓥ ⁹ ————————
23 ⁿ ⓒⓔ ⁸ ————————

"Fly it"--there must be a great deal
of air flow to keep this kind of
vibration going. If the flow of air
is not fast enough it will stall out,
eg. it sounds like it is sticking.

22 ⁿ ⓞ̸ ⁷ ————————
21 ⁿ ⓞ ⁶ ————————
20 ⁿ ⓥ ⁵ ————————
19 ⁿ Ⓨ ⁴ ————————

Variation: Sing the vowels indicated without the
hand over the mouth
but simulating that
feeling.

107

The Use of the Open Mouth Hum. Practice the open mouth hum frequently to strengthen the overtone of the Male voice and to
take off the dead weight starting on Note #19. Go as high as
is easy. At Note #30 the Super-Whistle or Head Mix comes in.
If the nasal passage sounds partially closed, pinch the nostrils
and allow the passage to blow open. If there is friction from
a partial closure, a singer's doctor should be seen. Many world
known singers have had deviated septums surgically repaired to
allow complete resonance. The test is to breath easily on a
metal mirror; if the moisture of the breath forms a two-winged
butterfly the septum is in proper position. If the moisture
forms a one-winged butterfly, the septum is deviated and should
be repaired. Allergies and health problems can occur from poor
air flow past the nasal turbinates. See p. 191.

On Note #19, sing the open mouth hum, ^{h} Ⓐ , on the descending
passage indicated. Sing as high as Note #25. This aids in reinforcing the sung pitch of the voice.

When Giovanni Martinelli, who sang at the Metropolitan Opera
Company for 33 seasons, was asked to what he attributed his
longevity, he replied, "First to learn well how to sing, do
not spread the voice, and particularly between the middle and
the high register, keep the voice collected at e, f, and f♯
[Notes #21, 22, 23]. This is the place where most singers,
especially tenors, run into trouble. Be sure of the good
support of deep breath and it is a must, a must I repeat, do
not attempt any role unsuitable to your voice." (Sounds of
Singing, p. 55.)

The Narrow Passaggio preceded by the Open Mouth Hum. Sing the open mouth hum on the first triplet then sing the "collected" (closed) vowel on the upper note and the more open vowel on the lower note. This exercise will establish a channel to the high notes of male voices.

The "collected" sounds at e, f, f# referred to by Martinelli are Mixed Voice. The same procedure should apply to all male singers on Notes #21, 22, and 23 in their voices. I have notated exercises above this point which should be vocalized each day if within the range of the singer. Do not slam down on the low notes--keep them high in the chest for full resonation.

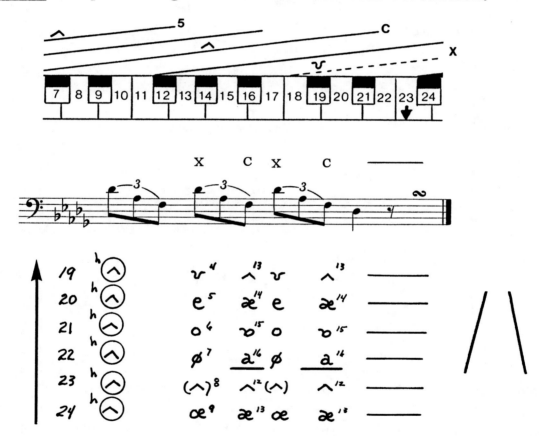

Let the tongue vault upwards and forwards on the closed Front and Umlaut Vowels.

Variation: Sing the last four notes in reverse three times.

M

Yodels at the Fourth from Upper to Mixed and Chest Voice.

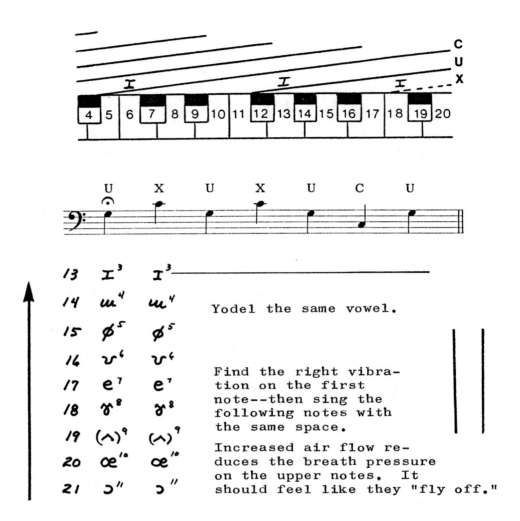

13   I^3 I^3 _____

14   μ^4 μ^4 Yodel the same vowel.

15   ϕ^5 ϕ^5

16   υ^6 υ^6

17   e^7 e^7 Find the right vibration on the first

18   γ^8 γ^8 note--then sing the
following notes with

19   $(\wedge)^9$ $(\wedge)^9$ the same space.

20   $œ^{10}$ $œ^{10}$ Increased air flow reduces the breath pressure

21   $\mathfrak{o}^{11}$ $\mathfrak{o}^{11}$ on the upper notes. It
should feel like they "fly off."

The larynx raises and lowers somewhat for pitch and for vowel.
In the case of a yodel on the same vowel the mouth position will
remain in very nearly the same position, but the larynx will be
found to make slight adjustments in height for pitch. This is
excellent for training a flexible positioning of the larynx and
for the changing of registers. The vowels and pitches are in
harmonic relationship.

M

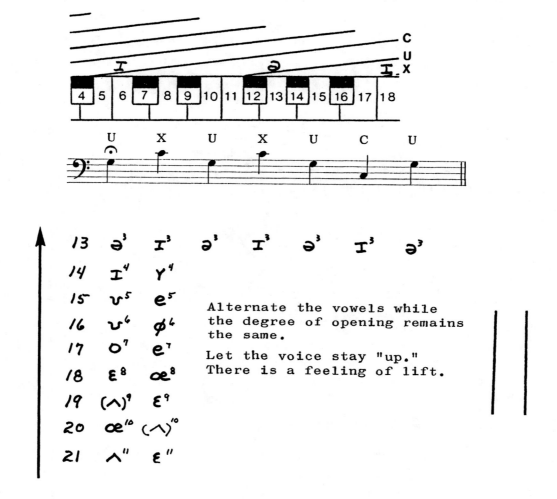

Alternate the vowels while
the degree of opening remains
the same.

Let the voice stay "up."
There is a feeling of lift.

Get into Notes #27, 28, and 29 by dimple Falsetto to avoid
weight.

In yodeling vowels harmonically on the same degree of opening,
one has to have the courage to sing the lower one closed
enough (it will want to open) and to sing the upper note
closed--it will also want to open.

M

<u>Mixed Voice High Notes for Male Voices</u>. Know where you are
going before you get there. Sing the first vowel and then the
second--develop your instinct as to how open the second note
should be. <u>The sense of greatest vibration</u> will tell you when
you are right, then sing the four-note passage to that sound
at the top. When using the Vowel Chart sing different vowel
series on this exercise.

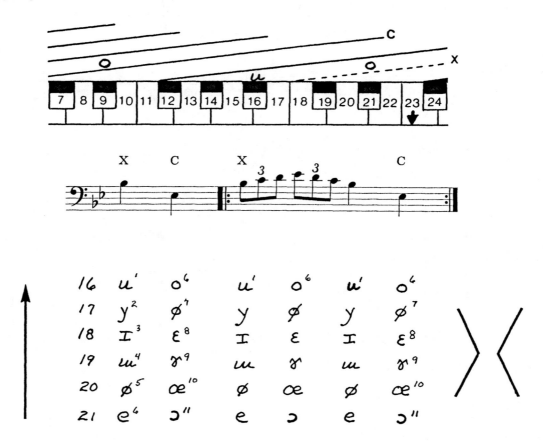

The <u>voix mixte</u> register exists and should be cultivated in all
singing voices. In the Female Voice it also exists between the
Chest and Vowel Registers.

M

Mixed Voice Crossovers to High Voice.

The same exercise crossing over between varied vowel series.

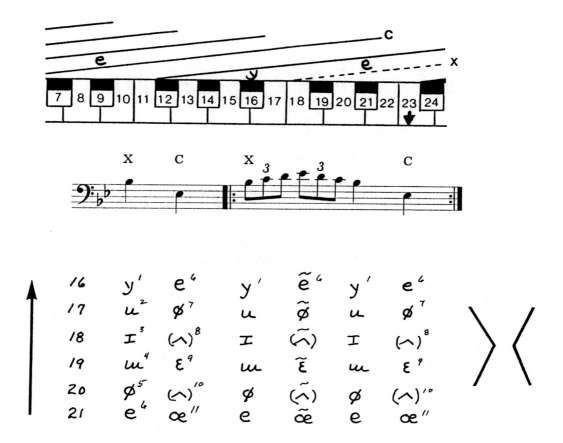

"In studying Italian vocal scores we are forced to the conclusion that in the days of the Old Masters the 'voix mixte' was cultivated to an extremely high degree; it would have been impossible, otherwise, for singers to make use of their high range as continually and skillfully as was called for, and yet have remained active in their art at what in our time seems a remarkable age. Nowadays, when the art of using the 'voix mixte' belongs, apparently, to the realm of fable, we can hardly find a singer capable of interpreting the old Italian compositions; we overcome this difficulty simply by contemptuously shrugging our shoulders at 'Italian acrobatic feats,' and content ourselves with bellowing out high tones with as much dignity as possible. Only a few seem to appreciate that the modern dearth of brilliant tenor voices is to be sought in the non-cultivation of the 'voix mixte.'" August Iffert of Dresden, Germany as translated by Lankow (1902, p. 37).

Low Notes for Basses, Baritones, and Tenors.

Strengthen the low notes by the use of bright vowels--in gold.
If the breath action is stiff, bounce by articulating the
couplets.

There must be muscular contractions in the vocal organ for low
notes--they are not gained by relaxation. The [w], [j], and
[y] contractions help construct low notes. For low notes,
lift the sternum--they take less breath pressure.

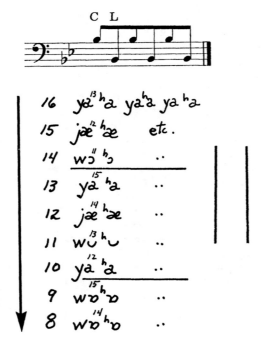

The growl register, sometimes
called strobass or contra-bass
register can be found and strengthened by 8ve leaps downward from
#12 on the first vowel indicated
for that pitch.

The ʰ on the lower note will
assist in establishing this unique vibration. The larynx rises
and there is little resonation--
there is a possibility that resonance comes in after this vibration is established. There is
a great deal of air flow and
little pinch of the glottis on
these notes. Garcia says (1841),
"In order to form this range, it
is necessary to raise the larynx
and enlarge the pharyngeal cavity."
Do not practice this to excess.

114

Yodels at the Fifth on Various Vowels of the Same Resonance
Pitch. Mixed, Vowel and Chest Registers. These are jumping
couplings--the vowels have the same degree of openness.

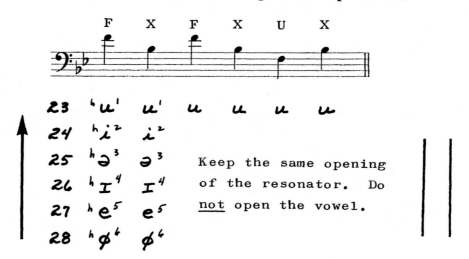

23 $'u'$ u' u u u u

24 $^h i^2$ i^2

25 $^h \partial^3$ ∂^3 Keep the same opening

26 $^h I^4$ I^4 of the resonator. Do

27 $^h e^5$ e^5 <u>not</u> open the vowel.

28 $^h \phi^6$ ϕ^6

Yodels at the Fifth on Related Vowels of the Same Resonance
Pitch. Mixed to Vowel Register. These are jumping couplings--
the vowels have the same degree of openness.

23 ∂' i' ∂' i' ∂' i'

24 y^2 ∂ y ∂ y ∂^2

25 I^3 Y I Y I Y^3

26 Y^4 υ Y υ Y υ^4

27 υ^5 e υ e υ e^5

28 e^6 υ e υ e υ^6

"From the physiological and phoniatric viewpoints it may be said
that correctly formed yodeling represents a natural use of the
voice. A good yodeling style cannot harm the vocal organ. Similar to any other vocal performances, yodeling may be produced
correctly or with faulty technique. Most of the yodelers studied in the course of these investigations were excellent artists.
Several of them had performed for 25 or 30 years without ever
suffering from vocal disorder...yodeling belongs among the physiologically natural styles of artistic singing." Luchsinger
(Switzerland) and Arnold, p. 110.

M

<u>Singing Proper Vowel Pitches in Chest Voice.</u> Establish round-
ness and brightness of low voice on open vowels. Sing different notes which resonate the indicated vowels by their overtones.

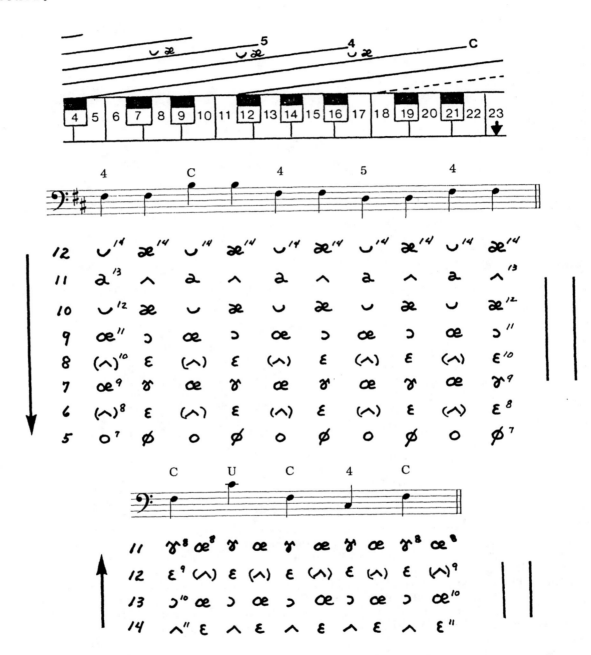

M

Yodeling between the Mixed, the Vowel, and the Upper Registers.
Loosen up the voice! This is the same as lip slurs for a
trumpet.

Yodeling between the Upper, Mixed,
and Chest Registers.

Reinforcing the instrumental vowel
resonance by the 1.5, 2nd, and 3rd
harmonics.

M

Agility Exercises of the Passaggio.

To keep the voice collected in the passaggio it is necessary to
close the vowels on Notes #20, #21 and #22 a bit more than
instinct would indicate. The first sounds of Exercises 19-22
are in Mixed Voice. Each exercise is on the same vowel series.

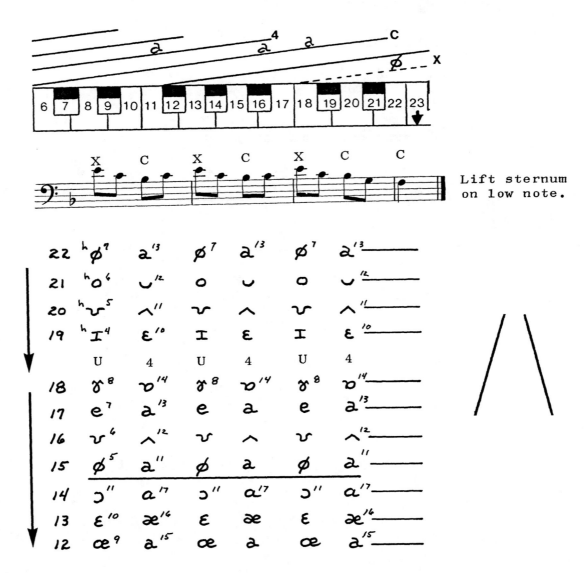

Lift sternum
on low note.

The outer muscles are involved with the tuning of the resonator
as well as the tuning of the vocal cords. Source and system
are one.

M

Crossover Exercises of the Passaggio.

This exercise has crossovers of related vowel series. It is an
excellent area of the voice in which to have dynamic contrasts.
Pianissimo singing should be cultivated after the voice is
placed in resonance and the throat structures have been strengthened by the vocal gymnastics used. Otherwise there is a
tendency to "grab" the throat in soft singing. Keep the air
moving between the vocal cords, and keep the vowels in resonance while making dynamic contrasts in this exercise.

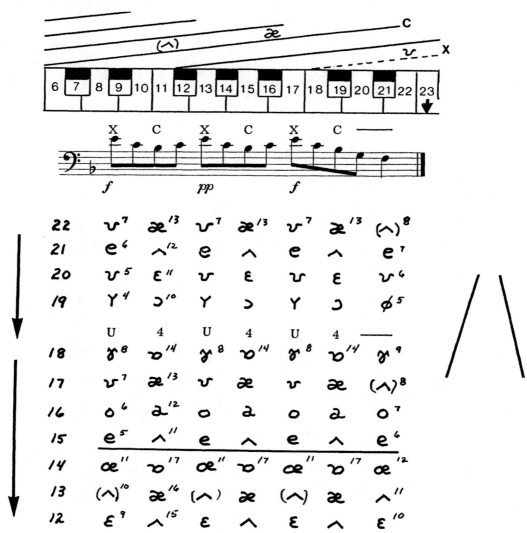

M

Yodels between Upper, Chest, and Vowel Registers at 5th and 4th. These exercises are extremely effective, but very few should be done at a time. DO NOTHING TO EXCESS!!! Move to a contrasting exercise before you feel fatigue.

By singing the vowel on the lower note the upper note is placed before going to it.

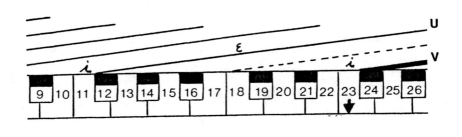

Same Vowel Series

The tongue vaults upward and forward on the Closed Front, and Umlaut Vowels.

120

M

<u>Variation Yodels between Upper and Vowel Registers</u> at 5th and 4th. Alternate between the vowels below.

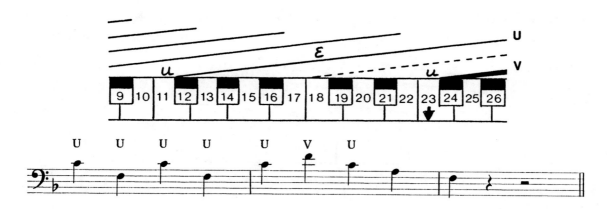

Italian Crossovers--Front and Back Vowels.

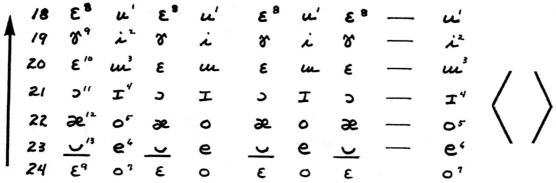

18	$ε^8$	u'	$ε^8$	u'		$ε^8$	u'	$ε^8$	—	u'
19	$γ^9$	i^2	$γ$	i		$γ$	i	$γ$	—	i^2
20	$ε^{10}$	$ɯ^3$	$ε$	$ɯ$		$ε$	$ɯ$	$ε$	—	$ɯ^3$
21	$ɔ^{11}$	I^4	$ɔ$	I		$ɔ$	I	$ɔ$	—	I^4
22	$æ^{12}$	o^5	$æ$	o		$æ$	o	$æ$	—	o^5
23	$ᴗ^{13}$	e^6	$ᴗ$	e		$ᴗ$	e	$ᴗ$	—	e^6
24	$ε^9$	o^7	$ε$	o		$ε$	o	$ε$		o^7

Varied Crossovers.

18	$(ʌ)^8$	i'	$(ʌ)^8$	i'		$(ʌ)^8$	i'	$(ʌ)^8$	—	i'
19	$γ^9$	y^2	$γ$	y		$γ$	y	$γ$	—	y^2
20	$ʌ^{10}$	I^3	$ʌ$	I		$ʌ$	I	$ʌ$	—	I^3
21	$ε^{11}$	Y^4	$ε$	Y		$ε$	Y	$ε$	—	Y^4
22	$ᴗ^{12}$	e^5	$ᴗ$	e		$ᴗ$	e	$ᴗ$	—	e^{5-}
23	$ʌ^{13}$	$ø^6$	$ʌ$	$ø$		$ʌ$	$ø$	$ʌ$	—	$ø^6$
24	$œ^9$	e^7	$œ$	e		$œ$	e	$œ$		e^7

121

M

Chest Voice to Mixed Voice arpeggios--closed Vowels.
Many times languages call for vowels which are not the most
natural to the throat. Use the most comfortable vowel nearest
to that which the language calls for. These placements and
yodels should be alternated with the more usual vowel openings.

Allow the voice to "escape" to the Falsetto in the last four
exercises. Later they can be increased in fullness.

122

Mixed Voice to Chest Register. When singing softly it is well to start with a dimple position of the larynx for Mixed Voice.

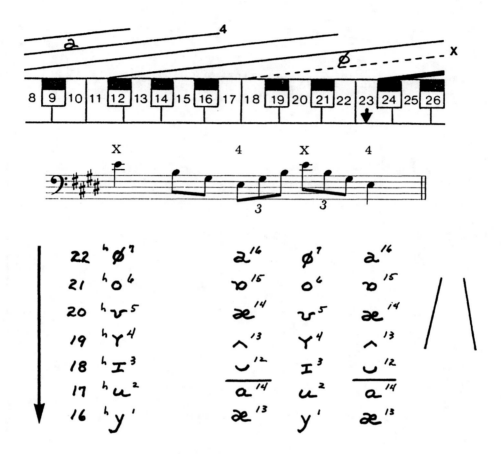

The low notes should feel very high in the body and the head should move well back to assist in the tuning. The gold notes on low notes have the highest degree of opening because the larynx has shifted downwards for the pitch.

Find the full Chest Voice from the breath flow and laryngeal position of the upper note in Mixed Voice. Keep the chest high and ringing. This was of prime importance to Sbriglia.

Crescendo and diminuendo on Mixed Voice sounds below the arrow on Note #23.

M

Falsetto to Mixed Voice. Mixed Voice has an equal distribution
of energy in the note being sung and in the overtone an octave
above. Use falsetto to add energy to the note being sung.

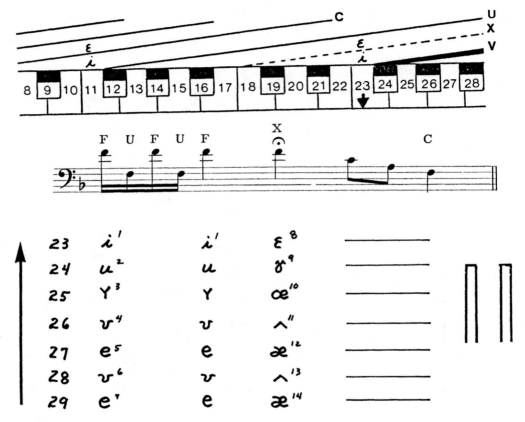

Opening from Falsetto to Mixed Voice.

"As for teaching high notes falsetto, that is only for tenors
who have trouble with their upper voice. Nobody seems to realize that a tenor's high notes are falsetto with breath under
them. Jean de Reszke was a baritone. I made him the greatest
tenor of his time." Sbriglia (Byers), p. 338.

Richard Miller has observed that the Italians do not teach falsetto at present. Something has been lost; Sbriglia was an
Italian tenor from Naples who became one of the greatest teachers of all time having taught the De Reszkes, Nordica, Plançon,
and Sybil Sanderson. I believe the falsetto should be used as
a teaching technique for all voices.

Vowels in blue and green on the Vowel Register are Falsetto for
Male Voices when sung softly.

124

M

Yodels between Upper and Vowel Register at Major 3rd. Do very
few of these at one time. Also alternate yodeling from top
down and bottom up.

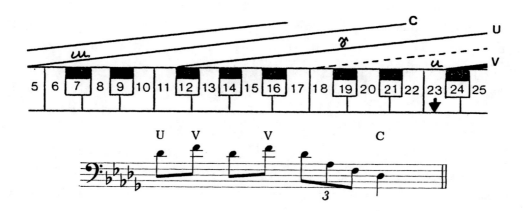

Same Vowel Series.

19	ɤ⁹ ʰu¹	ɤ⁹	u¹	ɤ⁹		u¹
20	ɛ¹⁰ ʰi²	ɛ	i	ɛ		i²
21	ɔ¹¹ ʰɯ³	ɔ	ɯ	ɔ		ɯ³
22	æ¹² ʰɪ⁴	æ	ɪ	æ		ɪ⁴
23	ʌ¹³ ʰʊ⁵	ʌ	ʊ	ʌ		ʊ⁵
24	æ¹⁴ ʰe⁶	æ	e	æ		e⁶

Varied Crossovers.

19	(ʌ)⁹ ʰi¹	ʌ⁹	i¹	ʌ⁹		i¹
20	ɛ¹⁰ ʰy²	ɛ	y	ɛ		y²
21	ʌ¹¹ ʰɪ³	ʌ	ɪ	ʌ		ɪ³
22	ʊ¹² ʰY⁴	ʊ	Y	ʊ		Y⁴
23	ʌ¹³ ʰe⁵	ʌ	e	ʌ		e⁵
24	æ¹⁴ ʰø⁶	æ	ø	æ		ø⁶

Variation: pp mf pp with dimple Vowel Register.

125

<u>Augmented Triad, Whole Tone Scale, and Chromatic Phonetics.</u>
Resonance tracking on the same Track and the same Vowel Ser-
ies--which gives a constant vibration of the lower resonance.
Vowels are usually different at the interval of a Major 3rd on
the Chromatic Vowel Scale. After the Augmented Triad and Whole
Tone Scales have been sung, heard and felt, then fill in the
half steps to hear and feel the subtle gradations in the Chromatic Vowel Scale. Chromatic phonetics are a necessity to the
singer--linguistic phonetics in singing cause atrocious sounds
and problems. I have warned of this in the Foreword of
<u>Phonetic Readings of Songs and Arias</u> which was published 15
years ago. Now we can tell the singer what should be done to
make the best wedding of language and music. In the process,
this is a discipline which will build a healthy and beautiful
voice. Exercises on Notes #6-10 are in what has been called
chest register. Exercises from Notes #11 to 16 are in what we
call "Upper Voice," Track 2.

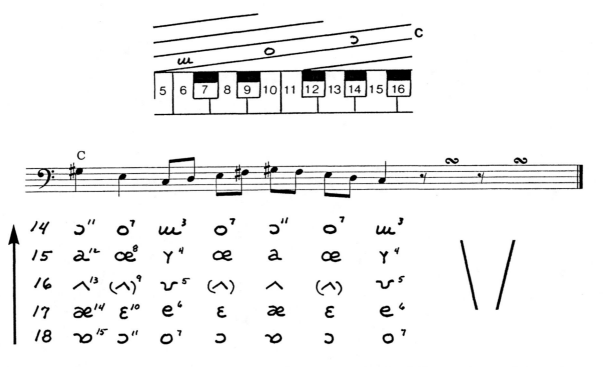

Keep chest up on last note and turn twice without breathing
on rest.

M

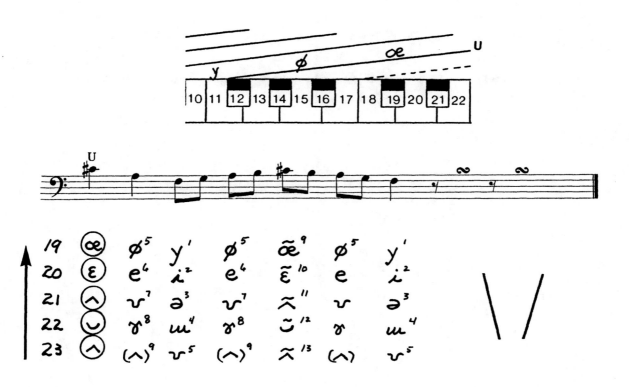

Resonance tracking of florid exercises in the same pipe act as a massage to the voice.

Keep the chest up on the last note.

Variation: Start the exercise without the hand over the mouth using the degrees of opening indicated.

Perhaps the word "piping" is more meaningful to singers than the term "resonance tracking." Whatever it is called, it is very obvious in treble singers because of the more critical overtone relationship to the resonator in their voices.

M

Messa di Voce High Notes.

There is a piano high voice that has a bit more space which a
singer can crescendo and diminuendo. It demands a flexible
breath starting lightly, becoming heavier and then becoming
lighter (or high, low and higher). The vowel centering must
be exact and both the larynx position and breath must be
supple. It should be practiced daily.

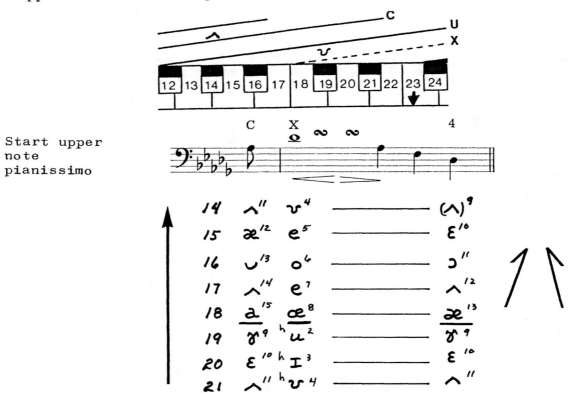

Start upper
note
pianissimo

Lengthen and shorten the velar-pharyngeal axis when making the
messa di voce. Pages 128, 129, 134, and 135 are studies in
breath management. They are basic to dynamic interest and vo
vocal coloring.

Variation--

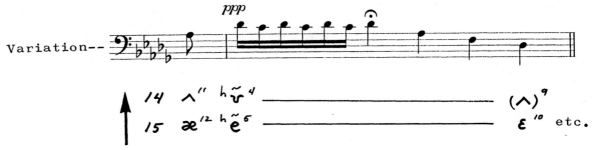

128

M

<u>Cercar la Nota</u>--which means "search for the note." This also involves finding the resonances and the shifting of registers. It might also be called a "reasonance suspension." Sing the first note as an <u>acciacatura</u> or hammered note.

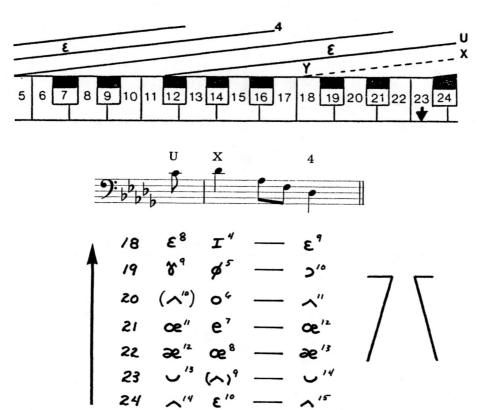

Variation: Sing the second vowel on the first two notes, sliding into resonance.

Back vowels do not work well on Notes #27, 28, and 29 because of the necessity for tongue elevation and fronting to make the higher resonance frequencies.

M

Singing the Bright Vowels for Low Voice. Resonance Tracking by
Yodeling. Vocalizing on the gold vowels will give brilliance
to the male voice. This is best done by yodeling the same
vowels on the indicated intervals. (They are sub-harmonics of
the vowel sung.) In other words, all pitches of the exercise
have the same vowel as their reinforced overtone.

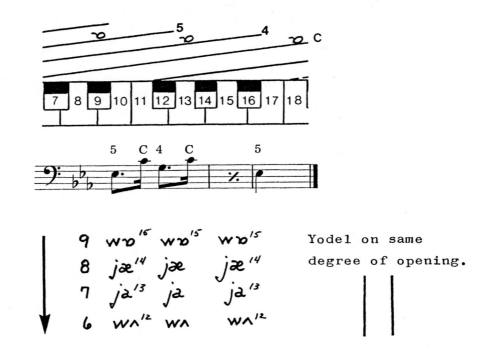

Yodel on same
degree of opening.

Alternate with Crossovers between Varied Vowel Series.

<u>Yodels between Chest, Upper and Mixed Registers</u>. These are
actually moving rhymes since the openings of the vowels in each
of the lines is the same. This is an easy way to find the
placement of extreme notes and facilitates the ability of the
voice to move up and down.

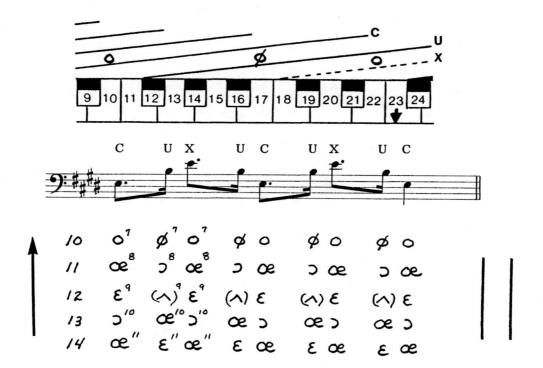

Where is pitch created? It is created <u>both</u> by the larynx and
the vocal tract. This is known as source and system. This is
the reason we have so much forced and out of tune singing--the
system is distuning the pitch of the vocal cords. This text
tells how to tune the system to vocal cord vibration.

It is believed by some that the intrinsic muscles of the vocal
cords themselves are involved with vowel formation. It is
safest to work a broad spectrum of vowel colors so that all
muscular systems will be activated.

M

Agility Exercise, Mixed Voice and Down.

Do not sing this exercise to the upper limit of your voice.
Also, do not practice this to excess. Keep moving from one
part of the voice to another.

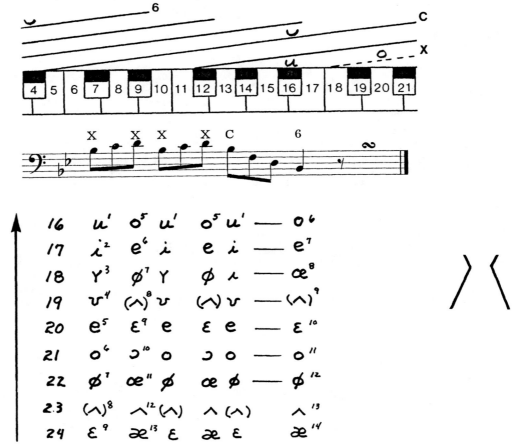

Variation: Sing chromatic thirds for the first two groups.
Keep the chest up on the turn at the end.

132

M

The Mixed Voice which shows on the dotted line is the way male voices can keep the tone collected at the e, f, and f# referred to by Martinelli. Learn to switch into it and out of it. This is one of the great techniques of a singer. In my observation it is a learned technique and is not a natural one. It must be practiced or the voice will spread at the wrong spot. Notice that register changes occur at different places for different vowels!

Sing this varied vowel series. This will do much to blend the vowel colors.

Variation: Also sing chromatics on the first two groups.

M

Pianissimo High Notes. Uncouple the voice for <u>sotto voce</u> high
notes. The word for "clutch" in German is "Kuppelung" or
coupler. When going to <u>sotto voce</u> high notes uncouple the
engine of the breath by use of a light [h]. Let the larynx feel
high and the soft palate low. The use of this is for color contrast and physical rest.

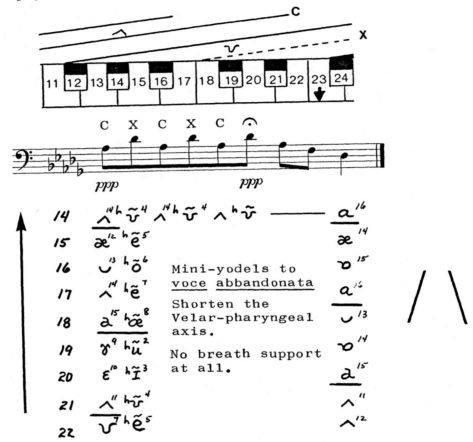

Alternate between natural voice on the lower note and a feeling
of falsetto on the upper on which there is a high larynx and a
slight flow of air through the nose.

Keep the chest up, the ribs very wide and the waist thin.

Make a smaller mouth cavity on the upper note by a slight closing of the jaw.

134

M

Forte High Notes. This exercise is for developing the Mixed Voice for High Notes. The larynx feels deeper because of darker vowels and the ascent is made in the same register. One sometimes has the feeling of grunting on this exercise. The engine of the breath is definitely coupled.

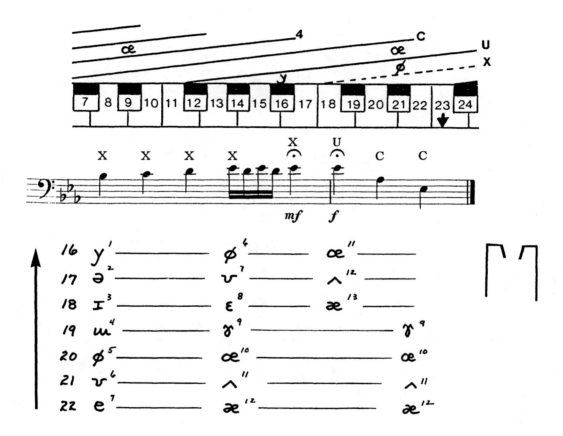

In the crescendo and diminuendo enlarge and diminish the size of the vowel cavity (lengthen and shorten the velar pharyngeal axis).

The vowels must fit the throat. This is necessary for them to have both fullness and ring.

Form the correct resonator through which you sing by inhaling on the vowel which you are just about to sing.

M

<u>Strengthening the Center of the Voice.</u>

Extremes of pronunciation. This is a physical workout because
the opposites are so extreme. Because of this it is excellent
for establishing flexibility of the articulators while maintaining resonance.

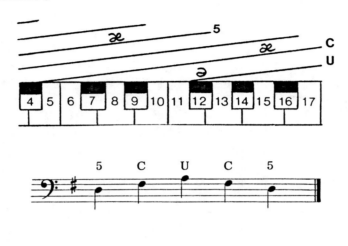

8 jæ^{14} wə^2 jæ^{12} wə^2 jæ^{14}

9 wɔ^{11} jʏ^3 wʊ^{13} jʏ wɔ^{11}

10 wʌ^{12} jɪ^4 wʌ^{14} jɪ wʌ^{12}

11 jɛ^8 wʊ^5 jɛ^8 wʊ jɛ^8

12 jœ^9 wu^1 jœ̃^{9} wu jœ^9

13 wɔ^{10} jy^2 wɔ̃^{10} jy wɔ^{10}

M

Strengthening the Center of the Voice.

Extremes of pronunciation which involve changes of registers.
The use of extreme alternate sounds develops strength and
articulatory skills.

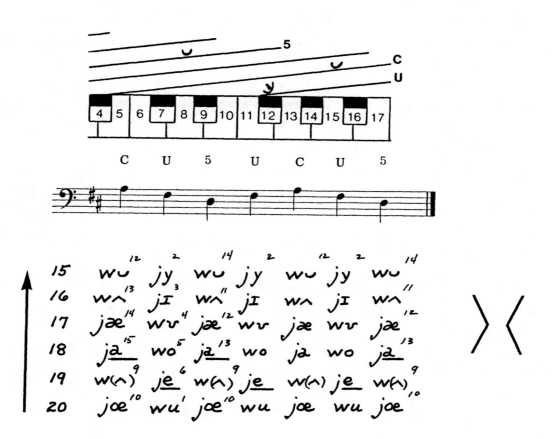

Substitute Vowels. On the notes just above the passaggio in
male voices the vowels, [i], [ə], [u], and [y] are so closed
that singers have difficulty in singing them because of breath
compression and muscular contractions of the throat. Therefore,
on the arrow ²↓³ and Notes #24, 25, and 26 the singer may
substitute the vowels on the dotted line just above on the Chromatic Vowel Chart. These are in Mixed Voice which extends to
the extreme high notes of the Male Voice. The Mixed Voice exists because of the ability to reinforce and resonate the vowels
on the Vowel Register, and the octave above. The [i] on Notes
#23 and 24 may be sung as [œ]. Garcia said the vowels should be
opened somewhat in this part of the male voice. My statement
indicates how to open these close vowels and retain some of
their color. (See p. 221 concerning the harmonic structure of
Mixed Voice.) The sound will have a more veiled and sympathetic
quality when these vowels are used. If intensity is desired in
the interpretation, the closed forms may be sung.

Hole in the Sky. I have called these vowels "Hole in the Sky."
At Cape Kennedy when astronauts were sent into orbit there was
an established hole in the sky through which the rocket had to
pass before orbit was possible, otherwise the flight was abort-
ed. This "Hole in the Sky" is the secret to the upper extension in male voices.

M

Low Voice. Resonance tracking while switching registers and changing vowel series.

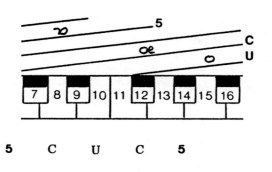

On Notes #23-#26 use equivalents:

23 - Substitute [ɤ] for [u]
24 - Substitute [œ] for [i]
25 - Substitute [œ] for [y]
26 - Substitute [ɔ] for [ɯ]

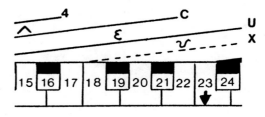

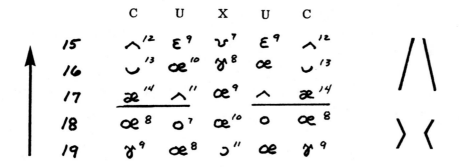

M

<u>Warm-ups by muscular and resonance contrasts in the middle</u>
<u>range of the voice</u>.

Opposite sets of muscles open and close the vocal tract, form
the four vowel series and act upon the vocal folds. All can
be activated early in vocalization in the middle range of the
voice. Use both slow and quick consonants.

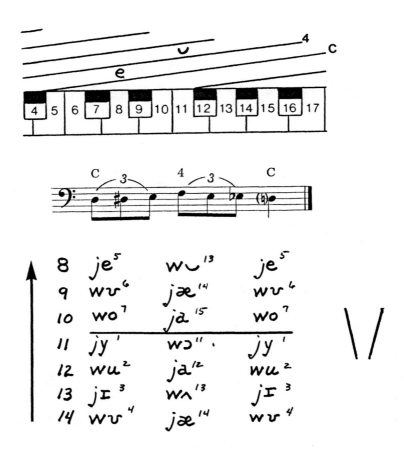

When the vowel of the last pitch is centered it is possible to
lean the breath against the arch of the chest and have a <u>messa</u>
<u>di voce</u>.

If there is a feeling of phlegm in the throat this exercise frequently removes this feeling.

M

Warm up both the laryngeal and articulatory muscles. Acoustical exercises in middle range. Solfeggio was used by the old
Italian teachers to make the articulatory muscles supple.
Flexibility of articulation and strength should be developed in
relationship to the ear which is the supreme control. This
equalizes what has been called the lower passaggio in male
voices. Change dynamics in this exercise, also making it a
study in the messa di voce. The low notes are quite full when
coming down from upper notes--there seems to be a better
air-flow.

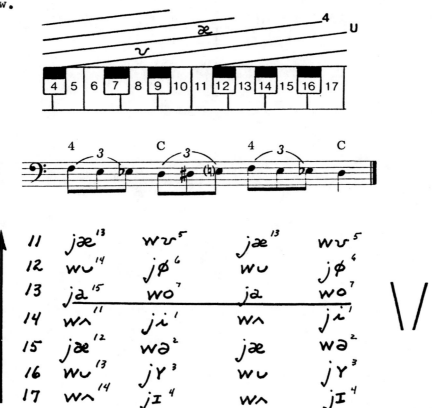

"In time many singers lose their voices through inflexibility
of the muscles of the tongue and larynx. As beauty of tone is
the foundation of vocal art, it should be the aim of every
singer to alter it as little as possible by means of a skillful
and flexible pronunciation without endangering the distinctness
of enunciation." Lilli Lehmann, p. 278.

141

M

Resonance Tracking in Scales.

Tune to the low and high vowels then make a quick run between
resonance points. The switch of tracks will be hardly noticed
by the listener and singer.

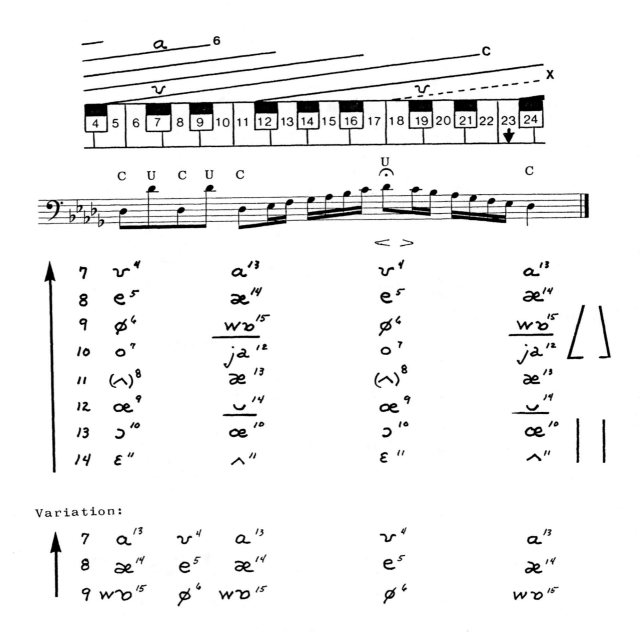

Variation:

Make a gradual change of opening in the runs.

142

M

Agility Exercises on Passaggio from Mixed to Chest Voice, Crossover Exercises.

M

Arpeggios--Switching Tracks to Mixed Voice.

Closed at top and bottom, more open in the middle.

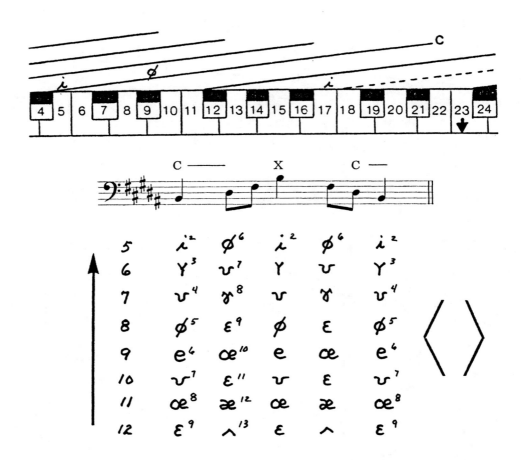

Various Vowel Series.

144

M

<u>Switching Tracks through the Passaggio</u>. More open at top and
and bottom, narrower in the middle of the arpeggio.

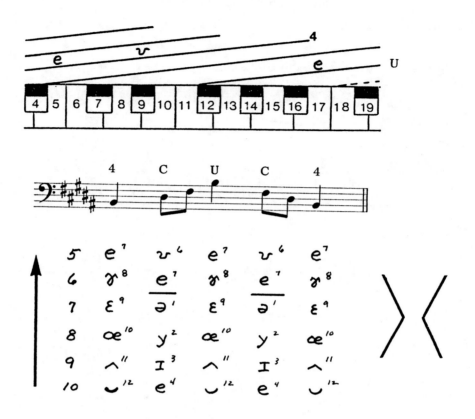

Crossovers of Various Vowel Series.

M

Tenor High Notes--Close.

There are two ways of resonance tracking to the tenor high notes. First, approach them with <u>close</u> vowels on the lower and upper octave with open vowels between. Be sure and BITE the high note to <u>close</u> it. Yodel several times on the first vowel at the octave before doing the exercise.

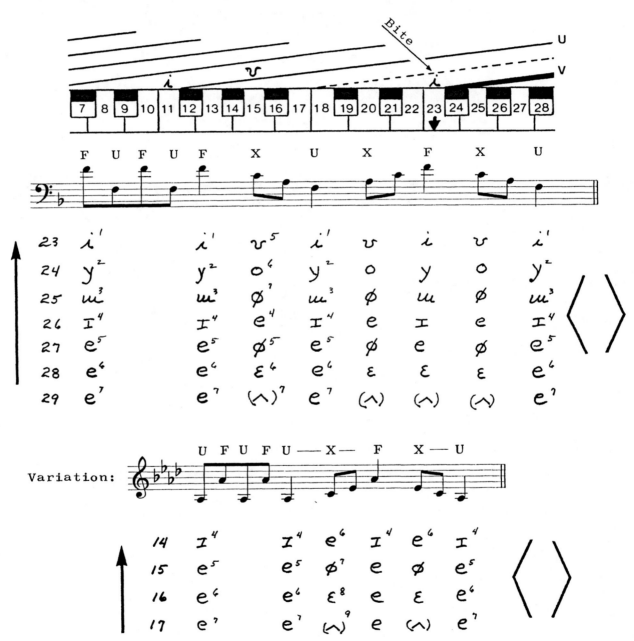

M

Tenor High Notes--Open. The second way is with <u>open</u> vowels on the lower and upper octave with <u>close</u> vowels between to make the switch of tracks. Yodel several times on the first vowel at the octave before doing the exercise.

<u>DO NOT OVERDO SUCCESS</u>!!!

At openings 5, 6, and 7 the Falsetto opens up enough to couple and becomes the upper extension of the Tenor Voice.

M

Baritone and Bass-Baritone High Notes--Close. There are two
ways to brilliant baritone and bass-baritone high notes. They
may be gained on close vowels on high notes; approach from
open vowels on the track of the high note and BITE for the
closure on the high note.

M

Baritone and Bass-Baritone High Notes--Open. Approach the open
vowels on high notes by yodeling proper open vowels then switch
to a close vowel on the same track by <u>biting</u> the closed vowel.
Then proceed up the track or channel to the proper open vowel
on top.

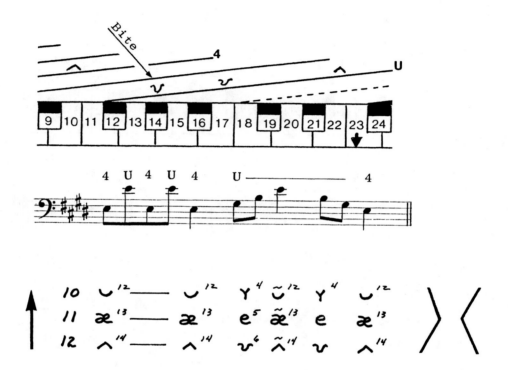

Let the larynx be flexible in yodeling. When singing the exercise, the ribs are wide and the waist thin.

DO NOT OVERDO SUCCESS!

Passaggio exercises to lower voice.

Find the placement of the lower tone by vowel rhyming before
singing downward to it. Preceed at times with open mouth hum
ʰⒶ which will lift the dead weight from the voice and help to
establish the Mixed voice of the passaggio. Rhyming green,
green, green vowels and going downward to one of them, thus also
tuning the lower note.

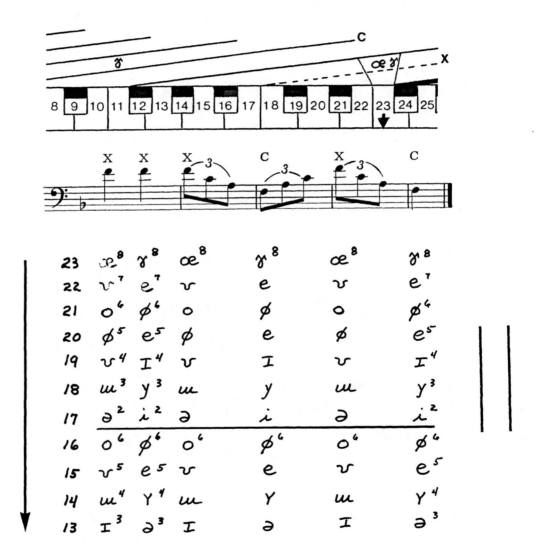

23	œ^8	ɤ^8	œ^8	ɤ^8	œ^8	ɤ^8
22	ʊ^7	e^7	ʊ	e	ʊ	e^7
21	o^6	ø^6	o	ø	o	ø^6
20	ø^5	e^5	ø	e	ø	e^5
19	ʊ^4	I^4	ʊ	I	ʊ	I^4
18	ɯ^3	y^3	ɯ	y	ɯ	y^3
17	ə^2	i^2	ə	i	ə	i^2
16	o^6	ø^6	o^6	ø^6	o^6	ø^4
15	ʊ^5	e^5	ʊ	e	ʊ	e^5
14	ɯ^4	Y^4	ɯ	Y	ɯ	Y^4
13	I^3	ə^3	I	ə	I	ə^3

Variation: Begin on second note.

M

Mixed Voice, Upper Voice, Mixed Voice Passaggio to Low Voice.
Switch tracks to a brighter vowel to get the feel and sound.
Then sing down to that vowel--you will know the placement before
you get there. Then return to the collected or rounded upper
tone before finishing the exercise. The fast notes are not
placed and do not need to be. Open the second note five degrees and change registers.

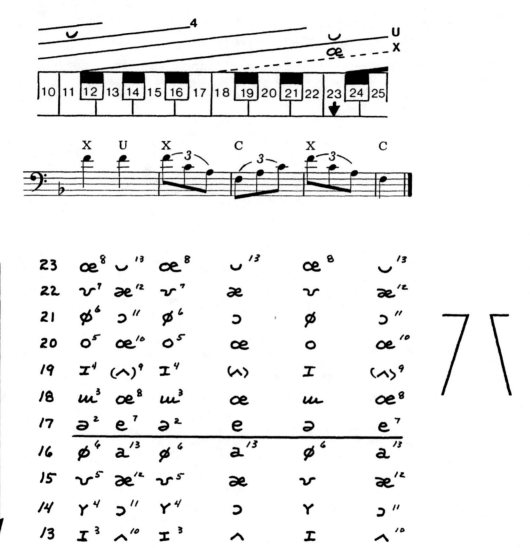

Variation: Begin on second note.

151

M

Sotto Voce. Dimple <u>Falsetto</u> in high voice and down.

Inhale through both nose and mouth with head back--when singing imagine you are inhaling in that manner.

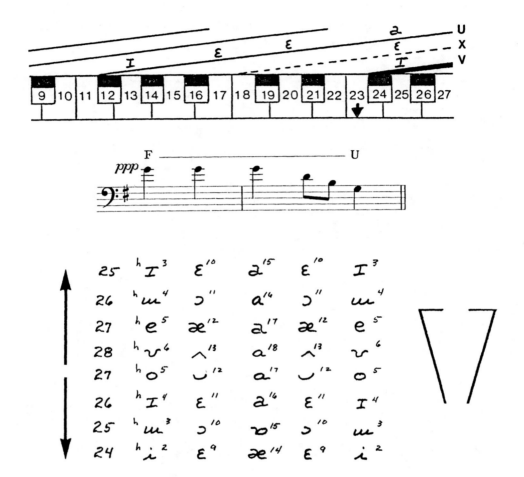

Variation: Start after the bar.

M

Half Voice in Mixed Voice. Although the voice is ascending in
the same channel. The upper note will be facilitated by a
slight [h]. The singer can crescendo and diminuendo this quality
to full voice.

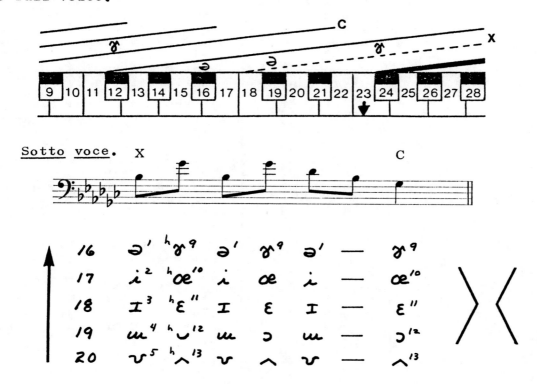

Although this is not a yodel, since it is on the same track,
the upper note becomes easier if preceded by an aspirate which
negates any tendency to carry up weight.

The upper falsetto is half dimple.

DIPHTHONG CHART

	æe	αo		ɔø	ei

Sing across on the same pitch so that there is a continuity of resonance. Each diphthong should have a diminuendo ‎>‎.

	æe	αo		ɔø	ei
29	æe	æʊ			æe
28	æe	æʊ			æe
27	æe	æʊ	1.5		æe
26	ʌɛ	ʌʊ		ɔœ	ɛɪ
25	ʌɛ	ɔʌ		ɔœ	ɛɪ
24	ʌɛ	ʌɣ		ɣœ	ɛi
23	ʌɛ	ʌɣ		ɣœ	ɛi
22	ʌe	ʌʊ	2	ʊø	eɪ
21	ʌe	ʌʊ		ɔø	eɪ
20	ʌe	ʌʊ		ɔø	eɪ
19	ʌɪ	αɣ		ɣœ	ɛɪ
18	aɪ	αɣ		ɣœ	ɛɪ
17	ae	ɒo	3	ʊø	ei
16	ae	ʌo		ʊø	ei
15	ae	ʌo		ʊø	ei
14	aɪ	ʌʊ		ɔɣ	ɛɪ
13	aɪ	ɒa		ɔɣ	ɛɪ
12	aɛ	ɒɣ	4	ʊœ	ɛi
11	ae	αɣ		⌣œ	ɛi
10	ae	αʊ		⌣œ	ei
9	ae	ɒa		ɔœ	ɛe
8	ae	ɒo		ɔœ	ɛe
7	aɛ	αʊ	5	ʊœ	ɛɪ
6	aɛ	ɒʊ		ʊœ	ɛɪ
5	aɛ	ɒɔ		ɔø	ei
4	aɛ	αɔ		ɔø	ei
3	aɛ	αɣ	6	ʊœ	ei
2	aɛ	αɣ		ɔœ	ɛɪ
1	aɛ	ɒɔ		ɔœ	ɛɪ
0	aɛ	ɒɔ		ɔœ	ɛe

(Register Shifts by Harmonic)

Fig. 21.

Diphthongs are glides which should be harmonic or they will be weak. They may occur between vowels on the same Track with the same or different vowel series, or on different tracks.

French and German are more rounded than English. English has 1/3rd rounded vowels--both French and German have 2/3rds of the vowels rounded. For long notes in singing, where standing waves are necessary, the rounded glides of diphthongs should be used in all languages. Diphthongs are <u>directions</u> of vowel shift --go to the nearest harmonic. This page should be practiced and used as a reference.

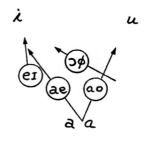

154

FRENCH NASAL CHART

With the nasal passage left open so that the air vibrates through both nose and mouth.

	ã	ẽ	ɔ̃	œ̃	
30					30
29	æ̃	æ̃			29
28	æ̃	æ̃			28
27	æ̃	æ̃			27
26	ᴧ̃	ẽ	ɔ̃	œ̃	26
25	ᴧ̃	ẽ	ɔ̃	œ̃	25
24	ᴧ̃	ẽ	ɣ̃	œ̃	24
23	ʊ̃	ẽ	ɣ̃	œ̃	23 →
22	ʊ̃	æ̃	õ	ᴧ̃	22
21	ᴧ̃	ẽ	õ	ᴧ̃	21
20	ᴧ̃	ẽ	õ	ᴧ̃	20
19	ᴧ̃	ẽ	ɣ̃	ᴧ̃	19
18	ʊ̃	ẽ	ɣ̃	ᴧ̃	18
17	ʊ̃	æ̃	õ	ᴧ̃	17
16	ʊ̃	æ̃	õ	ᴧ̃	16
15	ʊ̃	æ̃	õ	ᴧ̃	15
14	ɔ̃	ẽ	ɔ̃	ᴧ̃	14
13	ʊ̃	ẽ	ɔ̃	ᴧ̃	13
12	ʊ̃	æ̃	ɣ̃	ᴧ̃	12
11	ʊ̃	æ̃	ɣ̃	ᴧ̃	11
10	ʊ̃	æ̃	õ	ᴧ̃	10
9	ʊ̃	ẽ	ɔ̃	ᴧ̃	9
8	ʊ̃	æ̃	ɔ̃	ᴧ̃	8
7	ʊ̃	æ̃	ɣ̃	ᴧ̃	7
6	ʊ̃	æ̃	ɣ̃	ᴧ̃	6
5	ʊ̃	æ̃	ɔ̃	ᴧ̃	5
4	ʊ̃	æ̃	ɔ̃	ᴧ̃	4

Fig. 22.   Delattre

Nasal Vowels.
Notice the velum is lowered and the base of the tongue raised.

In nasal vowels the soft palate is lowered to allow the nasal passages to vibrate. This also creates a weaker resonance of R^1. Nasal vowels are for passaggio notes and head voice. If even one of the nasal passages is obstructed there is a <u>cul de sac</u> sound which reduces resonance and makes passaggios difficult. Professional singers attempt to cancel performances when the nose is closed. If there is a partial closure of either nasal passage it should be repaired by a singer's doctor. See pp. 192 and 193.

M

<u>The Scoring of Songs and Arias</u>. Vocalization on the exercises
in this text will do much to automate the singing senses of ear,
throat, and eye. A vowel and note on a pitch will cause the
singer to hear, see, and feel the sound before it is sung.
However, there are certain notes or passages which are worthy
of attention by the teacher and student because they are difficult due to register, opening, and vowel problems. These can
be scored before they are sung so that the singer's kinesthetic
memory will have a positive thing to do rather than being con-
fused by the memory of a poorly placed vowel. Do not learn
music with the throat! Score the most effective vowel-harmonic
in relationship to the rest of the vocal line.

The examples given are all operatic because they are written
for very specific voice classifications. Songs are transposed
and sung on differing pitches by different voices. To notate
a song for all voice classifications would be an exercise in
futility. However, a study of <u>how</u> scoring of arias for specific voices is done will show singers the way to score vowels
for their own individual throats in any music they sing.

I will classify voices by arrow placement--fortunately compo-
ers were writing for specific voices which could do certain
things on certain notes--otherwise they were changed (sometimes by the singer). Thus I will give examples for a tenor
whose arrow is on g^1--called <u>G</u> tenor. Other examples are for
<u>F#</u> tenor, <u>F</u> baritone, and <u>D</u> bass.

Scoring a song or aria may appear to be tedious but so is fingering wind instruments. The phenomenon is the same; <u>control
the resonance</u> and help the vocal cords. Scoring may be done
just on exposed notes or rather completely; you will know your
needs. A successful appearance is a much happier event than
an embarrassing one. Scoring, with growing skill, will improve your hearing and feeling, and will give you an overtone
control of your <u>bel canto</u>.

156

M

Scoring can be done only in questionable spots. The example is
for tenor with the arrow on F#.

F# Tenor

Or scoring can be done more extensively.

Or scoring can be complete according to individual needs of the
singer. I will score the examples rather completely. Watch the
numbers and notice the opening and closing; frequently most of
the opening is on the inside of the mouth being done by the
tongue where it cannot be seen. The numbers assist the singer
in resonance tracking and in knowing whether an overtone shift
is occuring (register change).

M

F# Tenor

Language has to be modified to sing this passage successfully.
The problem is basically with, _si_ and secondarily with _io_.

Register	Vowel Openings	
X	e o⁷	The diphthong will have ring is fund as _eo_, see diphthong chart, p. 154.
ʋ	(ʌ)⁹	_nar_. Sing sheltered _ah_ for resonance.
X	œ⁹	_si_. Sing [œ] which reinforces both the sung pitch and the octave when a vowel half way between the sung pitch and the 8ve is sung. This means there is an [i]--aural illusion.
X	ʋ⁵	n_u_nzio--open [u] to [ʋ] on pipe series.
4	∪¹²	Sing ∪ in Chest register.
c	a¹²	Sing an honest [a] where it is possible. It is the last note and emphatic.

M

un   dol - ce ri - sto - ro   al cor__ por - ge - rà,__   un

G Tenor

The largest problem with this aria is what to do with "dolce."
In changing registers, even if it can be a yodel on the same
vowel, shift to another series if possible so that there is a
change of articulation musculature when the sung pitch changes,
therefore:

Register   Vowel Openings

υ   ɔ¹⁰ ∧¹⁰   dol. This is a yodel on 10th degree of
X   (∧)¹⁰ ce   opening. Change the vowel series to
X   I⁴ ri   facilitate the melodic flow.
U   ɤ⁸ sto

The (∧) vowel gives a more frontal tongue
movement for the high note--so go to the
pipe vowel series and sing uh with lips
rounded (∧) coming down on that vowel.

U   ∪¹² co   Come down the track.

C   ɔ¹⁰ por   Ah porgerà should be sheltered ah [∧] so
C   ∧¹² 11 rà   that all resonators keep vibrating.

Breath: The ribs widen in support and the waist thins above d^1.
d^1. Below d^1 is just resting.

Since the vowels are known in many cases, a thought of <u>the
degree of opening</u> will suffice. In yodels, as in "dolce" a
crossover will facilitate the change of register.

159

M

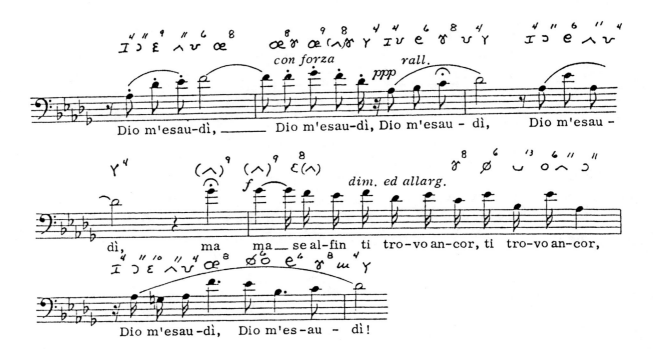

F Baritone

This is one of the most difficult passages for the baritone
voice. The primary problem is how to keep the voice resonating
without touching the throat. Mixed Voice must first be established by several months of vocalization. Notice how many of
the notes are in Mixed Voice, symbolized by X.

Register   Vowel

    X   œ ɤ ʌɤ all in Mixed Voice! Do they look like pure
                  Italian vowels? No--but they give instru-
                  mental Italian tone.

    X   hm(ʌ)[10] Use a puff of air through the nose before the
                  m to establish air flow for the consonant and
                  vowel. The singer must use the sheltered (ʌ)[10]
                  on the Ah.

    X   ɤ   Ending note--feel the vibration on the lips
                  and keep the air flowing.

160

M

I have scored this passage using Umlaut vowels for many of the modifications. It may be possible to think the Italian vowels with loose lips. They would make nearly the same sound. Be very conscious of the degrees of opening in problem places. Watch video tapes to see how Italian singers tune their vowels for instrumental tone. When scoring for voice, stay as near to the green as possible in the passaggio area.

In die - sen heil'-gen Hal -len kennt man die Ra-che nicht,

D Bass

Register	Vowel	
X	Y	The voice needs to be slightly closed for orotund voice in which there is both fullness and brilliance. This aria begins on a lower extension of Mixed Voice.
ʊ	ɔ¹⁰ø⁷	Use [Y] instead of in the beginning. There is a problem with the diphthong on <u>heil'gen</u>--round the ah to [ɔ] or [ʌ] and use [ø] for the vanish to keep the resonator vibrating.
4	(ʌ)¹⁰	<u>Hallen</u>. Round a sheltered ah [ʌ].
5	ʌ¹⁴	<u>Rache</u>.
∪	y²	<u>nicht</u>--use either y² or neutral lipped [i].

It is not necessary to score all vowels--just those whose resonance you have difficulty in finding.

161

M

Do these look like the German vowels in our text, <u>Phonetic</u> <u>Readings</u>? No. They have been treated for instrumental resonance and will sound like German. Coaches please take note of the singer's dilemma!!!

CHAPTER IV

SINGING MUSCULATURES AND RESONANCES

Observations on the physiological-acoustic basis of singing are
available from the early part of the last century. A contempor-
ary comprehension of the phonetic basis of artistic singing will
be best understood if a few muscular and sound occurrences are
narrated and described by both word and picture.

First I show the vocal cords as they would appear for silent
breathing in singing. A very large breath can be taken quickly
with this opening. When the cords are close together, forming
a narrow opening, a person can whisper and pronounce all of the

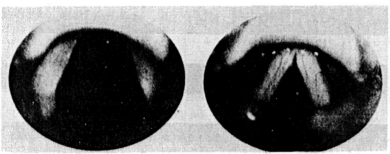

Forced inhalation. This subject
is demonstrating very nearly maximum abduction of the vocal folds.

Forced exhalation. In this condi-
tion the glottis does not appear
different from the glottis during
quiet breathing.

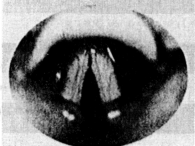

From SPEECH AND HEARING
SCIENCE by Willard R.
Zemlin. Reprinted by
permission of Prentice-
Hall, Inc., Englewood
Cliffs, NJ, 1968.

Fig. 23.

Normal inhalation. During quiet
breathing the glottis may remain
essentially unchanged from inhalation to exhalation.

Glottal configurations for forced inhalation and
exhalation and during quiet breathing.

163

sounds except those which are vocalized. However, enough sounds of language are present so that language can be understood. No harmonics appear in whispered speech.

It is not known what the vocal cords look like in the production of good sung tone, nor will it ever be known because any device inserted into the vocal tract upsets vocal function to such an extent that no good tone or variety of good tones can be made. This also pertains to insertion of fiberoptics through the nasal passage. As an example, try to speak while holding one of the nostrils closed. The waves formed upon the air particles are disturbed and they in turn disturb the action of the vocal folds. I show no pictures of vocal cords in singing vibration because I feel that none have or can be taken of good singing vibration. Furthermore, there is evidence that the vocal cords vibrate differently for vowels. As early as 1906 Scripture reported in the Carnegie Institute Publications (p. 164) that after experimentation with artificial resonators and rubber membranes it was observed that the membranes vibrated differently for vowels depending on the action of the air in the cavities above them.

Vowels in singing are brought about by articulations of the tongue, jaw, lips, soft palate, and movements of the head. The articulation of the front vowels is indicated in Fig. 24. Two things may be seen. [i] has a very closed space in the front of the mouth and a large space in the back. [ɪ] has a larger space in the front and a smaller space in the back. The tongue progresses backwards to [æ] which has a very large space in the front and a smaller space in the back. (This is closely related to the Italian Ah.) At the time the tongue action is occurring, the jaw is making a gradual opening. These are known as the Front vowels because the tongue hump is forward, approaching the hard palate. They are most important to the singer because if vocalization occurs only on Back vowels the voice becomes overly heavy. Balanced vocalization utilizes all vowel series.

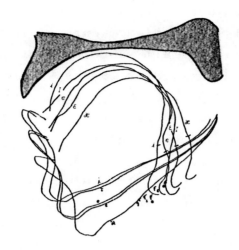

Fig. 24.

Permission of Peter Ladefoged.

In the back vowels the tongue hump approaches the back wall of
the throat with the largest opening in the throat being for
[u]. There is a <u>decrease</u> in openness--oo--oh--aw--ah. See
Fig. 6. All other vowels are mixed or altered positions of the
Front and the Back vowels. These are the Umlaut and Neutral
vowels which I have established by pitch on the Chromatic
Vowel Chart.

It so happens that the various tongue, jaw, lip, and palate
movements bring about certain frequencies in the throat which
vary slightly between male and female voices and between different voice classifications. There is a word <u>formant</u> created
by Hermann, the physicist in 1890. It is unknown why this
word was used unless he was referring to forms of the throat
which give these frequencies. I prefer the word <u>resonance</u> because a singer is very interested in resonance and so is his
audience because centered resonance carries better and is the
core of the voice. I have used the words <u>resonance</u> and <u>formant</u>
interchangeably.

165

Very intensive observations of vocal resonances were made by
Mackworth-Young (1953) who studied twenty-seven leading professional British singers of all voice classifications. It is
a work which has been unnoticed by many scholars of the vocal
art. The work is out of print, the publisher no longer in business, and the author deceased. It is a study which cannot be
repeated because he had as consultants Richard Paget, who was a
leader in the study of Human Speech (the title of his book),
and Daniel Jones, the leading influence of the International
Phonetic Society. Experiments and recordings were made at the
Phonetics Department, University College of London under the
direction of Dr. Dennis B. Fry an eminent phonetics authority
who is no longer at University College. Such resources and in-
ternationally known singers are no longer available in any
one place.

I publish the following Table with due credit and appreciation
to Gerald Mackworth-Young and Newman Neame Limited for their
great contribution which, unfortunately, is unknown to teachers of singing. Their endeavors must be made known because
the information gathered is the most valid concerning resonances of the singing voice. Fig. 25.

This Table brings together the observations of leading British
and American researchers prior to his work. This is a "Rosetta
Stone" to the mysteries of the instrumental resonances of the
human throat which can serve as a point of departure to those
who wish to pursue research in singing.

Fig. 25 illustrates the vowel values in four notations--musical,
keyboard, letter of note, and frequency which is on the Vowel
Chart when the arrow is placed on f^1. It also shows how the
lower "instrumental" resonances of the vowels vary between male
and female voices. This is the reason the arrow of the Chromatic Vowel Chart has different settings for the voice classifications. Values other than these need extensive explanation.
Notice the Front vowel sequence is i ɪ e ɛ and not i e
ɪ ɛ as found in a prominent diction text.

166

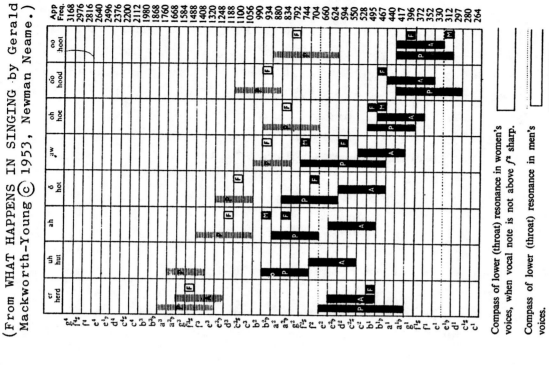

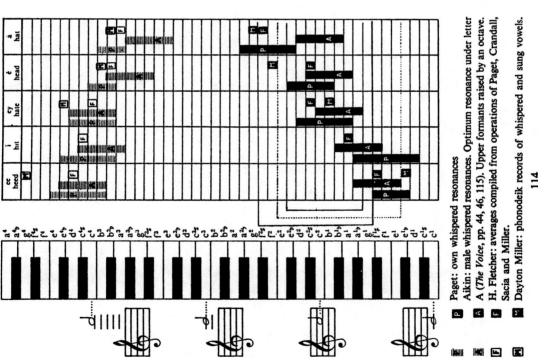

Fig. 25. Vowel formants and lower 'instrumental' resonances

P — Paget: own whispered resonances
Aikin: male whispered resonances. Optimum resonance under letter
A — A (*The Voice*, pp. 44, 46, 115). Upper formants raised by an octave.
F — H. Fletcher: averages compiled from operations of Paget, Crandall, Sacia and Miller.
M — Dayton Miller: phonodeik records of whispered and sung vowels.

Compass of lower (throat) resonance in women's voices, when vocal note is not above *f²* sharp.

Compass of lower (throat) resonance in men's voices.

167

114

Bartholemew has been quoted as saying that male voices of good quality reinforce partials around 500 Hz (b¹). The statement is simplistic and misleading. He stated (1940, p. 21) that "'good production' [vocal] has an aesthetic import....and vocal beauty, at least in Western civilization, has come to mean largely the presence of three things: (1) sustained vowels, containing (2) the proper smooth vibrato, and (3) a strong low formant in the general neighborhood of 400-600."

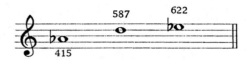

When the throat opening resonates in this area "a high formant appears, produced by a type of resonation in the semi-cavity formed by the glottis up to the aryteno-epiglottic rim." Mackworth-Young (1953), p. 76 found his throat resonances were from

which he said agreed with Paget's (1930, p. 86) whispered vowel resonances. This compares closely to the green of the Vowel Register on my Chromatic Vowel Chart.

The blues can be brought into resonance with training--the golds are more difficult. Blue and green vowels deal predominantly with the resonance of the vocal tract. That range on the Chart is from (f¹ to e♭²) compared with Mackworth-Young's throat reso-

nances of from (e¹ to e²). The Chromatic Vowel Chart relates the instrumental resonance phenomenon to the languages of singing.

168

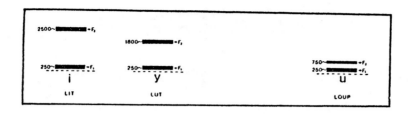

From "La radiographie des
voyelles française et sa
corrélation acoustique," by
Delattre. The French Review,
0. 1968. Permission of
French Review.

Fig. 26.

Although Delattre defined the first formant (R^1) of [i], [y],
and [u] as being 250 Hz in speech, see Fig. 26. He stated
(1962) that "For singing voice quality, the vowel structures at
the tongue and lips must be wider than for spoken vowels. This
applies more as the structure is nearer the front of the vocal
tract." This means that for these close vowels their pitch
must be higher for good singing quality. In a study with which
I was associated, Howie and Delattre established that vowels
tend to seriously lose intelligibility when the fundamental
reaches the frequencies in Fig. 27. This is the basis of his
statement (1958) that the "Singing quality and vowel color are
in articulatory conflict. The good production of one tends to
impair the good production of the other." This means that we
do not sing as we speak but that we do intend to give that ill-
usion. The vowels on the Chromatic Vowel Chart indicate the
pitches on which the standing waves for vowels occur as determined by sympathetic resonance. There is a further explanation
of this phenomenon, see p. 216 and 222.

æ	a	ɑ (750 cps)	roughly	g^2
ɛ	œ	ɔ (600 cps)	roughly	d^2
e	ø	o (456 cps)	roughly	a^1
i	y	u (350 cps)	roughly	f^1

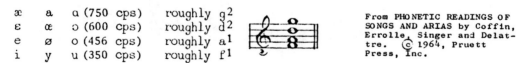

From PHONETIC READINGS OF
SONGS AND ARIAS by Coffin,
Errolle, Singer and Delat-
tre. © 1964, Pruett
Press, Inc.

Fig. 27. Where sung vowels tend to loose their intelligibility.
Howie and Delattre's values in musical notation.

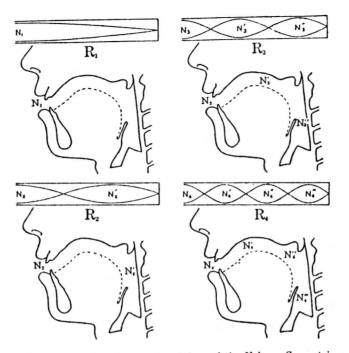

From THE VOWEL by Chiba &
Kajiyama. © 1958, Phon-
etic Society of Japan.

Fig. 28. Distribution of Maximum Points of the Volume Current in a
Uniform Pipe or in a Uniform Vocal Cavity

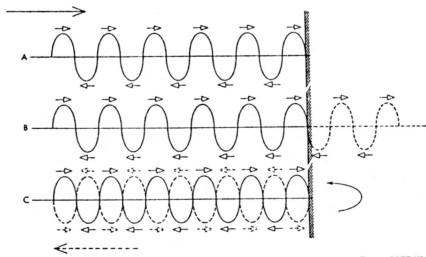

Fig. 29. *Illustration of particle movement in a standing wave.*

From SPEECH AND HEARING
SCIENCE by Willard R.
Zemlin. Reprinted by
permission of Prentice-
Hall, Inc., Englewood
Cliffs, NJ, 1968.

Note: The direction is reverse to that of
Chiba and Kajiama's illustration above.

Instrumental resonance is dependent upon a <u>standing wave</u> in the
singer's throat. Chiba and Kajiyama, Fig. 28 have shown how the
standing wave exists in the human throat--it exists in <u>all</u> wind
instruments. In the <u>standing wave</u> air pressures move from the
source to the mouth of the instrument and a portion of the
pressures is refelcted back upon the vibrating sound source
assisting it in its vibration. There is a resultant low and
high pressure variation below the vocal folds. This phenomenon can be seen sometimes in a pan of warm water on a stove in
which the pan of water vibrates and the waves seem to stand
still. The motion of the molecules is shown in Fig. 29. For
this phenomena to occur in the human throat, the vowels must
somewhat approach the form of a uniform stopped pipe--simply,
the vowels should be quite centralized as in Fig. 30. When compared to the vowels in the quadrilateral of Fig. 31 the vowels

Modified
raising
of
Tongue
Hump

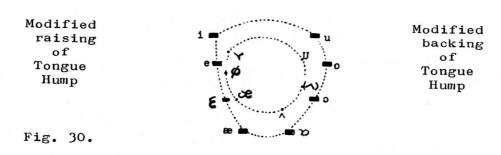

Modified
backing
of
Tongue
Hump

Fig. 30.

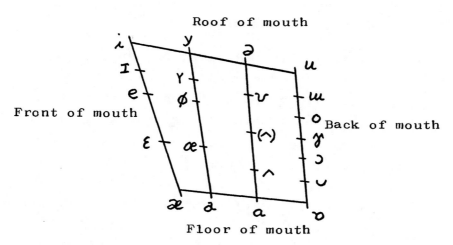

Fig. 31.   Diagram showing the Relative Positions of
the Highest Arched Portion of the Tongue
in the Mouth for the Vowels in this Text.

used on the Chromatic Vowel Chart, it will be seen that Ah becomes less ah and modifies towards [ʌ]; [i] opens and rounds a bit towards [y]; and [u] opens a bit towards [ʊ]. Rush (1827) gave a name to this pure tone voice--"orotund voice"--which means full, resonant and clear. Because of centralization, the lips are a bit more rounded than in speech and there is a feeling of vibration in the area of the lips because that is the point of greatest movement of the air particles. Melba said she knew she was singing well when she felt the vibrations on the lips. Sbriglia, an Italian tenor and teacher of singing, used the "loose rounded, pushed out lips," Byers (1942). However, this rounding varies with heights of vowel. Videotape replay of the best singers will help give you the "feel" of this phenomenon.

In recitative, speech-vowels and consonants are dominant. In singing lines, the instrumental values must be dominant or, in Garcia's words, the voice will bark. This occurs when the voice goes in and out of resonance. Manén (1974, p. 42) calls the difference between sung and speech vowels as "exclamatory vowels" and "articulated vowels." Dennis B. Fry (at the London NATS Workshop, 1977) described the difference--"Articulated vowels are what we use in language. Phonated vowels are ones that we use in emotion and also in singing....they probably come from different parts of the brain."

The famous phoneticist, Pierre Delattre, by means of a sonograph has identified the resonances of the vowels in spoken language. It must be stated that these are for speech and vary slightly in singing because of the standing wave and overtones. Otherwise, there should be no difficulty in the intelligibility of language in singing. But, since vowels are identified by pitch and singing is a matter of pitch, there are times when certain vowels work very well and other times when they are simply lacking in resonance because the

172

overtones of the sung pitch do not happen to lie in resonance
positions. There is a basic observation that as the mouth
opens, the lower resonance rises and the higher resonance
lowers. This can be seen in Fig. 32.

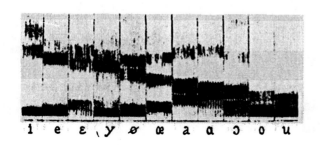

i e ɛ y ø œ a ɑ ɔ o u

High Front tongue hump posi-
    gives low R^1 and
    high R^2.

Low tongue hump position
    gives high R^1
    lower R^2.

High Back tongue position
    gives low R^1
    and low R^2.

Fig. 32.

From "The Physiological Interpretation of Sound Spectrograms" by Delattre. PMLA
66, 1951. Reprinted by permission of the Modern Language Association.

IN SINGING, WE ARE EXTREMELY INTERESTED IN THE LOWER FORMANT
BECAUSE IT IS THE TONE OR INSTRUMENTAL RESONANCE OF THE SING-
ING VOICE. When it is at its fullest, or as Helmholz has said,
loudest, the upper resonances become stronger and are better
heard. Fig. 32 has a Chart of Resonance [1] and Resonance [2]. It
will be noticed that the [i] vowel has a very strong Resonance[3]; this is the resonance which identifies that particular
vowel, however it is frequently rounded off to [y]. In singing we are interested in strengthening the lower resonance
which is gained by a larger opening in the throat when the
tongue is centered. Ah has a small space in the throat which
is opposite to what our senses tell us. In this system all
spaces are controlled phonetically--any other thoughts of
space should be discarded.

The standing wave in singing cannot occur as low as these
speech values. This accounts for the higher values of [i],
[y], and [u] on the Chromatic Vowel Charts. This can be tested by anyone by holding various tuning forks in front of the
mouth; the Echophone (Sounds of Singing); or any kind of artificial larynx device.

173

Fig. 9 shows that [i], [y], and [u] have the same lower resonance but have different high resonances. [e], [ø], and [o] have the same lower resonance but have different high resonances. Likewise [ɛ], [œ], and [ɔ]. I have used this device in what I have called "rhyming"--to help in the placement of the lower resonance of these vowels in singing.

Johan Sundberg of Stockholm has made a study of singers' resonances. This can best be done by establishing sympathetic resonance in the throat. Fig. 13 shows an artificial larynx device which plays against various frequencies at the side of the throat. In this situation, the vocal cords are held together and the vowel form is created by the tongue, lips, jaw, and soft palate. He shows pictures of [u] and [i] on 395 Hz, which is the arrow placement for the soprano voice. The usual value given for speech is lower than this for the female voice but if the mouth were closed enough to give the lower frequency there would not be a standing wave. Let us review. All reed and brass instruments utilize standing waves. They proceed from the vibrator, which is closed part of the time and represents the closed part of the tube, to the front of the mouth which represents the open part of the tube. At the mouth of the instrument, when the wave meets the outside air, there is a partial reflection of the wave back towards the vibrator, as well as a continuation of some of the wave energy into the auditorium. This vibration back upon the vocal cords assists them in their swing when it <u>is in phase with their vibration</u>. THIS IS THE REASON FOR THE CHROMATIC VOWEL CHARTS. CERTAIN VOWELS HELP THE VOCAL FOLDS IN THEIR VIBRATION ON VARIOUS PITCHES; OTHER VOWELS HINDER THE SWING. THIS IS THE SIMPLEST STATEMENT OF WHAT THE CHART IS ALL ABOUT.

Returning to Fig. 13 for the standing wave of [u] on the 525 Hz (c^2), the mouth would open (I think it would sound like [o]). The mouth for [u] on 700 Hz for f^2, would be more open and to my ears would sound like [ɔ]. On the lower example, of the pure [i] vowel, the mouth is almost closed and the throat opened for

174

the standing wave to occur. On 525 Hz (c²) the mouth opens more for the standing wave and I believe the sound to be quite a bit like the [e] vowel. When [i] is resonated on 700 Hz (f²), the mouth and the tongue take more open positions for the standing wave to occur. I believe the sound would be that of [ɛ]. I believe that a deaf person reading these pictures would say from the appearance of the lips that the upper sequence would be [u], [o], [ɔ] and the lower sequence to them would be [i], [e], and [ɛ].

We are in a time now where we can be helped more by visual appearances than ever before. With the assistance of video recorders with slow motion and stopped frames, it is possible to analyse live performances. The usual sight in singing is that the tongue lies forward, like in the lower right hand example of Sundberg. This is necessary for the upper frequencies to be heard. When the tongue lies too far back, as in the upper right picture of Sundberg, the tone will tend to turn towards a hoot and be lacking in high frequences and carrying power. However, it is a very helpful device for shifting to head voice when properly used.

I believe there is another difference between speech and singing. There are discontinuities of resonances between consonants and vowels. Classical singing requires a good singing line which is continuous in its harmonic resonation.

Let me re-emphasize that in using orotund voice the extreme vowels [i], [u], and [Ah] are slightly modified so that a standing wave can exist in the throat--the [i] and [u] have higher values than speech because the tongue humps are slightly centered and the mid-tongue becomes more active. With Ah there is a tendency for "spreading" so the extreme position (in red on the Vowel Chart) is to be avoided and either [ʌ] or [ʊ] are usually used. These vowels appear at all passaggios. Difficulties will arise if the pure open Ah is used except in sotto voce. The pure open Ah, contrary to feeling and belief, has a very small space in the throat. Shading the Ah toward [ʌ] or [ʊ] slightly adjusts the tongue hump and allows the standing wave to exist in the resonating cavity.

The Chromatic Vowel Chart states the most favorable compromise towards language while observing the acoustical laws which give the best tuning formations of the throat for instrumental singing. The Chart is NOT concerned with "speech singing"--a technique to which all singers must resort at times in recitative, fast passages in middle voice, and breathy-folk-like singing in which resonance, gained by the standing wave, is of less importance.

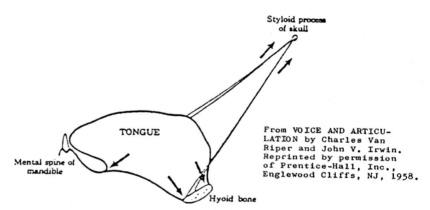

From VOICE AND ARTICU-
LATION by Charles Van
Riper and John V. Irwin.
Reprinted by permission
of Prentice-Hall, Inc.,
Englewood Cliffs, NJ, 1958.

Fig. 33. Diagram Showing Three Directions in Which Tongue Can Be Pulled by Its External Attachments. Heavy Arrows Show Direction of Pull.

Fig. 33 shows the tongue pulls which form the various vowels. In the Front vowels, both the pull towards the front teeth and towards the hyoid bone are prevalent. And in the Back vowels, the prevalent pulls are towards the ear (the styloid process) and towards the hyoid bone. There is no use in speaking to the student of the mechanisms involved because the amount of muscular pull can be controlled by the ear. This is very fortunate for us and enables us to communicate without thinking of all of the occurrences in the throat.

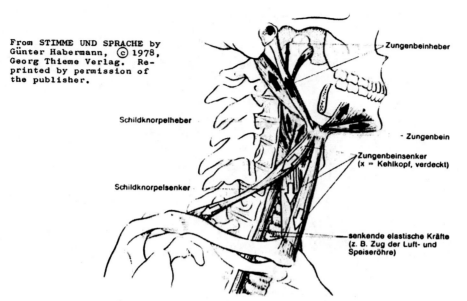

Fig. 34. Bewegungsapparat des Zungenbeins und Aufhängung des
Kehlkopfs: ➡ hebende Kräfte, ⇨ senkende Kräfte (nach *Wustrow*)

Fig. 34 indicates the strap muscle pulls which are involved
with the vowel formations. Some of the pulls are upwards and
some down. (Those which are upward are in dark arrows and those
which are downward are in the light arrows.) If there is too
much pull downward and the head comes forward the tone will become dark, lacking in overtone, and will not carry. If there
is a balanced pull between the downward pulling muscles and the
upward pulling muscles, we have what is called freedom because
the musculature is balanced.

Fig. 35. In addition to the muscles of which I have spoken
there are muscles which pull the base of the skull downwards
in such a way that the head raises. Muscle No. 1 and No. 20
must pull downward on the back of the head to offset the contraction of the muscles in Fig. 34. Muscle No. 1 in Fig. 35
tends to elevate the chest. In some singers these pulls are
so powerful against each other that the head can be seen to
bob up and down. In this case, the singer is attempting to
sing very dramatically, the larynx is being pulled down to a

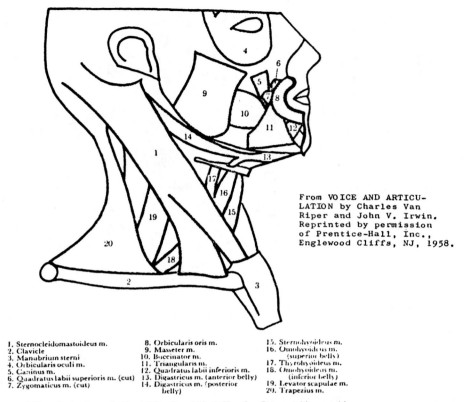

From VOICE AND ARTICU-
LATION by Charles Van
Riper and John V. Irwin.
Reprinted by permission
of Prentice-Hall, Inc.,
Englewood Cliffs, NJ, 1958.

1. Sternocleidomastoideus m.
2. Clavicle
3. Manubrium sterni
4. Orbicularis oculi m.
5. Caninus m.
6. Quadratus labii superioris m. (cut)
7. Zygomaticus m. (cut)

8. Orbicularis oris m.
9. Masseter m.
10. Buccinator m.
11. Triangularis m.
12. Quadratus labii inferioris m.
13. Digastricus m. (anterior belly)
14. Digastricus m. (posterior belly)

15. Sternohyoideus m.
16. Omohyoideus m. (superior belly)
17. Thyrohyoideus m.
18. Omohyoideus m. (inferior belly)
19. Levator scapulae m.
20. Trapezius m.

Fig. 35. Right Lateral View of Head and Neck Showing Sternocleidomastoideus Muscle Plus Other Cervical and Facial Muscles

lower position for more resonance. Muscles No. 1 and No. 20 must pull downward to elevate the head enough so that lowering of the larynx can occur. When the head is bowed in singing the larynx comes to a place where it can no longer be lowered except by the collapse of the chest. Sbriglia (the teacher of Jean and Eduard de Reszke, Plançon, and Nordica) points out that as singers become older there is a tendency for them to allow the chest to drop. When this occurs, the head comes down, and the tone becomes dull. This happens to be seen frequently among European singers (regardless of age) and may be due to three factors: 1) the acoustics of their smaller opera houses; 2) the fact that the German language has many sounds which are very closed, for instance [ø], [y], [e], [o], and

178

[u]; and 3) the fact that when these singers in advanced age begin teaching, they teach as they were singing at the end of
their careers.

Sbriglia's thought was that "the new pushing method of singing
with the [bowed] back of your neck, sunk in chest, and muscularly pushed-out diaphragm is a quick way to get results in singing, and only a little less of a quick way to ruin a voice and
that it takes three years to train a voice properly with a beautiful overtone," Byers 1942, p. 307. My belief is that extreme
activity of the depressor muscles leads to a wobble and to a
dull sound, which only the singer can hear.

Fig. 36 is a picture of the world famous tenor Gigli. It will
be seen that his head is in an upward posture which offers a

Fig. 36. Beniamino Gigli.

Herbert-Caesari in <u>Voice of the
Mind</u> speaks of a "vertically
soaring sound beam." I believe
it is involved with the upward
and downward pulls of Fig.
The head position appears to be
best for the muscles to operate
on the green and gold vowels on
the Vowel Chart.

From VOICE OF THE MIND by
E. Herbert-Caesari. Per-
mission of Robert Hale, Ltd.

better opportunity for a balance between the upward and the
downward pulls of the muscles attached to the hyoid bone (Fig.
35). This is also exemplified in a poster I have of Nilsson in
Stockholm announcing her TV appearance (so she must have thought
that indicated her art). I have pictures of many other international artists depicting the same posture of the head. Jean
de Reszke (Leiser, p. 315) sang with his head to the Gallery

except when he was using mask resonance and then he felt like he was butting his head into a wall. Upon close observation of video tapes, it will be seen that the head tends to tilt backwards on the open vowels and move forward as the vowels are closed; during a phrase the head position will change for open and closed vowels. I have illustrated this many times when vocalizing voices of the same classification on the diagonals of the Vowel Chart--their heads will move upward and downward together. The head will also be higher for sotto voce.

My observation is that there is definitely a relationship between acoustics and posture. Nathan, a student of Porpora, wrote in 1836, "The larynx...is distinctly seen rising in the production of acute tones, and descending in low ones. For the purpose, therefore, of effecting the greatest elevation of this organ, we almost involuntarily throw the head back in great efforts in singing [also in laughter]."

Duval (1958, p. 170) has written more explicitly about posture. "The chin must be held in, and the upper part of the neck, just where it meets the head should be kept well back... to make that position as natural as possible, a series of exercises to develop the neck, chest and upper back should be assiduously followed." This allows room for the larynx to take a lower position. Delattre and I observed in X-Ray motion pictures that there is a compensation for full sound. Below the upper passaggios in a male voice, the larynx is sometimes lowered between 2 and 3 cm. from speech position. An additional opening is frequently gained by the backward tilt of the head by international singers.

At the upper passaggios of both men and women the tongue is vaulted upward and forward. As a result the Back Vowel series is not successful on the highest notes of tenors and coloratura sopranos. The most successful vowels, it will be found, are the Forward and Neutral Vowels in green on the Chromatic Vowel Chart. As a consequence the teeth show more on high notes, more so with sopranos than tenors because they are in a higher register.

180

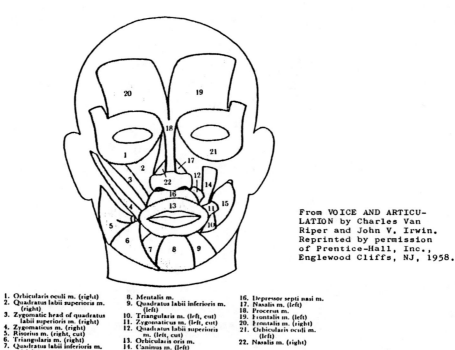

From VOICE AND ARTICU-
LATION by Charles Van
Riper and John V. Irwin.
Reprinted by permission
of Prentice-Hall, Inc.,
Englewood Cliffs, NJ, 1958.

1. Orbicularis oculi m. (right)
2. Quadratus labii superioris m. (right)
3. Zygomatic head of quadratus labii superioris m. (right)
4. Zygomaticus m. (right)
5. Risorius m. (right, cut)
6. Triangularis m. (right)
7. Quadratus labii inferioris m. (right)
8. Mentalis m.
9. Quadratus labii inferioris m. (left)
10. Triangularis m. (left, cut)
11. Zygomaticus m. (left, cut)
12. Quadratus labii superioris m. (left, cut)
13. Orbicularis oris m.
14. Caninus m. (left)
15. Buccinator m. (left)
16. Depressor septi nasi m.
17. Nasalis m. (left)
18. Procerus m.
19. Frontalis m. (left)
20. Frontalis m. (right)
21. Orbicularis oculi m. (left)
22. Nasalis m. (right)

Fig. 37.   Frontal View of Superficial and Deep Facial Muscles

Fig. 37 indicates the facial muscles which do much to control
resonance. Muscle 13 is especially involved because the fronting of the lips actually lengthens the vocal tract and lowers
its pitch. The widening of the mouth and the raising of the
cheeks come about by contractions of Muscles 3, 4, 6, 11, 14,
and 15. Opening the mouth of the resonator raises the pitch of
the tone resonance, R^1. When watching TV, in slow motion, these
muscular pulls can be identified. Speech is so fast that
we cannot identify the muscular pulls, but those who are
deaf can lip read and tongue read sufficiently well to understand language. We who hear understand because these movements
affect the pitches of resonance which come to our ears.

To Sbriglia looseness of the lip muscles, slightly rounded, and
an elevation of the cheeks (Muscles 3, 4, 14, and 15) gave a
highly desirable form for singing. The cheeks raise, the mouth
spreads slightly, and the upper and lower jaws separate for
high notes.

Relating to Fig. 16, I have spoken frequently of the activity of the soft palate. The larger picture is a side view--the dotted line indicates the position of the soft palate when it is lowered as by the open mouth hum ⒶThe solid line indicates the usual position of the soft palate in vowels and consonants. The dotted position occurs during inhalation and is an indication of when breath is taken in motion picture X-rays. It occurs when singing the French nasals or when other vowels and consonants are nasalized. The small picture on the right is an indication of what this opening looks like from above. The No. 2 muscles are the pillars of the fauces which narrow for high notes and widen for singing in the mouth.

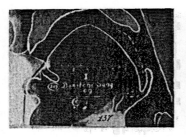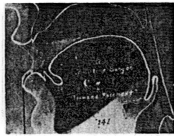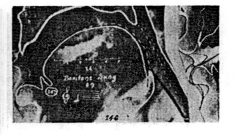

Fig. 38. Pasquale Amato's singing of [ɪ], [ɑ], and [u].

From SPEECH AND VOICE by G.O. Russell. Macmillan Publishing Co. Permission by Gallaudet College.

The illustrations Fig. 38 are from Russell's Speech and Voice (1931) which he indicated later (ca 1959) were X-rays of the throat of the Italian baritone, Pasquale Amato. The [ɪ] is nearly an evenly stopped pipe--equally open in bore from the larynx to the front of the mouth. A string was swallowed so that the midline of the tongue could be identified. One end of it can be seen in front of the chin and the other end going down the esophagus. The dotted lines are the edges of the tongue in a higher position and the back walls of the throat forwarding in such a manner as to form a round pipe. Most interesting of all the persons X-rayed, the palatal passage is open in all of Amato's pictures with the exception of the [ɑ] which has been described as having a forward placement. Phonetically [ɪ] is a Forward Vowel, [u] is a Back Vowel, and [ɑ] is a Back Vowel which lies low in the throat. Notice that the tongue is relatively high. The so-called huge space of [ɑ] in the throat is fiction--notice the small opening between the epiglottis and the back wall of the throat. As a consequence, there is high pressure in this area which is probably felt as being space.

Dr. Russell later (ca 1959, p. 4) identified Fig. 39abc as being X-rays of Enrico Caruso. Again the Front Vowel, in this case [i], is open enough so that there can be a standing wave. Again notice the small opening in the throat for [ɑ]. Caruso was dismayed at not seeing his velum open--he thought it should be open to show the "'resonance' of the nasal passages 'properly utilized'," p. 4. Because of this he would not allow his

 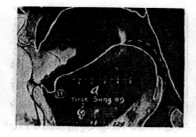 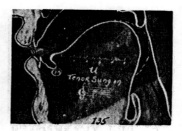

Fig. 39. Enrico Caruso's singing of [i], [ɑ], and [u].

From SPEECH AND VOICE by G.O. Russell. Macmillan Publishing Co. Permission by Gallaudet College.

name to be associated with these pictures. He could not accept the truth of the matter--fancy being stronger than fact. My feeling is that much harm has been done in attempting to form spaces which are spurious and misleading. It is better to allow the spaces to form as they will. Bartholemew (1935) said, "With many students merely thinking of the vocal organs while singing is enough to produce involuntary tension. It is much safer to use phonetics, such as <u>oh</u>, <u>ee</u>, <u>ng</u>, or whatever is nec-

essary, to secure change of setting." I object to the word
"setting" since the positions taken are very flexible. The gold-
en truth is that all spaces are controlled by the ear and vowel
color thought. No thought of space is necessary--in fact, it
will usually cause problems. The Caruso pictures are devastating to the "open throat" theory. Look how small the opening
is on the mouthpiece of a brilliant trumpet. They are related.
Vowels can have large spaces in the throat--closed vowels. Or
vowels can have large spaces in front of the tongue hump--open
vowels. They cannot have large spaces both in front and behind
the tongue hump--the throat is not constructed that way. Openings 7, 8, and 9 on the Vowel Chart are nearly even in openness
in front and behind the tongue hump, but neither space is
especially large.

Dr. Russell's (1932) pictures, Fig. 40abcdef, are of Lucrezia
Bori, Spanish soprano, and show the vocal tract from the vocal
cords to the front of the mouth. They constitute a progression
of ah vowels on d^2, e^2, f^2, a^2, $c\#^3$, and e^3.

It will be noticed that there is a big forward swing of the
tongue between e^2, f^2, and a^2 which is in the area of the upper
passaggio in the soprano voice. The space becomes smaller on
$c\#^3$ and yet smaller for the e^3. Yodeling on vowels will
assist in finding these vowel sounds and positions.

Vennard (1967, p. 109), "I must guard against the impression
that the larynx should never rise in singing. It is bound to
follow the motion of the tongue in forming vowels and consonants, for example, because the thyroid is suspended from the
hyoid bone which is in the root of the tongue. Also the larynx
may rise for high notes. Almost all singers need the assistance
of the extrinsic muscles for the highest and loudest notes in
any register, although one's objective should be to avoid it."
[The opposing muscles should be at play.] Furthermore, the
raised head position as used in First Aid is for the purpose
of opening the wind tract.

MTNA Proceedings of 1932.
Permission of The American Music Teacher.

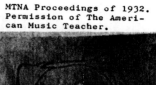

Fig. 352

Vowel ah (a). Sung on 2 D/C (d"- 2nd d above middle C), 574 cycles per second

or

Fig. 360

Vowel ah (a). Sung on 2 E/C (e" - 2nd e above middle C), 645 cycles per second

or

Fig. 354

Vowel ah (a) verging towards uh (ə). Sung on 2 F/C (f"- 2nd f above middle C), 683 cycles per second

or

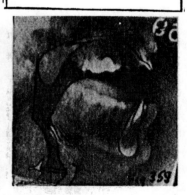

Fig. 355

Vowel ah (a) verging towards uh (ə). Sung on 2 A/C (a" - 2nd a above middle C), 861 cycles per second

or

Fig. 353

Vowel ah (a) verging towards aw (ɔ). Sung on 2#C/C (#C"' - 2nd C# above middle C), 1084 cycles per second.

or

Fig. 359

Vowel ah (a) verging towards at (æ). Sung on 3 E/C (e"' - third e above middle C), 1290 cycles per second

or

Fig. 40. abcdef

185

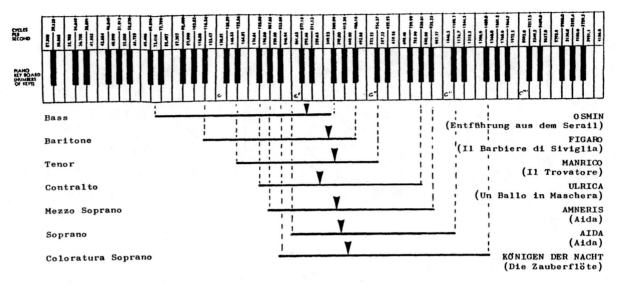

Fig. 41.   Ranges of Roles and settings of
the arrow of the Chromatic Vowel
Chart for different voice classifications (after Ruth).

From STIMME UND SPRACHE by
Günter Habermann, © 1978,
Georg Thieme Verlag. Re-
printed by permission of
the publisher.

Fig. 41 indicates that in singing operatic roles, extended
ranges are required. Professional voices must have extensive
ranges either by nature or by cultivation. Usually they are
gained through instruction or imitation. The arrow placement
for the voices is indicated.

Fig. 42 shows the registers which should be established to extend the range for operatic singing. Again, folk singing and
chamber music singing do not require such large ranges. There
has been an historical extension of ranges to the extremes of
Richard Strauss. Of course, Mozart had some extreme ranges in
his operas also (influenced by unusual voices of the 18th century Bolognese school of singing), but those roles were written
for smaller houses than the great 20th century Strauss operas.

Fig. 43 indicates what is most frequently thought of as giving
range extension. In the example to the left, the two arrows
represent the location of two crico-thyroid muscles which draw
the upper cartilege towards the lower--when they contract the

186

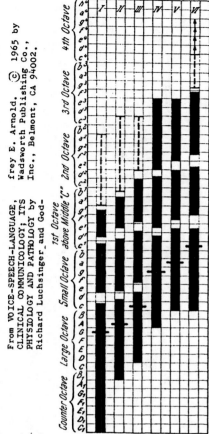

From VOICE-SPEECH-LANGUAGE, CLINICAL COMMUNICOLOGY; ITS PHYSIOLOGY AND PATHOLOGY by Richard Luchsinger and Godfrey E. Arnold, © 1965 by Wadsworth Publishing Co., Inc., Belmont, CA 94002.

Fig. 42. *Average vocal ranges* in the six voice types: I, Basso; II, Baritone; III, Tenor; IV, Contralto; V, Mezzo-soprano; VI, Soprano. Speaking pitch at cross bars.

the vocal cords are stretched and give a higher pitch. On the example to the right, the upper cartilege moves forward on the lower to further stretch the vocal cords to give the highest pitches. This can be seen in pictures as forming a dimple below the thyroid cartileges, especially in female voices in which the neck happens to be thin. In the yodeling exercises, between lower register and higher register, this dimple occurrence can be seen to occur. The oblique crico-thyroid muscles pull the upper cartilege forward as in the right example, and the vertical crico-thyroid muscles pull it downwards as in the left picture. In the teaching of singing these muscles and the other intrinsic muscles of the larynx must be strengthened in an orderly and balanced way at the same time that the resonator tuning muscles and postural muscles of the larynx are utilized.

Fig. 43. *Illustration of the mechanism by which the crico-thyroid may function to tense the vocal folds.*

From STIMME UND SPRACHE by Günter Habermann, © 1978, Georg Thieme Verlag. Reprinted by permission of the publisher.

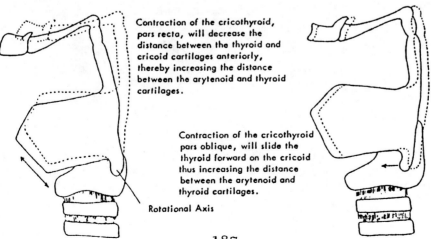

Contraction of the cricothyroid, pars recta, will decrease the distance between the thyroid and cricoid cartilages anteriorly, thereby increasing the distance between the arytenoid and thyroid cartilages.

Contraction of the cricothyroid pars oblique, will slide the thyroid forward on the cricoid thus increasing the distance between the arytenoid and thyroid cartilages.

Rotational Axis

187

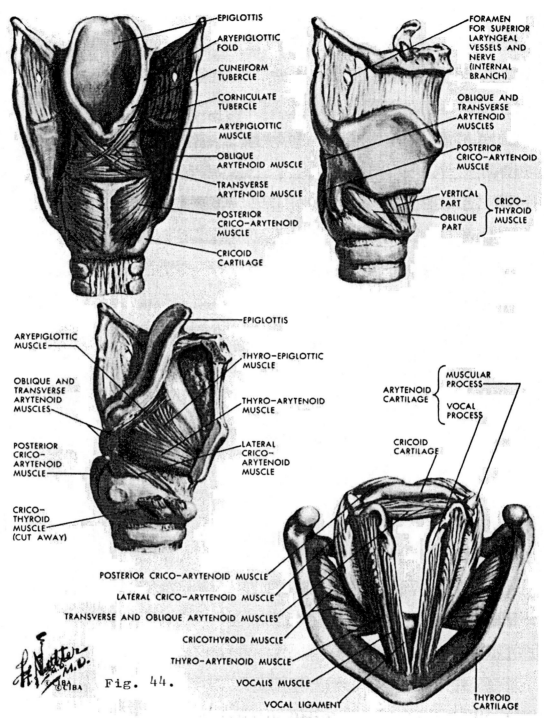

Fig. 44.

Fig. 44. The intrinsic muscles of the larynx. Of special interest is that a side view is given of the vertical and oblique parts of the crico-thyroid muscle.

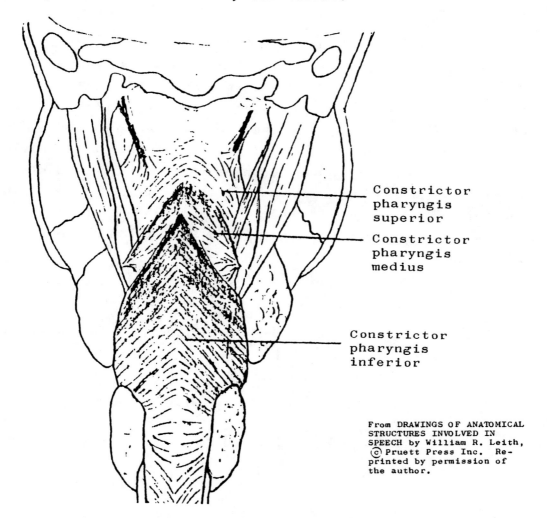

Constrictor
pharyngis
superior

Constrictor
pharyngis
medius

Constrictor
pharyngis
inferior

From DRAWINGS OF ANATOMICAL
STRUCTURES INVOLVED IN
SPEECH by William R. Leith,
ⓒPruett Press Inc. Re-
printed by permission of
the author.

Fig. 45. The Swallowing Muscles Seen From Behind.

Fig. 45 shows the swallowing muscles of the throat. There are from top to bottom 3 muscles. The top one relaxes to allow nasality, but in swallowing it has a closing action against the back of the throat. In swallowing, the upper muscle contracts first then the middle closes, and finally the lower muscle contracts. Thus there is a one-two-three firing of the muscles by which swallowing takes place. These muscles are relaxed at the time

189

of inhalation. The open mouth hum Ⓐ and vowels behind the hand
remove excessive tension in the superior constrictor muscle to
allow the elevator muscles to function better in singing.

Fig. 46 is a view from behind looking out the front of the
mouth. We can see the back of the tongue and the epiglottis
which is in the form of a leaf. In the variable vocal tract
there is great play between the muscles shown. Muscle (4)
shortens for the high notes and muscle (2) contracts to denasal-
ize, and relaxes to nasalize. All of the muscles are involved
in varying timbres, degrees of opening, and falsetto techniques.
When watching in a mirror one can see the uvula shorten and the
soft palate raise and narrow when singing high notes. This
narrowness is brought about by the action of the upper muscles
pulling towards the skull.

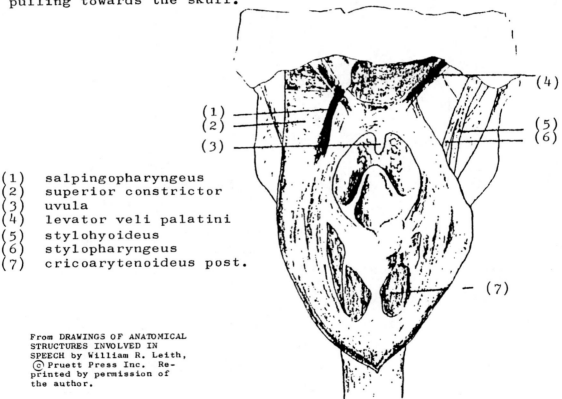

(1)   salpingopharyngeus
(2)   superior constrictor
(3)   uvula
(4)   levator veli palatini
(5)   stylohyoideus
(6)   stylopharyngeus
(7)   cricoarytenoideus post.

From DRAWINGS OF ANATOMICAL
STRUCTURES INVOLVED IN
SPEECH by William R. Leith,
ⓒ Pruett Press Inc. Re-
printed by permission of
the author.

Fig. 46. Throat muscles seen from behind.

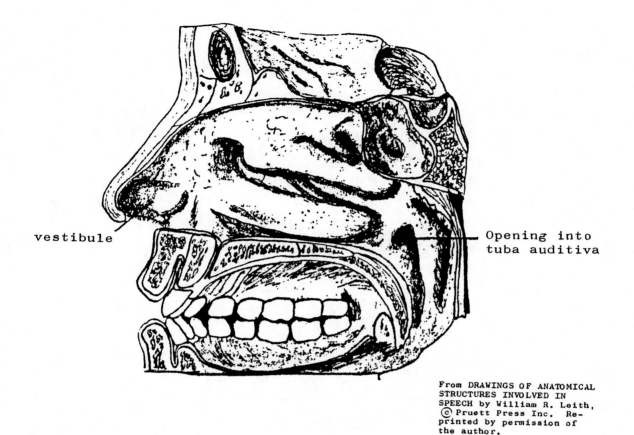

vestibule   Opening into
tuba auditiva

From DRAWINGS OF ANATOMICAL
STRUCTURES INVOLVED IN
SPEECH by William R. Leith,
© Pruett Press Inc. Re-
printed by permission of
the author.

Fig. 47. Turbinates Seen From the Side.

Fig. 47 indicates the turbinates in the nasal passages which
are radiator devices covered by mucuous membrane that warms,
moistens, and cleanses the inhaled air. Moisture is extremely
important because the vocal cords must be lubricated to run.
Excised vocal cords which have been vibrated artificially
crackle unless the air used has high humidity. The singer will
have the same feeling when he is singing in dry and musty
rooms or halls. Whenever it is possible to control the humidity,
have it high. Of especial interest in the jet age is that humidity is reduced in high altitude flights to such an extent that

the singer can become dehydrated. A person should drink a glass
of water an hour to protect his mucous membranes and voice.
Also, never take drying medicants before singing a performance.
There are medicants which will increase saliva flow. Frequently
the dry throats of public performance come more from the atmos-
phere in which a singer performs than from excitement. Nose
breathing which gives the turbinates a chance to moisten and
purify the air is highly beneficial whenever there is a time to
use it. Novikova indicated the time of nose breathing in music
by $\sqrt{}$ with the length of the line indicating the time
allotted in the music for breathing. It is a device that is
very helpful. Nose breathing has been recommended by many of
the great singers when time allows.

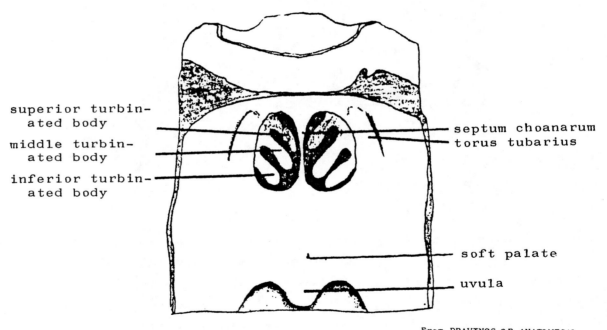

superior turbin-
ated body

middle turbin-
ated body

inferior turbin-
ated body

septum choanarum
torus tubarius

soft palate

uvula

From DRAWINGS OF ANATOMICAL
STRUCTURES INVOLVED IN
SPEECH by William R. Leith,
ⓒ Pruett Press Inc. Re-
printed by permission of
the author.

Fig. 48.   Turbinates Seen From Behind

Many of the world's famous singers have had their nasal passages surgically repaird to allow free passage of air. Some-

times the turbinates obstruct the air flow and need to be short-
ened; sometimes the septum is deviated. Sometimes both septum
and turbinates are obstructive. Dr. J.B. van Deinse of Den
Haag, Holland has said that is especially important to tenors
and sopranos at their upper passaggios around e, f, and f#.
I believe this to be true of all voices and have marked Notes
#22, 23, 24, and Notes #31-35 with the nasal symbol [~] on the
Chromatic Vowel Chart. The nasalization assists in changing to
Mixed and Head Voice.

Fig. 48 shows how turbinates extend into the nasal passages.
The thin line in the middle is known as the septum and contains
the ethmoid bone which frequently bends towards one side or the
other in such a way as to block the nasal passage. When such a
septum is repaired (operated on) the voice sounds clearer.
This can be tested by singing with cotton in the nose to show
the difference in sound between an obstructed nasal passage and
one which is freely open. Dr. Punt of London states that the
nasal passages should be free for clear articulation. When
they are not open there is a cul-de-sac sound. [m] tends to
sound like [b]; [ŋ] tends to sound like [g]; and [n] tends to
sound like [d]--like a cold-id-de-dose. This is most important
to singers who wish to sing in the upper extension of the range,
for three reasons--1) if it is not open there is a possibility
of poor drainage upon the vocal cords; 2) there is a possibility of infections and allergies which would not occur if there
were good flow of air; and 3) there is not the effect of nasality upon the standing wave which is necessary to go into the
upper extensions of the voice.

Delattre, p. 33 shows what occurs with nasality. R^2, R^3, and
R^4 tend to become farther apart and the lower resonance R^1 is
weakened. This is exactly what a singer does when he goes to
the upper register. He weakens the lower resonance and inten-
sifies overtones of the upper resonances. This occurs at the
area of the d^1-g^1 passaggio of male voices and at the d^2-g^2
range of female voices. How nasality can be trained into a
voice by means of vowels behind the hand and Ⓐ is shown on

p. 37 . Nasality cannot be controlled mechanistically, only by
the sound in the ear and by the sensation. A test for whether
the nasal passages are open is to hold a metal mirror below the
nostrils, blow on it; if butterfly wings are formed everything
is in order. If one wing is longer than another, there is a
problem and it should be corrected. Sometimes the turbinates
extend so far towards the septum that they close the passage.
In rare cases these have been shortened by surgery. One teacher I knew in the past said such a case could be corrected by
singing [ŋ]. I simply ask the question, is it possible to
change a bone by singing [ŋ]? Answer--NO! The repair work
should be done by a doctor who is knowledgeable of singers
problems.

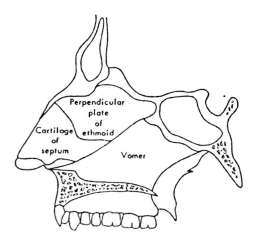

From SPEECH AND HEARING
SCIENCE by Willard R.
Zemlin. Reprinted by
permission of Prentice-
Hall, Inc., Englewood
Cliffs, NJ, 1968.

Fig. 49. *Schematic of medial
wall of nasal cavity showing vomer
bone, perpendicular plate of the
ethmoid, and the articulation of
the nasal bone with the septum.*

Fig. 49 indicates the ethmoid bone which can be deviated towards the right or left because of growth or injury. In many
of the world's great singers this operation has been done to
allow the beautiful [m], [n], and [ng] sounds. One who can no
longer say this was John Charles Thomas. Very seldom is the
septum perfectly straight, but for the singer it must allow good
air flow.

Fig. 50. Speaking of range, there is an extension known as the whistle register. I bring to your attention the syrinx which is the vocal organ of song birds, located at the base of the trachea. It is a thin membrane which fluctuates in the passage of air. The change of pitch is by air flow and bill opening.

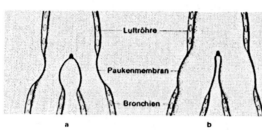

Fig. 50. a u b Schema einer Vogelsyrinx mit ihren Paukenmembranen. Die schwingungsfähigen Paukenmembranen liegen an der Gabelung der Luftröhre in der Wand der beiden Hauptbronchien. Sie schwingen senkrecht zum anblasenden Luftstrom, ohne sich zu berühren. a) Phase der maximalen Einwärtsschwingung, b) Phase der maximalen Auswärtsschwingung der Membran (nach *Paulsen* u. *Lullies*)

The picture on the left shows the membrane in its most closed position, and the picture on the right when the membrane is most open. It is like the Bernoulli effect, which can be shown by blowing between two sheets of paper; they vibrate vigorously. By this means the songbird makes his tone. The whistle register has been referred to as Vogetstimme, or bird voice. I submit that a type of mechanism like this exists between the vocal cords, when they vibrate without touching, in high voice. In the middle and lower voice the cords either slap each other or wave at each other (as in sotto voce).

Garcia (ab 1855, p. 7) describes the mechanism of the whistle register in this manner, "The lips of the glottis are stretched, and perfectly, though gently touch one another, while the space between the vocal tendons is considerably lessened. In this state of the organ, the least pressure of air will rush through a minute aperture of the glottis, which, however narrow, serves to produce the most rapid beats with extreme facility. The pressure of the air, however, should be very slight, when the aperture of the glottis is to be minute." The same phenomenon should occur in male falsetto at Note #23 and above. These high notes are gained by knowledge rather than strength!!

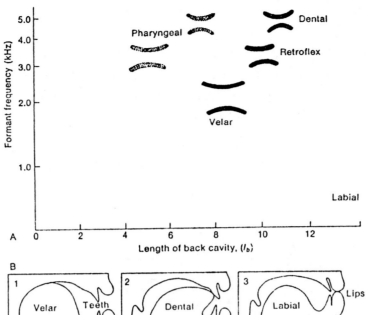

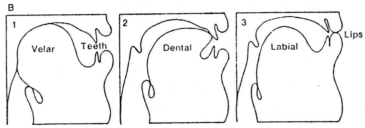

Fig. 51. *Results of a computer modeling of the model of Figure 8-10. The curved bars indicate the* quantal *acoustic signals that are produced at particular "points of articulation."*
FIGURE 8-11(B) *Sketches of supralaryngeal vocal tract for labial, dental, and velar stops (the stop sounds [p], [t], and [k]). The retroflex and pharyngeal quantal regions shown in Figure 8-11(A) are not used in English. Further anatomical "landmarks" can be seen in Figure 6-17.*

Fig. 51. There are very few songs without words, so vowels in combination with consonants communicate meaning to the listener. The nature of consonants is less easily understood but they come from contacts in various parts of the mouth. So bah, pah, mah come from the touching of the lips; dah, tah, nah come from the touching of the tongue and teeth, or front of the hard palate; and nah, gah, kah come from touching the tongue and the palatal structure. In the process there are certain frequencies which tend to occur. These are shown in the upper example as determined by a computer. It will be noticed that the labial frequency is extremely low, whereas the [d] and [t] are extremely high which allow higher frequencies to pass.

The retroflexive, like in the American [r], gives a lower fre-

quency or dull sound, and the [ŋ] gives a lower sound yet.
It will be seen from this why the dental consonants have been
used in the teaching of singing--to give higher frequencies.
I think that [ŋ] should be exercised sufficiently for agility
of articulation but that it is only partially effective for add-
ing height to a tone thus limiting the high voice. The open
mouth hum Ⓐ is more advantageous because a standing wave can
be established. Most of the other consonants are whistles
and buzzes between the places of articulation mentioned. The
famous Graun syllables used by Sieber in his vocalizes are seen
to have great value--da me ɲi po ʈu ʎa be. The dentals
front the tone, the nasal consonants of Italian cause articulation of the soft palate and the labials [p] and [b] also
bring about forward vibration. The p and t are non plosive
in Italian. A feeling of vibration near the front of the mouth
was a guide to great singers of the past. THE PLACE OF GREAT-
EST VIBRATION IN R¹, R², R³, and R⁴ IS AT THE FRONT OF THE
MOUTH AND LIPS.

Fig. 52 shows the influence of the various consonants upon
vowel pitches. It must be said that we comprehend in large
auditoriums and over heavy accompaniment more by the consonant
effects on vowel resonances than by consonantal sounds. In
fact, consonants can be softened or even omitted provided the
"little curves" are placed on the vowel resonances. This is
what is meant by silent consonants and is a way of sustaining
vocal line and at the same time being comprehended. This may
not work as well when a singer is close to a microphone where
consonant sounds are picked up. Such a situation is a bit
false--singers are not heard that way in large halls. But in
Head Voice, consonants must be softened regardless of singing
locale. Incidentally, try to stop a videotape on a consonant
by an Italian singer. The movement is so short and the vowel
so long that it is almost impossible to "catch" a consonant
on the TV screen.

197

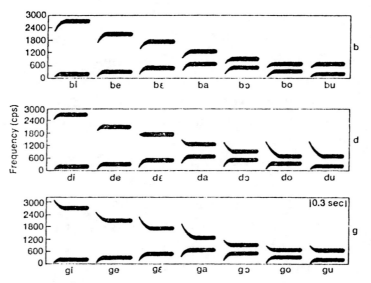

From "Loci and Transitional
Cues for Consonants," by
Delattre, Liberman, and
Cooper. JASA, Vol. 27,
1955. Permission granted
American Institute of
Physics.

Fig. 52. *Synthetic spectrograms using only F_1 and F_2 information that produce the voiced stops before various vowels. (After Delattre et al., 1955.)*

Fig. 53 is my explanation of vowel color in terms of wavelength of light. Both light and sound are wave forms which are
processed physically and psychologically by the mind of man in
his communication and in his living (and in TV). As light of
certain wavelengths (and frequencies) has colors, so do vocal
sounds of certain wavelengths (and frequencies) have vowel
color. The Chart is after the values of Miller (1916) which he
established with his invention, the Phonodeik. He did not take
into consideration that there are several formants in the voice,
but he did establish that when energy was in a certain region
or combination of regions there was a tendency towards that
vowel color. I believe that this is near enough to the truth
to be accepted as a general fact. I give his values in musical
and frequency notation. The values which I have found by sympathetic resonation over a period of years and with many voices
is indicated on the Chromatic Vowel Chart. In the exercises
I have shown those vowels which will be most favorable and
which will best communicate the language intent of the singer.

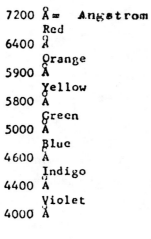

7200 Å = Angstrom
Red
6400 Å
Orange
5900 Å
Yellow
5800 Å
Green
5000 Å
Blue
4600 Å
Indigo
4400 Å
Violet
4000 Å

The shorter wavelengths give violet (a sombre color) and the longer wave lengths give red (a bright color) while gold is somewhere in the middle with medium wavelength. It is interesting that the eye is most sensitive to the frequencies which are strongest in the radiation from the sun. This is involved with the psychology of man.

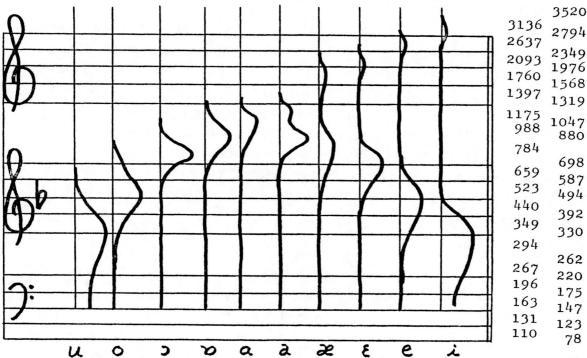

Fig. 53.

The spectra of Miller's vowels in musical notation and their frequencies.

Fig. 7, p. 11 indicates that the higher the voice, the fewer the overtones. Lily Pons is singing about b^2-natural in the upper example, whereas Lawrence Tibbett in the lower example, is singing an [i] vowel falsetto--"Figaro," in which the fundamental is

199

seen with a total of 5 partials. When he goes to regular voice
voice, more partials are seen but no energy is shown in the
fundamental which should be halfway between the bottom line
(zero line) and the next line up. Energy was there, but I know
from my Viennese studies (p. 224) that there was not sufficient
energy to show on the Sonagram, and was not intense enough to
actually be heard by the ear. The missing sung pitch is heard
because of what is known as difference tone. Because of this
the ear created the lower pitch which was actually very weak in
his singing voice. (See "subjective tone" or "difference tone"
in an acoustics text or dictionary.) The phenomenon is of ut-
most importance to singers and explains why a "fat" voice will
not carry in an auditorium and why a voice with brilliant overtones will. A voice feels heavy when there is too much low in
the voice and feels free when the lower resonance (R^1) is just
right to allow a great deal of the high frequences "to pass."
Also remember--a pushed voice will become smaller--allow
the vocal cords to vibrate easily in the oscillation of high
and low pressures above and below the vocal cords. The
sensation of leaning against the arch of the chest is related
to the vibrating pressure (rumble) in the chest. This is a
mark of great singing.

Fig. 54 indicates that we hear extremely well in the upper
overtones of the voice, especially around the region of Ah
which is between 800 and 1400 Hz. This may be the reason that
the Italians taught so predominantly on their Ah vowel. If one
teaches on the [u] vowel extensively the voice will become weak
since [u] has very few overtones and lies around 300-500 Hz; a
range in which the ear does not hear very well. What can be
done--open [u] until a standing wave exists and allows high
overtones to pass. But do not train on [u] or any single vowel
alone. It should be pointed out that the frequency of the ear
canal has been found to be between 2800-3800 Hz which is the
area of the singer's formant. This is a unique way a singer
has of being heard over an orchestra. When the so-called

"ring" is missing from the voice, the singer should cancel
until another day. For some harmonic or laryngeal reason it
begins to disappear from treble voices around c². Check the
frequencies on the Chromatic Vowel Chart to actually see where
the ears are most sensitive.

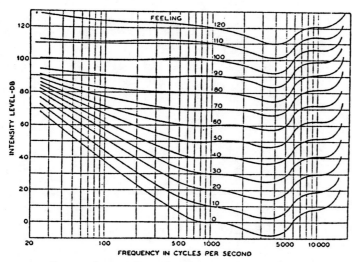

FIG. 135.—LOUDNESS LEVEL CONTOURS VERSUS INTENSITY LEVEL.

Fig. 54.

Before we look at resonance peaks and overtones in the next
chapter, let me point out the difference between an instrument,
such as a trumpet, in solid lines, and the resonance peak as it
appears in the flesh-walled vowel tube of a human throat. You
will notice it is a much wider--there upon hangs much of the
magic and mysteries of languages and of singing.

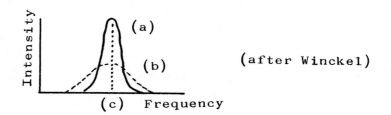

Fig. 55. Resonance curves.
(a) Resonance peak of Wind Instruments.
(b) Resonance peak of the Voice.
(c) Center of resonance peak heard
     with Echophone.

201

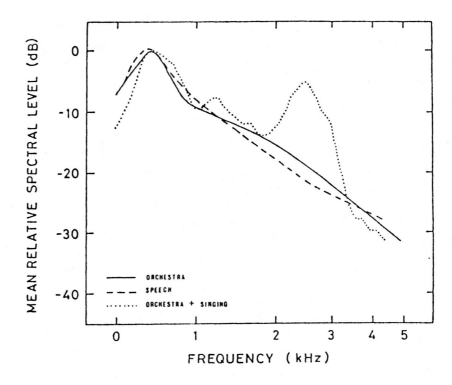

Fig. 56. Averaged spectra of the sound of a symphony orchestra
(solid curve), normal speech (dashed curve), and a
singer accompanied by an orchestra (dotted curve).
The average spectrum of the orchestra is strikingly
similar to that of normal speech. The "singing formant" is seen as a broad peak being the only major
difference between orchestra with and without a
singer soloist. A singer's voice accompanied by an
orchestra is easier to discern when it has a "singing formant" than when it lacks it, as is the case
in the normal speaking voice. From Sundberg (1972),
Report of the 11th Congress of the International
Musicological Society.

Fig. 56 . is a comparison of the energies of the voice of the
late Jussi Björling with orchestra and speech. It can be seen
how a brilliant voice carries over an orchestra--the energies
of the voice are above those of the accompaniment and in the
area which is most sensitive to the human ear.

CHAPTER V

THE OVERTONES, REGISTERS, AND PHONETICS OF BEL CANTO

Mackinlay (1908, p. 131) stated that Garcia in his Method of Teaching Singing "cleared up the confusion which had hitherto existed between 'timbre' and 'registers'." He defined register "as being a series of consecutive homogeneous sounds, differing essentially from another series of sounds equally homogeneous produced by another mechanism....Each of the registers has its own extent and sonority...." My study indicates that the mechanism is a physiological-acoustical phenomenon of vowel coincidence with certain overtone relationships. I will state that the main register is the Vowel Register (V) where the vibrations of the vocal cords and of the lower resonance of the Vowel tract have a 1:1 relationship. Middle Voice (M) for women and Upper Voice (U) for male voices are the same and have a 1 to 2 relationship of the vibrations of the vocal folds and of the resonator. Chest Register (C) for both Female and Male Voices has a 1 to 3 vibrational relationship of vocal folds and the vowel tract. Other Chest Registers exist which have 1 to 4, 1 to 5, 1 to 6, and 1 to 8 relationships of vibrations to vowel tract resonation. A Mixed Voice (X) appears midway between Middle Register and Vowel Register in Female Voices and Upper Register and Vowel Register in Male Voices. The relationship of vocal cord vibration to resonation is 1:1.5. As a consequence the Fundamental (sung pitch) and the second partial are equally reinforced.

Head Register (H) exists a perfect 5th above the Vowel Register in Female Voices and Counter Tenors. The ratio of vocal cord vibration and vowel tract resonation is 1 to .75. This is midway between the Whistle Register (W) and the Vowel Register in Female Voices. Falsetto, in Male Voices, is an uncoupled sound in the Vowel Register. Most of my conclusions are evidenced in the following materials.

203

The registers are the harmonic diagonals on the Chromatic Vowel
Chart each of which when sung below its lower extreme extin-
guishes the voice and when sung into the red of the upper extremes spreads the voice. The registers of the diagonals have
have their own homogeneous quality. The Vowel Register is ringing (towards the metallic). The Head Register has a soft and
pure sound. The Mixed Voice has a mellow sound. The Middle
Voice needs to be trained so that it has a somewhat metallic
sound to bridge the e^1 passaggio. The Chest Voice has a more
masculine sound as do the registers below which reinforce the
Vowel Register by the 4th, 5th, 6th, and 8th harmonics.

Open and close timbres are register contrasts with the open
vowel directly over the close form on any note on the Vowel
Chart with the exception of Notes #23, 24, 25, and 26 in Male
Voices of which Garcia says the timbres are the same. In reality Overtones of Bel Canto is an update of Garcia's statements
made possible by more sophisticated observation techniques.

Does this by-pass the laryngeal bases of registers? Half way.
I believe the vocal folds are assisted or disrupted in their
vibration by the pressure of the resonating air particles. The
vocal cords are little more than thin membranes as the lips of
a trumpet player. Has any one examined by means of fiber optics
the regimes of oscillation of a bugler as the lips change vibration? The tubing remains the same but all kinds of calls can
be made--reveille, charge, taps, etc. These all occur by thin-
ning or thickening the lips. The voice has thin and thick
mechanisms also but in addition can change tubing by phonetic
processes. In reality we are phonetic trumpets which talk.
Thus I hope I have further clarified the relationship of timbre
and register in the singing voice and that it will further ad-
vance the art of singing.

The Chromatic Vowel Chart is a logarithmic device as is the
piano keyboard (and the clefs of musical notation). They are

involved with the frequency numbers which musicians know as
pitch. The Chromatic Vowel Chart forms the C scale of a slide
rule--and--the piano the D scale. Frequencies of vowel colors
and register events are notated on the Chromatic Vowel Chart.
Vowel resonances have been considered as being around 15% higher
in Female voices than in Male voices. There is also a variation
within Male voices and within Female voices. By means of the
Chromatic Vowel Chart the vowel colors and their register relationships can be taught, equalized and strengthened in all
voices from the highest soprano through the counter tenor, to
the lowest bass.

I have been challenged as to the vowel values in singing and
will continue to be until visual evidence is presented. I have
told in The Sounds of Singing how anyone can determine the pitch
of vowels by means of sympathetic vibration. However, the magic
and infallibility of the printed page holds sway. Several
statements are misleading and require reinterpretation. With
the availability of more sophisticated measuring and visual devices, I present further illumination on vowel-pitch-register
phenomena in singing. Some of the sonagrams are from the Sound
Laboratory of the University of Colorado. Other sonagrams and
Long Term Mean Spectrums were made at the Academy of Sciences,
Kommision für Schallforschung in Vienna, Austria with technology
made possible by Fonds zur Förderung der Wissenschaftlichen For-
schung on a Signal Processor SD 306, with the assistance of
Dr. Werner Deutsch.

First let me explain in Fig. 57 how overtones are seen in sonagrams in relationship to music notation and piano keyboard notation, both of which are logarithmic scales. If a pitch is sung
on A-110 Hz, the first 16 partials involved are indicated in
music notation and where they would appear in a sonagram with
the overtones equal distance apart. This is called a linear or
arithmetic scale. The zero line is the end of the ruler and
the sung pitch is always the second line. It is called the
first partial or first harmonic. Everything above is a harmonic

overtone if it is related by multiples of 1, 2, 3, etc. If not
the overtones are non-harmonic (noise).

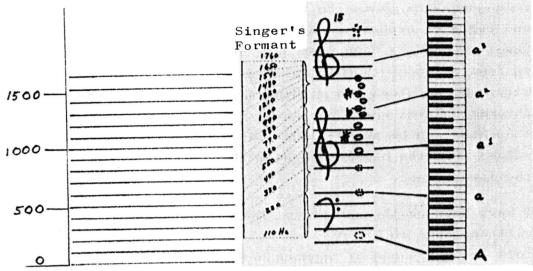

Fig. 57. Overtone structure of A 110 Hz in Key-
          board music notation and sonagraph scale.

Fig. 58 is a case in which a <u>pure</u> <u>tone</u> (sine wave) was played
against the side of the throat. The reverberations in the vocal
tract are such that overtones are created--see the lines come
into existence. Overtones are a pipe phenomenon--the vocal folds
were immobile, being held together to form a stopped pipe.
Notice that no fundamental or overtones appear until 440 Hz--
the vocal tract is not long enough to resonate loudly the dotted

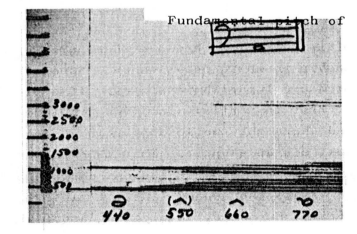

Fig. 58.

whole notes in the musical notation. However, overtones between
the 4th and 12th harmonics vary in strength according to the
vowels which were mouthed. The lower resonance, R^1, rises
through the overtones and the second resonance, R^2, lowers
through the overtone structure as the vowels ə, (ʌ), ʌ,
and ɒ are mouthed by a baritone. This is Note #8 on the Vowel
Chart. Notice also there are overtones sounding around 3000 Hz.
There is a cavity in the throat which resonates overtones which
lie in this region. Notice also the 3000 Hz resonance is more
prominent as the open vowels are pronounced. The same can be
seen in Fig. 2 where an artificial larynx with a broad spectrum
is played against the side of the throat while pronouncing [ah].
The overtones center around 800 and 1200 Hz.

Fig. 59 shows what happens when an artificial larynx with a
broad spectrum, rich in harmonic and non-harmonic overtones,
was played against the side of the throat while pronouncing
[ah]. Again the vocal cords are held together--what is seen is
the resonance quality of the [ah] vowel. Two resonace centers
are seen around 800 and 1200 Hz. Most amazing is that there is
resonance in the area of 3000 Hz. This is called the singer's
formant--but there was no vibration from the vocal cords--only
the artificial larynx. This would seem to be proof that there
is a cavity in the throat which will resonate these frequencies
expecially on the open vowels.

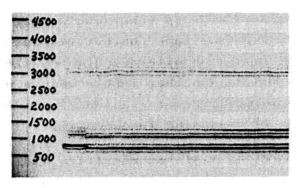

Fig. 59. Ah   vowel being pronounced while a wide spectrum
          artificial larynx is played against the side of
          the throat.

207

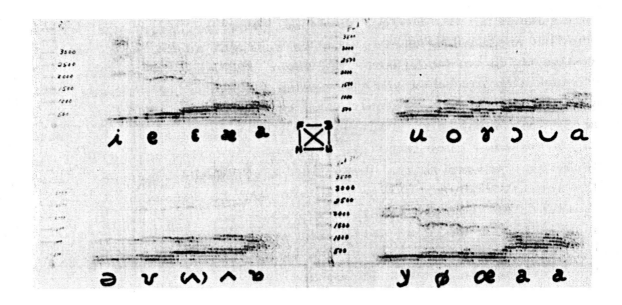

Fig. 60. Speech-droning fundamental with overtone characteris-
          tics of vowels.

Let me conclude this introduction with a Male speaking voice in
the four vowel series. As in all of the illustrations the Front
Vowel is in the upper left picture. The Neutral Vowels in the
lower left, the Back Vowels in the upper right, and the Umlauts
are in the lower left. This is so the vowels can be better related to the Chromatic Vowel Chart. The speaking voice drones
along between c and d below middle c, while the overtones
are selected and amplified by the vowel resonances (formants).
More formants are seen in the Front and Umlaut Vowels so more
overtones are present. There are fewer and weaker ones in the
Neutral and Back Vowels. The same characteristics exist in
sung vowels and they should be alternated to equalize the
voice. This may be the reason that treble voices prefer to run
on Neutral Vowels--there are fewer overtones to interfere with
the sung pitch which is a running fundamental.

Next the phonetic overtone basis of registers.

208

Vowel Register--Female Voices

Fig. 61 shows an LTM (long term mean value--1.6 seconds) spectrum of a Mezzo Soprano singing [œ] on e♭²-622 Hz. The left picture is on a logarithmic scale as is the piano keyboard and Chromatic Vowel Chart. Sung pitch, the fundamental is always the first peak from the left. The resonance peak of R^1 falls on the sung pitch. A more usual visual picture of the same tone is in the right picture in which the overtones are closely grouped in an arithmetic (linear) scale. This is the scale used in sonagrams, only in sonagrams the movement of overtones can be seen while in the Long Term Mean Value Spectrum the <u>frequency</u> of the overtones and their intensity can be compared in decibels (the scale on the left side). We are interested both in the frequency and the intensity of the lower formant which I call R^1. Intensity is interpreted by the ear in terms of loudness though the relationship between the two is very complicated as we have seen in Fletcher's loudness contours, p. 201.

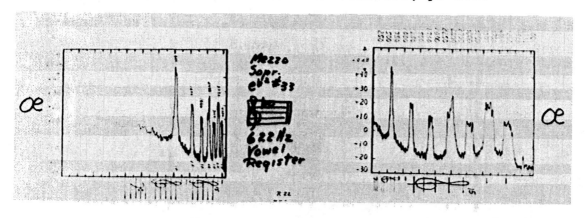

Fig. 61. The same Vowel-Pitch in logarithmic (musical) and arithmetic (mathematical) notation.

Fig. 62 of an operatic soprano shows the centering of the lower resonance of i, u, and y on g^1, the proper pitch of those vowels in her voice and the pitch on which her arrow, Note #23, was placed. The decibel scale on the left side indicates that the resonance of sung pitch is much more intense than any of the other overtones including the singer's formant around 3500 Hz. Vowel Register.

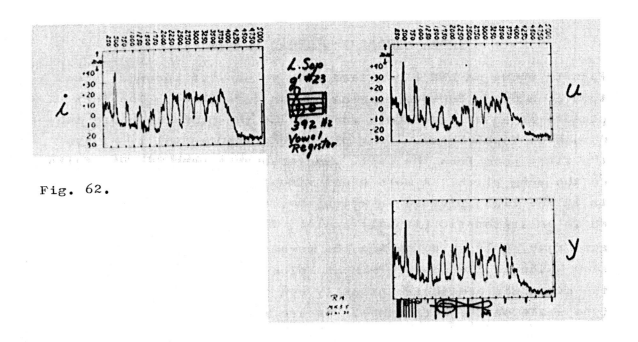

Fig. 62.

Fig. 63 of an operatic mezzo soprano shows the lower resonance of i, ə, u, and y centered on f^1, the proper pitch of those vowels in her voice. The lower resonance is more intense than on other overtones with the possible exception of the singer's formant which in her case centers around 3700 Hz. Vowel Register.

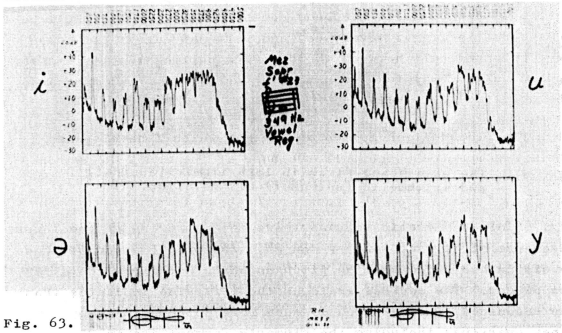

Fig. 63.

Fig. 64 is the g¹ soprano singing c² with vowels of that
proper pitch. The [ø] vowel is well placed, however, the [o]
is a bit open, sounding towards [ɔ]--the type of thing which can
cause instability and weakness because the vowel is not precise-
ly centered. The [e] vowel is slightly open towards [ε]--never-
theless the fundamental is strong. Vowel Register.

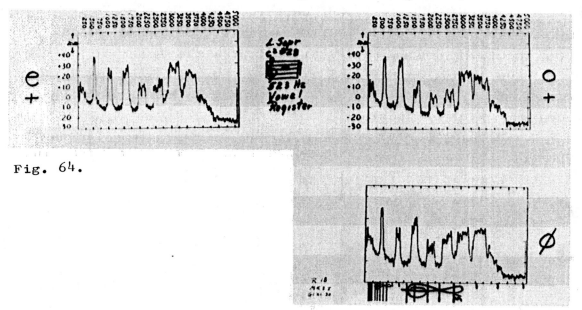

Fig. 64.

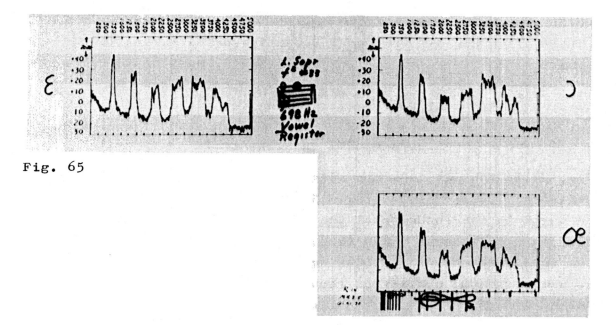

Fig. 65

211

Fig. 65 is the g^1 soprano singing f^2 with vowels on their proper pitch. All of the fundamentals are strong but the overtones are also increasing in strength. One note higher rounding should occur for Head Voice. Vowel Register.

Fig. 66 is an illustration of an analysis of a rather open [o] vowel on c^2 by the g^1 soprano. The upper example on the right shows what happens when the sound is cut off at 60 dB down; the lower one on the right indicates the sound cut off at 40 dB down. This explains missing overtones in sonagrams--they are too weak to show and possibly too weak to hear. Vowel Register.

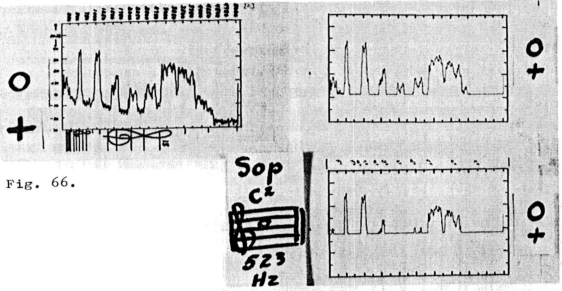

Fig. 66.

Head Register--Female Voices

Fig. 67 is the g^1 soprano singing g^2 Note #35 in her Head Register. Compared with Fig. 15 there has been an increase of strength in the fundamental and the 6th harmonic has disappeared. As a consequence, the sound is purer and more bell like. The sung pitch has an astounding reinforcement--no wonder there is a more limpid quality of sound. At about Note #40 the 5th harmonic falls out to make a purer sound. At about Note #44 another harmonic disappears--so there is a still purer sound

212

and at Note #51 the 3rd harmonic usually drops out. No wonder
the voice of a coloratura soprano sounds flutelike. Head Voice.

Incidentally, Figures 4, 16, and 17 are of a soprano singing
vowels on their proper pitches of the Sundberg picture, p. 25.
I think _either_ the degree of opening or vowels shown will place
and strengthen the voice on these pitches. When one has the
feelings of openings well enough in mind, the charting of openings in the score can also direct the singer to a good modification of the vowel.

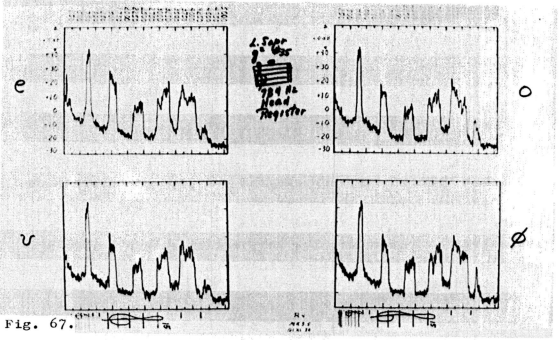

Fig. 67.

Fig. 68 is the f^1 mezzo soprano singing Note #35 in her Head
Register. Compare these spectra with those of the soprano in
Fig. 67. There is a quality difference but the pattern of
strong fundamental and weakened overtones is characteristic of
Head Voice. She does have one higher overtone and the voice is
less pure.

213

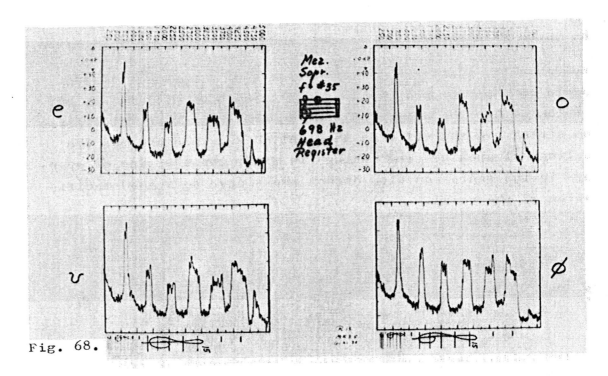

Fig. 68.

Fig. 69 is of the g¹ soprano singing the indicated vowels on
d² - 587 Hz--Note #30 which is her first note of Head Voice.
Notice that in all cases the fundamental has been reinforced
and the overtones weakened. The only strong second harmonic is
on the [u] which has a low second formant, R^2. Head Register.

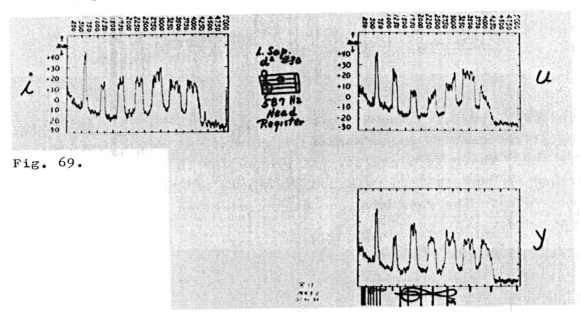

Fig. 69.

214

Fig. 70 is of the f^1 mezzo soprano singing the indicated
vowels on c^2 - 523 Hz which is her first note of Head Voice.
Because of the vowel closure, all sounds have a very strongly
reinforced sung pitch and slightly muted overtones. The result
is that the tone sounds much purer. Head Register.

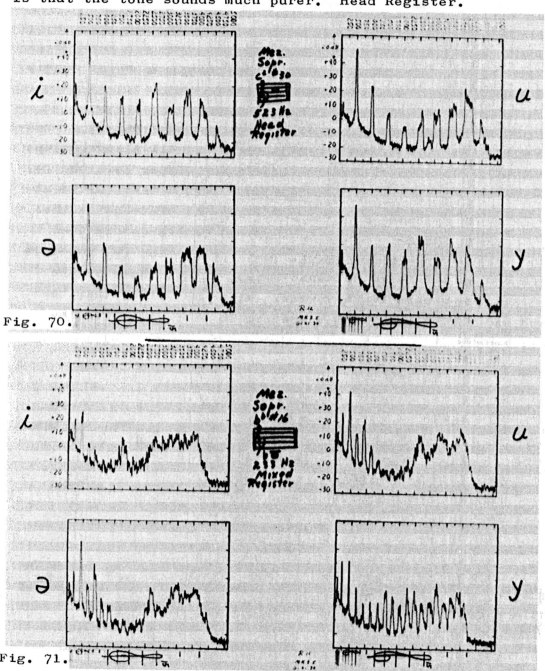

Fig. 70.

Fig. 71.

215

Mixed Register--Female Voices

Fig. 71 of the f^1 operatic mezzo soprano shows Note #16 b♭ - 233 Hz as her first note of Mixed Voice. The [y] is in ideal placement with the first and second harmonics equally strong-- indicating the vowel resonance peak is midway between the two harmonics. [u] is a little too open, sounding more than an [u] and the [ə] sounds like an [u]. These closures are very diffi- cult to teach. The placement of the [i] vowel is about ideal. Mixed Register.

Fig. 72 probably tells more about the acoustical nature of reg- isters than all of the other illustrations. All illustrations are on the [ʊ] vowel, between ɔ and ɒ . Upper left the [ʊ] is on its proper pitch--Vowel Register. Lower left [ʊ] is al- most centered between the sung pitch and the overtone at the octave--Mixed Voice. Upper right [ʊ] is reinforced by the second harmonic--Chest Register. Lower right the [ʊ] vowel is reinforced by its third harmonic--Chest Voice. Some people teach sounds--others teach vowels. It is my belief that the colors and registers of the voice can be best controlled by vowel thought.

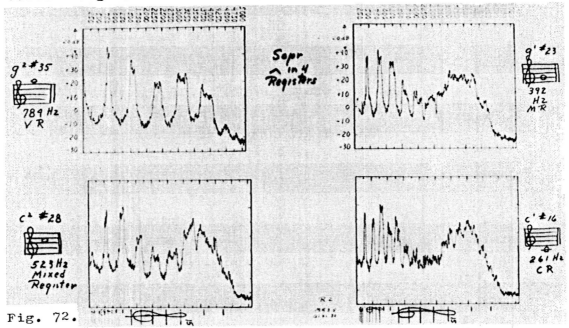

Fig. 72.

216

Vowel Register--Male Voices

In the case of the registers of the Male Voice, I will begin with vowel spectra of the different registers.

Fig. 73 of an f^1 - 349 Hz concert baritone indicates much more energy at the octave when f - 175 Hz is sung because of the proper pitch of the [i] vowel, Upper Register [U]. The b♭ - 233 Hz indicates an ideal placement for Mixed Voice (X) because the proper pitch of the vowel is midway between sung pitch and the second harmonic--as a consequence both are equally rein- forced. This may be the reason that Howie and Delattre said the pitch of the [i] vowel was up to the vicinity of f^1 - 349 Hz, and Delattre said that [i] could be as low as 250 Hz which was the value he used in synthetic speech. The pitch of a resonator can reinforce other notes than its own when it lies halfway between harmonics 1 and 2. This is the secret of Mixed Voice and the 1.5 scale on the Vowel Chart. The f^1 - 349 Hz falsetto, Vowel Register, on the proper pitch of [i] shows it is almost all fundamental with the next strongest resonance being about 30 dB down. The full voiced [i] on f^1 - 349 Hz, Vowel Register, shows the strongest overtone as being 10 dB down from sung pitch.

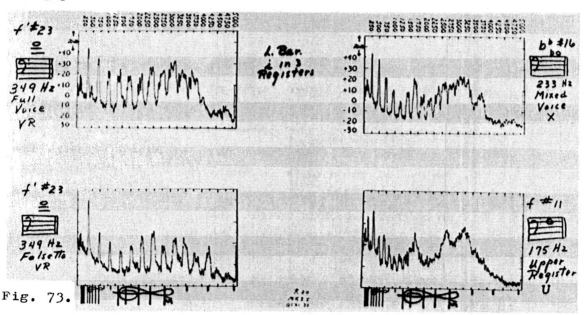

Fig. 73.

217

Fig. 74 shows the concert baritone singing [u] an octave below its proper pitch, Upper Register, with the sung pitch having much less energy than the second harmonic, the proper pitch of [u]. The attempt at <u>Mixed Voice</u> on b♭ - 233 Hz is a little bit open and is overly strong at the octave. It is necessary to have a feeling of too much closure for best placement of Mixed Voice in the loop area. The [u] f^1 - 349 Hz is sung on its proper pitch, Vowel Register. The strong second harmonic is due to the low R^2 of [u].

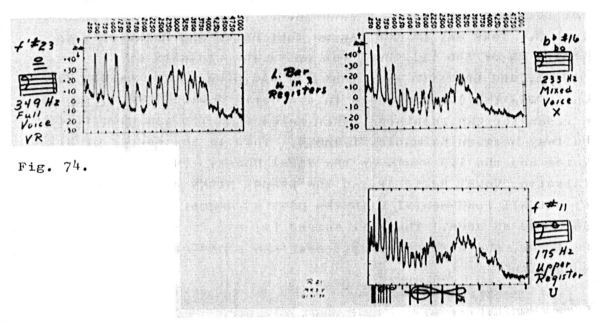

Fig. 74.

Fig. 75 of the g^1 operatic tenor shows a picture of [u] sung in three registers. In the lower right picture g - 196 Hz is being sung in Upper Register, but there is more energy at the octave because g - 392 Hz is the proper pitch of [u]. The [u] on c^1 - 262 Hz is Note #16, the first note of Mixed Voice. The energy of the first two harmonics is about equal as expected in Mixed Voice. The 3rd and 4th overtones are affected by R^2 because R^2 is the octave in this vowel. The falsetto note on g^1 - 392 Hz Vowel Register indicates about equal energy on the first two harmonics because R^2 is low on the [u] vowel. Other harmonics have little energy in falsetto but much greater energy in full voiced Vowel Register.

218

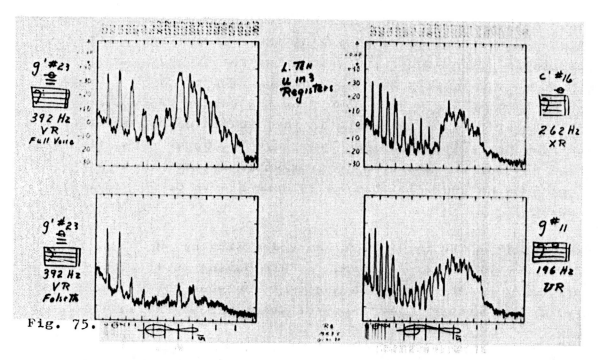

Fig. 75.

Fig. 76 of a concert baritone shows how the lower resonance of i, u, and y center on f^1 - 350 Hz an octave above the f - 176 Hz pitch being sung in Upper Register. In fact, according to the decibel scale the octave resonance, second harmonic, is louder than sung pitch. There is a possibility that the [i] vowel might have a lower proper pitch in this voice.

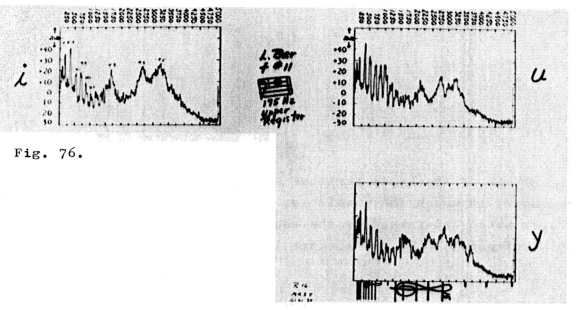

Fig. 76.

219

Fig. 76 indicates the dB variance from fundamental pitch. In this case the baritone was singing the [i] vowel an octave below its proper pitch--the reinforcement of the second harmonic had 5.3 dB more intensity than sung pitch. The singer's formant at around 3000 Hz was 9.5 dB down from the energy of sung pitch. BUT the ear is more sensitive in that region of the spectrum. See Fletcher's illustration, Fig. 46. The upper right figure shows how far the measuring equipment is valid. Those events about 4000 Hz and more than 45 dB down are to be considered unreliable.

Fig. 77 shows the Lyric Baritone voice singing d^1 - 294 Hz in which the vowels ε, ɔ, and œ are having their proper pitch reinforced by the second harmonic of the sung tone. This is a typical pattern of Upper Register which Garcia called Middle Voice.

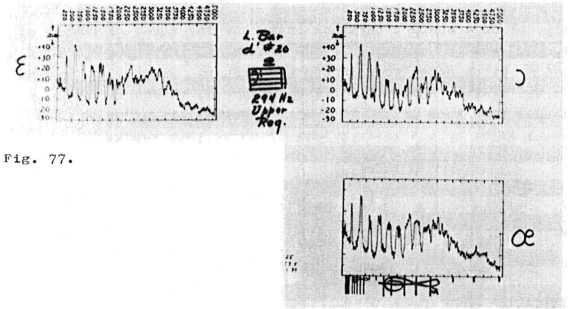

Fig. 77.

Fig. 78 is of the Lyric Baritone singing b♭ - 233 Hz, Upper Register, in which the vowels e, o, and ø are having their proper pitch reinforced by the second harmonic of the sung tone. The configuration of the spectra is the same as for Figures 76 and 77.

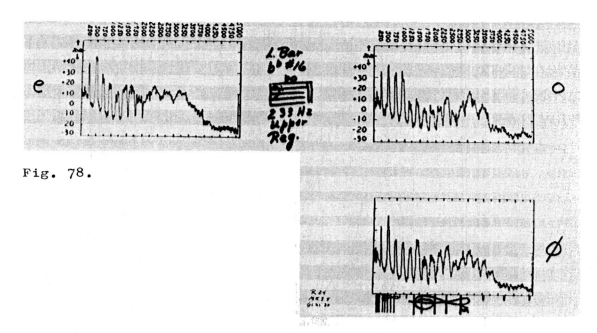

Fig. 78.

Fig. 79 is the baritone singing Note #16--the first note of
Mixed Voice in which the lower vowel resonance, R^1, is midway
between the first and second harmonic (an octave apart). The
placement is quite good since both are rather equal in energy.

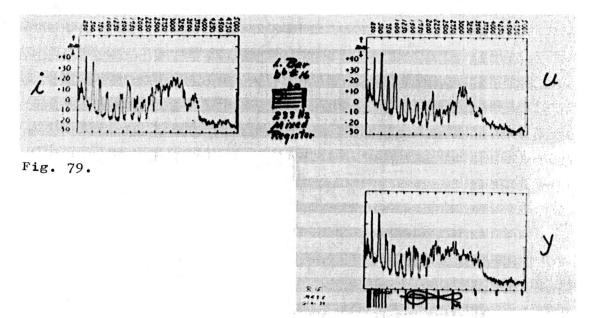

Fig. 79.

Fig. 80 is of the baritone singing [i] on Note #16 in a scale which relates directly to music notation (logarithmic). It shows that the left peak--the sung pitch and fundamental--is equally strong with the second harmonic. In this case the proper pitch of the [i] vowel is halfway between the fundamental and the overtone at the octave. As a consequence both have high and even intensity levels in decibels. This is Mixed Voice--the first two harmonics equally balanced. This exists in nature--I merely report it. This is the secret of <u>Mixed Voice</u> in both Male and Female voices. In a way it is unnatural and has to be taught. It is the secret to the upper extension of male voices and to the bridging over the eη occurrence in female voices.

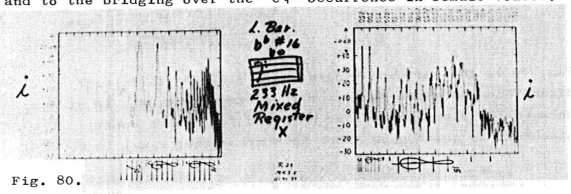

Fig. 80.

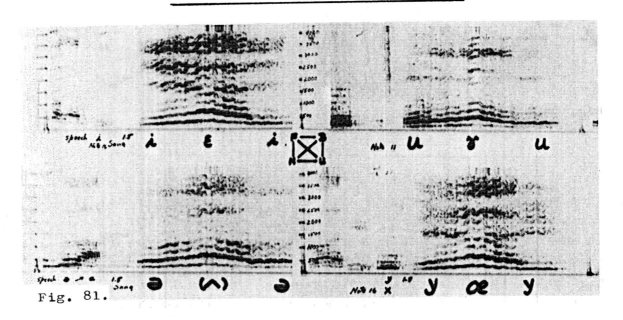

Fig. 81.

Fig. 81 is an illustration of the baritone singing a five-note
scale in Mixed Voice beginning on the vowels and note in Fig.
79, i, u, and y on bb - 233 Hz. In addition, the Neutral
Vowels were added. As in the spoken vowels, Fig. 60, there are
more overtones in the Front and Umlaut Vowels, less in the Back
Vowels and the least in the Umlauts. Overtones are colors.
Learn how to mix them and use them to equalize the scale and
for use in intelligibility.

The upper note is what I have called the "Hole in the Sky."

Fig. 82 shows the "Hole in the Sky" in Mixed Voice on Note #23
of the Tenor. The resonance being midway between the first two
harmonics reinforces them both. The "placement" is relatively
good with the exception of the [ε] vowel which is too open.
[ε] is the most difficult vowel on Note #23 because it wants to
spread to [æ]. Think of it as half [e] for equalization of the
two harmonic sounds of Mixed Voice. Mixed Register.

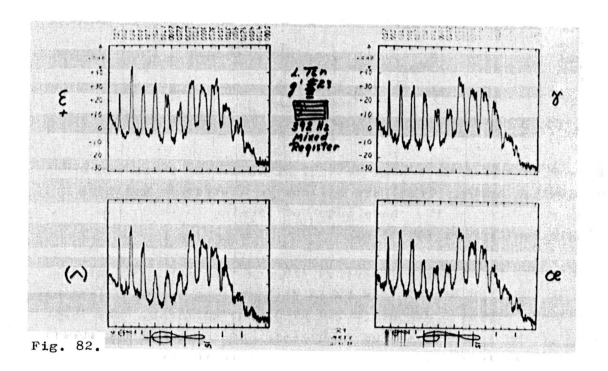

Fig. 82.

Fig. 83 is an illustration of a Helden Baritone singing the [ε]
vowel in four Registers. Upper left is [ε] on Note #23 in Mixed
Voice, which for him is one of the "Hole in the Sky" vowel-
pitches. Lower left is Upper Register in which the vowel is reinforced by the second harmonic. Upper right is in Chest Register in which [ε] is reinforced by the third harmonic, and lower
right is another Chest Voice which reinforces the [ε] vowel by
the fourth harmonic.

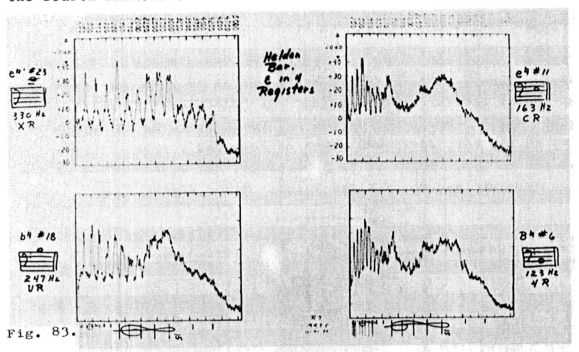

Fig. 83.

To end this book on a high note, I am including three sonagrams
of ovation notes. These are not due to histrionic ability;
they are three of the "home runs" of singing in which the
singer really hits the notes.

Figure 84. is of Edita Gruberova singing the high eb^2 at the
end of the "Mad Scene" from Lucia di Lammermoor. The definitely
outlined harmonics are her voice with four partials. The foggy
part of the spectrum is the orchestra. Her approach was thrill-
ing and was in the form of a slight leap to the upper note. Of
great interest is the scallop type vibrato at about 3800 Hz

224

which is probably her singer's formant. Also of interest is a
faint harmonic at around 5000 Hz. Density of darkness indicates loudness in sonagrams.

Fig. 84.

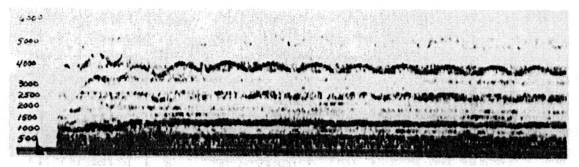

Figure 85. is of Birgit Nilsson on the ending B♭ of "Vissi
d'arte" from Tosca. The intensity of the fundamental at 932 Hz
indicates a great amount of voice. She too has a strong third
harmonic which may or may not be related to the singer's formant. She also shows a very high fourth harmonic at around
4000 Hz. The vibrato is less obvious but is present.

Fig. 85.

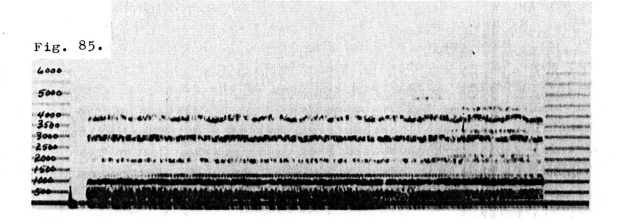

Figure 86. is of Jerome Pruett on the high c of "Salut demeure"
from Faust. The sung pitch is 523 Hz but the greatest energy is
at the octave in the vicinity of [ah] at 2800 Hz in the area of
the singer's formant. Of interest is the vibrato which is quite
even and at the end of the note which glides to the a$\flat^1$ the
overtones change in the constant singer's formant, and in its
octave around 5600 Hz.

Fig. 86.

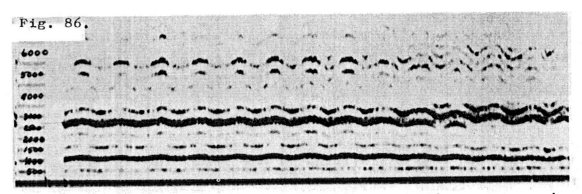

These were all ovation notes in performance. They were psycho-
acoustical events to both the singer and the audience. They
are evidence of physical phenomena which are the bases of the
great art of singing.

In conclusion I hope others will pursue observations along these
lines. My belief is that we are at a very interesting time in
our art. More people are hearing live performances of opera
than ever before because of the stimulation of television. On
TV they are able to hear and see some of the greatest artists of
our times as never before--sometimes from a distance of two or
three feet. The subtle acoustical-physiological observations
of vowel modifications should lead us to another Golden Age of
Singing. I hope this text will assist teachers and singers to
see and hear what is going on and to better realize their
potentialities.

BIBLIOGRAPHY

Aikin, W.A. The Voice, An Introduction to Practical Phonology. London: Longmans, Green & Co., 1927

Appelman, D. Ralph. The Science of Vocal Pedagogy (Theory & Application). Bloomington, Ind. & London: Indiana University Press, 1967.

Backus, John. The Acoustical Foundations of Music. New York: Norton & Co., 1969.

Bartholemew, Wilmer T. Physical Definition of "Good Voice Quality." JASA, Vol. 6, No. 25, 1934.

Bartholemew, Wilmer T. "The Role of Imagery in Voice Teaching and the Paradox in Voice Teaching." Chicago: NATS Bulletin, May, 1951 (reprint from MTNA Proceed., 1935 & reprint from JASA, Vol. II, No. 4, 1940).

Benade, Arthur H. Fundamentals of Musical Acoustics. London: Oxford, 1976.

Brown, William Earl. (G.B. Lamperti) Vocal Wisdom. Boston: Crescendo Publishers, 1957.

Byers, M.C. "Sbriglia's Method of Singing." Philadelphia: Etude 60: 307+ May, 1942

Chiba, T. & M. Kajiyama. The Vowel, Its Nature and Structure. Tokyo: Phonetic Society of Japan, 1958.

Coffin, Berton. "Articulation for Opera, Oratorio, and Recital." Chicago: NATS Bulletin, Feb., 1976.

Coffin, Berton. "The Instrumental Resonance of the Singing Voice." Chicago: NATS Bulletin, Dec., 1974.

Coffin, Berton. "The Relationship of Breath, Phonation and Resonance in Singing." Chicago: NATS Bulletin, Dec., 1975.

Coffin, Berton. "The Relationship of Phonation and Resonation." Chicago: NATS Bulletin, Feb., 1975.

Coffin, B., Errole, R., Singer, W., Delattre, P. Phonetic Readings of Songs and Arias (The Singer's Repertoire Series). Boulder, CO: Pruett Publishing Co., 1964.

Coffin, Berton. The Sounds of Singing. Boulder, CO: Pruett Publishing Co., 1977.

Cooke, James Francis. Great Singers on the Art of Singing. Philadelphia: Presser, 1921.

Corri, Domenico. The Singer's Preceptor. London: Chappell & Co., 1810. Reprinted, Editor, Edward Foreman, The Porpora Tradition. Minneapolis: Pro Musica Press, 1968.

Culver, Charles A. Musical Acoustics. New York: McGraw-Hill Book Co., 1956.

Delattre, Pierre. "Acoustic cues for the perception of initial w, j, r, l in English." New York: WORD, 13, 1: 24-43, 1957.

Delattre, Pierre. "Change as a correlate of the vowel-consonant distinction." Studia Linguistica. Vol. 18, 1965.

Delattre, Pierre. Comparing the Phonetic Features of English, French, German, and Spanish. Heidelberg: Julius Groos Verlag, 1965.

Delattre, Pierre & John Howie. "An Experimental Study of the Effect of Pitch on the Intelligibility of Vowels." Chicago: NATS Bulletin, May, 1962.

Delattre, P., Liberman, A.M., Cooper, F.S., Gerstman, C.J. "An Experimental Study of the Acoustic Determinants of Vowel Color; Observations on One & Two-Formant Vowels Synthesized from Spectrographic Patterns." New York: Haskins Laboratories, reprinted from WORD, 1952.

Delattre, P., Liberman, A.M., Cooper, F.S. "Formant transitions and loci as acoustical correlates of place of articulation in American fricatives." Studia Linguistica. Vol. 15, 1961-62.

Delattre, Pierre. "La radiographie des voyelles françaises et sa corrélation acoustique." The French Review, 42, 1: 48-65, 1968.

Delattre, Pierre. "Vowel Color and Voice Quality (An Acoustic and Articulatory Comparison)." Chicago: NATS Bulletin, Oct., 1958.

Denes, Peter B. & Elliot N. Pinson. The Speech Chain. Baltimore: (printed by Waverly Press, 1963) (Bell Telephone Laboratories) (distrib. Wms. & Wilkins Co. Science Series, Baltimore).

DeReszke, Jean (Chapter by Walter Johnstone-Douglas on "Jean DeReszke's Principles of Singing" in the book - Jean DeReszke - Clara Leiser.) New York: Minton, Balch & Co., 1934.

Duval, J.H. Svengali's Secrets & Memoirs of the Golden Age. New York: Robert Speller & Sons, Publishers, Inc., 1958.

Fant, Gunnar. Acoustic Theory of Speech Production. S'Gravenhage: Mouton, 1960.

Fletcher, H. Speech and Hearing. New York: Van Nostrand Co., Inc., 1953.

Fritzell, Björn. The Velopharyngeal Muscles in Speech. Göteborg: Orstadius Boktryckeri Aktiebolag, 1969.

Fry, Dennis B. (Editor) Acoustic Phonetics. Cambridge, England: New York: Cambridge University Press, 1976.

Fucito, Salvatore & S. Beyer. Caruso and the Art of Singing (reprint). New York: F.A. Stokes Co., 1929.

Garcia, Manuel. The Art of Singing, Part I. Boston: Oliver
    Ditson, ab. 1855.

Garcia, Manuel (pere) (Popolo Vicenti). Exercises pour la voix
    (avec un Discours Preliminaire). Paris: Ph. Petit, 1819.

Garcia, Manuel P.R. Hints on Singing. London: Ascherberg &
    Co.; New York: Schuberth & Co., 1894. Available in
    H. Klein 1911 revision from Chappell, London, 50 New
    Bond St., W1.

Garcia, Manuel. Memoire on the Human Voice. Paris: 1841.
    Translated & copyrighted, Donald V. Paschke, Eastern New
    Mexico University, Portales, N.M., 1970.

Garcia, Manuel (Paschke, Donald V.-trans.). A Complete Treat-
    ise on The Art of Singing, Part II. New York: DaCapo
    Press, 1975.

Goldschmidt, Hugo. Handbuch der deutschen Gesangspädagogik.

Helmholtz, Hermann L.F. On the Sensations of Tone (fourth &
    last edition). New York: Dover Publications, Inc.,
    1954 (new); 1877 (old); 1885 (A. Ellis trans.).

Henley, Homer. "Sbriglia' Method." Philadelphia: Etude 51:
    50-51, Jan., 1933.

Howard, John. Physiology of Artistic Singing. Boston: 1886.

Husler, Frederick & Yvonne Rodd-Marling. Singing: The Physical
    Nature of the Vocal Organ. London: Faber & Faber, 1965.

Husson, Raoul. La Voix Chantée. Paris: Gauthier-Villars,
    Editeur, 1960.

Iffert, August. Allgemeine Gesangschule. Leipzig: Breitköpf
    & Härtel.

International Phonetic Association. The Principles of the Int-
    national Phonetic Association. London: International
    Phonetic Association, Phonetics Department, University
    College, London: Gower Street, WC 1E 6BT; reprinted 1978.

Jeans, Sir James. Science and Music. New York: Macmillan Co.;
    Cambridge, England: University Press, 1937. Reprint,
    New York: Dover Publications, Inc., 1968.

Joal, Dr. On Respiration in Singing. London: F.J. Rebman,
    1895.

Kay, Elster. Bel Canto and the Sixth Sense (The Student's
    Music Library Series). London: Dobson Books, Ltd.,
    1963. Chester Springs, PA: Dufour Editions, Inc., 1963.

Klein, Joseph J. Singing Technique. Princeton, N.J.: D. Van
    Nostrand, 1967.

Ladefoged, Peter. Elements of Acoustical Phonetics. Chicago:
    University of Chicago, 1964.

Lamperti, Francesco. The Art of Singing (revised, edited, translated, J.C. Griffith), Vol. 1587, Schirmer's Library of Musical Classics. New York: G. Schirmer, Inc., 1890.

Lamperti, Giovanni Battista with Maximilian Heidrich. The Technics of Bel Canto (translated, Th. Baker). New York: G. Schirmer, Inc., 1905; Berlin: Albert Stahl.

Lamperti, Giovanni Battista (see Brown, W.E.). Vocal Wisdom enlarged edition; supplement edit., L. Strongin). Dresden: (notes to W.E. Brown, 1891-93); New York: Crescendo Publishers, 1957.

Lankow, Anna. The Science of the Art of Singing. New York, London, Leipzig: Breitköpf & Härtel, 1902.

Large, John, Editor. Vocal Registers in Singing. Proceedings of a Symposium. 78th Mtg., Acoustical Society of America, San Diego, CA, Nov. 7, 1969 & Silver Jubilee Convention of NATS, Cleveland, OH, Dec. 28, 1969. The Hague & Paris: Mouton & Co. N.V. Publishers, 1973.

Lehiste, Ilse. Readings in Acoustic Phonation. Cambridge, MA: MIT Press, 1967.

Lehmann, Lilli (translated, Richard Aldrich). How To Sing (Meine Gesangskunst). New York: Macmillan Co., 1902 & 1914.

Leiser, Clara. Jean de Reszke, and the Great Days of Opera. New York: Minton, Balch & Co., 1934.

Leith, William R. Drawings of Anatomical Structures Involved in Speech. Boulder, CO: Pruett Publishing Co., 1974.

Lieberman, Philip. Speech Physiology and Acoustic Phonetics. New York: Macmillan Publishing Co., Inc., 1977.

Luchsinger, Richard & Godfrey E. Arnold. Voice-Speech-Language (Clinical Communicology; Its Physiology & Pathology). Vienna: Springer-Verlag (German), 1949; London: Constable & Co., 1959 (Belmont, CA: Wadsworth Publishing Co., 1965).

Mackworth-Young, Gerald. What Happens in Singing. London: Newman Neame, 1953.

Mancini, Giambattista. Practical Reflections on the Figurative Art of Singing. Boston: (translation of the 1777 edition), The Gorham Press, 1912.

Manén, Lucie. The Art of Singing. London: Faber Music Ltd., 1974. Bryn Mawr, PA: Theodore Presser, Inc., 1976.

Marchesi, Mathilde. The Art of Singing, Op. 21, BK. I & II. New York: G. Schirmer, 1890 (reprint after 1939).

Marchesi, Mathilde. Marchesi Vocal Method, Pt. I & II, Op. 31. Schirmer Library Series. New York: G. Schirmer, Inc., 1905.

Miller, Dayton Clarence. Science of Musical Sounds (2nd edition). New York: Macmillan Co., 1934.

Miller, Richard. English, French, German and Italian Techniques of Singing. Metuchen, N.J.: The Scarecrow Press, Inc., 1977.

Monahan, Brent Jeffrey. The Art of Singing. Metuchen, N.J.: The Scarecrow Press, Inc., 1978.

Moriarty, John. Diction. Boston: E.C. Schirmer, 1975.

Nathan, Isaac. Musurgia Vocalis. London: Fentum, 76, Strand, 1836. Reprinted, Editor, Edward Foreman. The Porpora Tradition. Minneapolis: Pro Musica Press, 1968.

Paget, Sir Richard. Human Speech. London: Paul, Trench Publishers, 1930. New York: Harcourt, Brace Publishing Co., 1930.

Pleasants, Henry. The Great Singers. New York: Simon & Schuster, 1966.

Potter, R., G.A. Kopp & H.G. Kopp. Visible Speech. New York: Dover Publications, 1966.

Robinson, Francis. Caruso (His Life in Pictures). New York: Bramhall House, 1957.

Rush, James. The Philosophy of Voice. Philadelphia: J. Maxwell Publishing Co., 1827.

Russell, G. Oscar. Causes of Good and Bad Voices. Washington, D.C.: National Research Foundation and Carnegie Institute of Washington, catalogued, 1959.

Russell, G. Oscar. "The Consonant - an X-Ray Analysis of Its Vocal Organ Modifications by Other Sounds." Proceedings of 10th mtg., JASA, 1934.

Russell, G. Oscar. Speech and Voice. New York: Macmillan Co., 1931.

Saunders, William H. The Larynx. Summit, N.J.: Ciba Corporation, 1964.

Scripture, E.W. "Analysis and Interpretation of Vowel Tracks." JASA, Vol. 5, 1933.

Scripture, E.W. Researches in Experimental Phonetics. Washington, D.C.: Carnegie Studies, 1906.

Shakespeare, William. The Art of Singing. Boston: Oliver Ditson, 1921.

Stockhausen, Julius. Method of Singing. London: Novello, 1884 1884.

Stratton, John. "Operatic Singing Style and the Gramophone." Recorded Sound, #22-23, April-July, 1966.

Sundberg, Johan. "Articulatory Differences between Spoken and Sung Vowels, in Singers." Speech Technical Laboratory, QPSR. Stockholm: 1969.

Sundberg, Johan. Music Room Acoustics. Stockholm: The Royal Swedish Academy of Music 17, 1977.

Tetrazzini, Louisa. How to Sing. Philadelphia: Theodore Presser Co., 1923.

Tosi, Francesco. Observations on the Florid Song.(trans. M. Galliard). London: J. Wilcox Co., 1723. (Available in reprint from William Reeves Bookseller, London, WC 2.)

van Deinse, J.B., Lucy Frateur, and J. Keyzer. "Problems of the Singing Voice." Folia Phoniatrica 26: 428-434, 1974.

Van Riper, Charles & John V. Irwin. Voice and Articulation. New York: Prentice-Hall, Inc., 1958.

Vennard, William. Developing Voices. New York: Carl Fischer, Inc., 1973.

Vennard, William. Singing, the Mechanism and the Technic. New York: Carl Fischer, Inc. (revised), 1967.

Wangemann, A. Theo. E. & Dr. Frank E. Miller. Observations about the Human Voice. New York.

Winckel, Fritz W. (trans. Thomas Binkley). Music, Sound and Sensation (A Modern Exposition). Berlin: 1960. New York: (trans.) Dover Publications, 1967.

Witherspoon, Herbert. Singing. New York: G. Schirmer, Inc., 1925.

Wood, Alexander. Acoustics. New York: Dover Publications, Inc. (orig. 1940), 1966.

Wood, Alexander. The Physics of Music. London: University Paperbacks, Methuen, 1962.

Yersin, Marie & Jeanne. The Yersin Phono-Rhythmic Method of French Pronunciation. Philadelphia: J.B. Lippincott Co., 1924.

Zemlin, Willard R. Speech and Hearing Science (Anatomy & Physiology). Englewood Cliffs, N.Y.: Prentice-Hall Inc., 1968.

INDEX of PROPER NAMES